Chicken Soup for the Soul®

Christmas Magic

With Love, to _____

From _____

Date _____

Chicken Soup for the Soul.

Christmas Magic

Chicken Soup for the Soul: Christmas Magic
101 Holiday Tales of Inspiration, Love, and Wonder
Jack Canfield, Mark Victor Hansen, and Amy Newmark

Published by Chicken Soup for the Soul Publishing, LLC   www.chickensoup.com

The publisher gratefully acknowledges the many publishers and individuals who granted Chicken Soup for the Soul permission to reprint the cited material.

Front and back cover, and interior illustration courtesy of iStockphoto.com/ Dirtydog_Creative (© Paul Bartlett). Back cover illustration courtesy of iStockphoto.com/ Toonhead

Cover and Interior Design & Layout by Pneuma Books, LLC
For more info on Pneuma Books, visit www.pneumabooks.com

Distributed to the booktrade by Simon & Schuster. SAN: 200-2442

Publisher's Cataloging-in-Publication Data
(Prepared by The Donohue Group)

Chicken soup for the soul : Christmas magic : 101 holiday tales of inspiration,
    love, and wonder / [compiled by] Jack Canfield, Mark Victor Hansen, [and] Amy
    Newmark.
        p. ; cm.
    Summary: A collection of 101 true personal stories from regular people about
Christmas and the holiday season.
    ISBN: 978-1-935096-54-2

    1. Christmas--Literary collections. 2. Christmas--Anecdotes. 3. Holidays--Literary
collections. 4. Holidays--Anecdotes. I. Canfield, Jack, 1944- II. Hansen, Mark Victor.
III. Newmark, Amy. IV. Title: Christmas magic

PN6071.C6 C45 2010
808.8/02/03942663   2010931537

PRINTED IN THE UNITED STATES OF AMERICA
on acid∞free paper
19 18 17 16 15 14 13 12 11   04 05 06 07 08 09 10

Chicken Soup for the Soul® Christmas Magic

101 Holiday Tales
of Inspiration,
Love, and Wonder

Jack Canfield
Mark Victor Hansen
Amy Newmark

Chicken Soup for the Soul Publishing, LLC
Cos Cob, CT

Contents

❶
~It's Beginning to Look a Lot Like Christmas~

❷
~Have Yourself a Merry Little Christmas~

❸
~Away in a Manger~

❹
~Deck the Halls~

❺
~There's No Place Like Home for the Holidays~

❻

~Joy to the World~

❼

~Holly Jolly Christmas~

❽

~O' Christmas Tree~

❾

~All I Want for Christmas~

❿

~Santa Claus Is Coming to Town~

⓫

~It's the Most Wonderful Time of the Year~

Foreword

The elves at Chicken Soup for the Soul have done it again! I'm writing this foreword during my less-busy season, the summer, and I must say that these stories are making me look forward so much to the Christmas season. Mrs. Claus and I have been passing this manuscript back and forth and commenting to each other on our favorite stories.

By the time you read this, the Mrs. and I and the whole gang up at the North Pole will be in full production mode — the factory will be running 24/7, the lists will have been triple-checked, and the reindeer will be practicing their flying maneuvers. Those satellite dishes have complicated matters for us a bit in recent years.

And we know that you will all be rushing about too. Mrs. Claus and I are not alone in loving the Christmas holiday season. We watch as you reunite scattered family members, enjoy the wonder on the face of a child, feel the joy of gift giving, and remember the true meaning of Christmas. The rituals of the holiday season give a rhythm to the years and create a foundation for your family lives. We watch you gather with your communities at church, at school, and even at the mall, to share the special spirit of the season, brightening those long winter days.

As I write this foreword, I know that many of you are sweltering in above-average heat and humidity. It has been a hot summer up here at the North Pole too. But despite the heat, the Christmas spirit lives in all of us year-round. Wouldn't it be nice if it were Christmas all the time? How about leaving a couple of those decorations up all year?

I hope you will find the time this busy holiday season to curl up in front of the fire and have a good read. And remember that Chicken Soup for the Soul's Christmas books are always appropriate for young readers or listeners — their editors work closely with Mrs. Claus and me to keep the magic alive.

I hope you will enjoy *Chicken Soup for the Soul: Christmas Magic* as much we are enjoying our advance copy. Have a wonderful Christmas season and keep those cookies coming!

~Santa Claus

P.S. Please do not listen to Mrs. Claus about the cookies. My cholesterol is fine. And I get plenty of exercise on Christmas Eve. I like the cookies. I depend on you for the cookies. She won't let me have any cookies the rest of the year....

Christmas Magic

It's Beginning to
Look a Lot Like Christmas

When Angels Sing

Angels can fly directly into the heart of the matter.
~Author Unknown

Two days before her school program, my youngest announced, "I'm singing 'Silent Night.'" Having raised two daughters ahead of her, I knew nine-year-olds aren't particularly great on details. I delved deeper.

"Right now?" I asked.

"Nope, in the play. I'm singing solo," she proudly proclaimed.

"What is solo?"—doing a vocab check to see if she knew what she was saying. Turns out she did. And that puzzled me. Charlotte loved to sing. She sang in the shower and the car and just about everywhere else. But, my baby had been partially tone deaf since she first opened her mouth. She could carry a tune a bit better now than last year or even the year before. Actually, I fully expected her musical ear to reach a level very close to normalcy as she grew older, but I didn't think she'd improved enough yet to sing a solo. Not wanting to voice any lack of confidence in her abilities and reminding myself that all things are indeed possible, especially in grade school, I stopped questioning.

•••

Even though our oldest had already moved away from home, I still housed two teenagers. We picked up an extra one along the way. Due to her family's sudden and unavoidable job relocation, my middle daughter's best friend was living with us until the end of the school year. Forty-eight hours after Charlotte's announcement, the proverbial plot thickened. I temporarily forgot teenagers can be worse than nine-year-olds when it comes to details. Both Monica, my daughter, and Corina, our temporary daughter, admitted that they also were to take part in a Christmas program on the same night as Charlotte. Corina was to sing a solo as well. Monica was to play a piano piece. The new question formed: how was I to be in two places at one time? My break came when I found out the older girls would be performing an hour later than the younger. I could try for both!

• • •

Something had gone dreadfully wrong. Charlotte stood facing me in the auditorium five minutes after I had dropped her backstage. Her little eyes glistened with unshed tears and her mouth quivered so violently she couldn't speak.

"What happened, baby?" I couldn't imagine.

Just then the teacher approached.

"Mrs. Stiles, there's been a mistake. Charlotte wasn't picked to sing with the choir tonight and somehow she's gotten the idea she is to sing a solo. I'm afraid there is no part cast for her. I feel just terrible about this."

Looking into my child's grief-stricken face and feeling a mother's rage, I thought: You don't know how terrible you're about to feel after I get done with you!

"Mama, can we go?" Her little voice finally broke through in utter anguish.

"Of course we can, baby," I said, tossing the teacher an I'll-deal-with-you-later look. My first concern now was how to mend my daughter's wounded heart.

• • •

Teenagers may be lousy at time with details, but they tend to pay attention to those who enter and leave their immediate environment. I think that comes from a wariness that they might get caught doing what they ought not to be doing. It took all of three minutes for both girls to figure out that we were in the high school auditorium. I offered to skip the program and take Charlotte for an ice cream, but she wanted to see her sister and Corina perform.

"You guys are here early." They resembled two parrots. Their heads darted back and forth between Charlotte and me in unison. Perched on the backs of the seats in front of us they waited, clearly expecting an explanation. I quickly and briefly hit the high points, wary of starting a new avalanche of tears. Sincere sympathy splashed up from the countenance of both girls.

"Come with us, Charlotte. You can see backstage and meet our friends."

The invitation to go hang out with the "cool" kids beat any flavor of ice cream—anywhere. I nodded my blessing and they disappeared.

• • •

I completely forgot about picking up a program when I entered the building. I had no way of knowing in what order the girls would be performing. But, after the second act, Corina walked out to center stage. Then, she looked left and held out her hand. Out walked Charlotte. The auditorium fell silent at the sight of a younger child. The music started, Charlotte looked up and at Corina's nod, my baby began to softly sing "Silent Night." Corina's smooth soprano joined her in just enough volume to cover any mistakes. The combination was ethereal. Both sang to a captivated audience. I wasn't the only one with tears running down my cheeks.

Somewhere during their duet, Monica's hand slipped into mine and we celebrated the true meaning of Christmas together. All of my previous agitation slipped away as I watched this magnificent moment orchestrated by God.

They simply and silently walked off stage when they were done, receiving a standing ovation as they went. Corina returned alone to do her originally planned solo. It was then I realized there was more to this Christ-filled moment than we saw being performed.

"Monica, why aren't you backstage?" I whispered.

"Don't need to be," she said grinning. "I gave up my piano piece so the squirt could sing."

How many times had I seen my two girls argue, bicker and fight? Too many to count. I couldn't recall one time when I'd heard one tell the other "I love you" with any sort of sincerity in their voices. Until now. Not in words, but deed. My Christmas was complete before we ever went to church or opened gifts or shared our family meal. I had already witnessed the miracle of three angels singing.

~Melanie Stiles

Making Christmas Memories

Each day of our lives we make deposits in the memory banks of our children.
~Charles R. Swindoll, The Strong Family

"I've been to that hotel, Grandma."

My seven-year-old grandson, Brandon, and I are driving to my mother's house to celebrate Thanksgiving when he spots a Radisson Hotel out the car window. Realizing that all Radissons look the same, my curiosity is nevertheless piqued and I ask, "Really? When did you go there?"

"You know," he replies. "You and Grandpa took me and Maddie there for ice cream after the music without words."

I'm silent for a moment, mulling over "music without words."

Ah, the symphony, I think, and glance at him in amazement. My husband Gary and I had taken two of our grandchildren to the symphony and then to the Radisson for their famous profiteroles—two years ago. Brandon is remembering an enjoyable but hardly monumental afternoon that happened when he was only five years old. I realize this is important; a small child's pleasant memory from what to him would be the distant past deserves attention and, although I still don't know exactly how, I know that this conversation will forever change the way our family celebrates Christmas.

My husband and I have a beautiful cornucopia of children, their spouses, and grandchildren. Our kids were essentially grown by the time we married so we bypassed many of the problems typical of "blending a family." The issue of holidays, however, has always required creative planning. It has grown more complex as the children married and new family members and traditions were introduced into their lives.

We've tried traditional Christmases. I would bake and cook for days in order to prepare a typical American feast—but when to enjoy this family meal eluded us. We've tried feasting on Christmas evening, then Christmas afternoon and then Christmas Eve. One year we tried Christmas brunch, but there always seemed to be a scheduling conflict with an in-law family. Our children would come to a table that was resplendent with turkeys, hams, platters of side dishes and scrumptious desserts, nibble a bit and be on their way to the next family home and the next feast.

I worried that, in a world where one in seven people go to bed hungry, it is wickedly wasteful to prepare such a feast when it can't be fully enjoyed. We longed for the company of our children for more than a couple of hours as we celebrated the season of family togetherness.

Grandchildren began to arrive, one-by-one until they numbered thirteen, and the issue of gifts took on an onerous dimension.

Then came the conversation with a little boy who remembered a fun afternoon spent with his grandparents and a cousin two years before.

Although the details were still fuzzy, we began to plan a special kind of Christmas. First, Gary and I agreed to stop giving them "things." Instead, we undertook to find a way to offer them opportunities to make memories. We needed some uninterrupted time and that meant that, most likely, Christmas would have to fall on a different day and traditions would have to be swept away like used gift wrap.

We decided to rent a cabin at Shaver Lake in central California, where we'd likely find snowy winter weather. The location is fairly convenient for everyone and we are there for a week that includes Christmas Day.

"Christmas is no longer on December 25th," we announced that year. "Whenever any family members can be there with us, that day will be Christmas." The plan was an adjustment for our more traditional children, but our grandchildren immediately embraced the adventure of it.

We never know exactly who will be there, when or for how long. In fact, there are days when we are alone — we use the time to put our feet up, read by the fire or nap. When someone is there, I cook Christmas dinner. It's not a feast, just a nice dinner featuring the favorite foods of those who are celebrating with us. Dessert is more likely to be someone's favorite treat than traditional holiday fare. The money we used to spend on trucks, Barbies or the latest TV toy now pays the rent and buys food for the week.

We are a large, noisy bunch. We have a "game box" and I love sitting with a cup of coffee, watching our children and grandchildren playing board games, working puzzles or playing Uno with the cards Gary, who is blind, has brailed. Often, groups of skiers head up the mountain to spend the afternoon on the slopes, a graduation from the "Daddy-built" sled runs of years past.

There is a "boot box" with extra snow gear and we take a box full of photo albums crammed with family pictures — and memories — of hairstyles and Christmases past.

Someone always brings up a Christmas tree. These days, it is decked out with traditional lights and decorations, but when the grandchildren were little, we provided a "crafts box" full of glitter and glue and they made decorations. Some years, silver stars, glittering angels, cotton snowmen and pipe-cleaner reindeer adorned only the bottom two or three feet of the tree.

One year the tree didn't arrive until late in the week and a tall 1970s orange lamp was pressed into service. When the grandchildren are asked to name their favorite Christmas tree, they always laugh and shout, "The Christmas Lamp." The Christmas Lamp is a silly, happy memory shared by all.

Each year brings a different configuration of family members together to ski, play in the snow, thaw out in front of the fire or take long, icy walks. Generally, everyone is able to be there for at least a couple of days. Relaxed, uninterrupted time together has allowed our children to become as close as biological brothers and sisters. Relationships among the thirteen cousins have formed and reformed as the years pass and each has found a special bond with the others.

Last year, a grown-up Brandon arrived at the cabin with his enchanting new wife. The joy of the season will come full circle this year when they bring their new son to play with his cousin, Maddie's daughter, and to help our ever-expanding family make Christmas memories.

~Irene Morse

The Cookie Party

Nobody can make you feel inferior without your consent.
~Eleanor Roosevelt

I set my briefcase on my gritty kitchen counter and traced the raised gold lettering on the thick ivory card. "You are Invited to a Holiday Cookie Party," the card read. The invitation was from a fascinating, creative, high-powered executive I had met only months ago. I was surprised and thrilled that she had invited me to such a gathering.

Each woman would bring a batch of home-baked cookies, she explained in her note. We would then get to sample all the cookies and take a bag of treats home to our families. I adored the idea of bringing my teenage daughters such an array of home-baked sweets. I envisioned a room filled with charming baskets of star-shaped sugar cookies, generously topped with red or green frosting. I imagined a jolly basket of Santa cookies, and a fragrant ginger-scented array of reindeer cookies. I wanted to bite into rum balls, sinfully rich fudge and even nibble a piece of golden raisin fruitcake. I fantasized about thumbprint cookies, gooey with jam, and about silky buttery sandies melting in my mouth.

Then I realized the implications. Given the nature of the invitation and the fact that its sender worked at such an innovative company, these holiday cookies would not only be beautiful, creative and delicious, they would be presented in festive and unusual ways. I didn't even have time to worry about what I would wear—I could only think about what I would bake.

Given the fact I had never really baked anything other than the occasional clumpy chocolate chip, peanut butter or oatmeal cookie, I figured my offerings would be ignored and I would feel left out, inadequate and disgraced. Why hadn't my mother been a more glamorous baker, I fretted, as I turned on the kettle and rummaged in the refrigerator for something to make for dinner. She only made the plainest of cookies—date crumbs, peanut butter and chocolate chip. As I sipped my tea, boiled water for pasta and heated up the jar of Mamma Somebody's Secret Marinara Sauce with Mushrooms, I analyzed the situation. Right before the pasta was ready to pour into the colander, a number floated into my head and I dialed it.

"If I decide to go to this cookie party, will you help me come up with a recipe and a cute idea for presenting the cookies?" I asked my friend Judith, who was graced with five-star baking abilities.

"Of course," she said. Judith had the kind of aplomb and panache that would fit right in at such a gathering. Briefly, I wondered if she could go to the party in my place, and just deliver my treats to me.

I told my daughters the good news—in several weeks we would have our own private holiday cookie festival. Since our sweets were usually the mass-produced variety, made by some giant corporate entity, they were ultra excited.

A week later, I received a thick packet in the mail. Judith had selected a number of "easy" recipes for me to consider. I smiled as I looked over the pictures. These cookies were adorable, with just the sort of cute holiday twist that would help me blend in. I frowned as I read through the baking instructions. These cookies required a kind of culinary acumen I had never been able to achieve. Plus, each cookie demanded its own specialized pan, gourmet tool, thermometer or esoteric ingredient. This would never work for me.

The day of the cookie party neared and I had no recipe, no cookies, no plan and nothing to wear.

That night at dinner, I said, "I don't think I can go to the cookie party."

"Why not?" Sarah said sharply. She was thirteen and took promises and plans very seriously. Plus, she had a highly sophisticated taste for sweets and was looking forward to expanding her repertoire.

"I don't have anything cute to make. I can't just walk in carrying a paltry tray of blobby-looking chocolate chip cookies." My throat constricted and I wished I was the sort of mother who could whip up a chocolate soufflé from ingredients that just happened to be in my kitchen cabinets.

"Why not?" my older daughter Jessica said. Even during the holiday season, she kept to her black-themed wardrobe. She looked Gothic and serious as she coached me. "Everyone else will be all silver bells and fancy sprinkles. You will represent the good old-fashioned approach to the holidays—the working middle class and all that. Your simplicity will be a breath of fresh air."

I took a breath and took in her words. If worse came to worst, I could always pretend I never saw those cookies before in my life.

That evening, my daughters and I made chocolate chip cookies. We put them, as usual, in a simple tin lined with aluminum foil. In honor of the holiday season, I unearthed a shiny red bow to top the tin. They analyzed my clothes and helped me select something reasonably festive to wear.

Walking into the party was like walking into a fairyland. Christmas lights lined the windows and a sparkling tree spread its branches in the living room. The dining room table looked like the December cover of *Gourmet* magazine. Stars, hearts, Christmas trees, snowmen, all the icons of the season were out and glowing with icing and sprinkles. Some cookies were nestled in handmade wreathes. Others shone from star-shaped or tree-shaped boxes. A fruitcake was surrounded by a miniature set of reindeer. A charming wicker basket lined with red velvet cradled a mound of delicate meringues. Walnut-topped fudge nestled in a wrapping paper covered box and a galaxy of colorful star-shaped cookies decorated a tiered silver-server. I admired each display, all the while looking for a quiet corner where I could tuck in my tin of chocolate chips. I finally settled them between candy cane cookies and the gingerbread Santas.

My hostess offered me a glass of champagne and introduced me to several women. The conversation flowed. Then our hostess announced, "It's time to gather the cookies." She had a large silver gift sack for each of us and encouraged us to take several of each cookie. As I began the table tour, I sneaked a look at my humble confection. What if no one took any? What if I had to take the whole batch home? What if... I thought as I filled my sack with samples of every delectable cookie there.

"Who made the chocolate chip cookies?" someone asked. The room quieted. I concentrated on the rum balls in front of me, considering my options. The silence spread and finally I said, "I did."

Though I spoke softly, I felt like the announcement blasted into the room from a bullhorn.

"What an interesting idea," someone said.

"Yes, I never would have thought of it. It's comforting, you know, it reminds me of my mother and home."

I smiled as I put three rum balls in my sack and headed for the reindeer.

That evening my daughters and I had a magnificent holiday feast, consisting of cookies, cookies and cookies.

"Here's the strange thing, Mom," Jessica said, as she leaned back, sated. "Your cookies are really just as good as any of them. Not as cute, but just as delicious."

"More delicious," Sarah said.

I smiled, thinking that about my mom's cookies when I was growing up. Maybe there was something to say about the plain old recipes offered in the plain old way, so sturdy, so unglamorous and yet so deliciously comforting... like coming home.

~Deborah Shouse

Christmas Blues

There is no psychiatrist in the world like a puppy licking your face.
~Ben Williams

I f you have married children you most likely watch them juggle parents at Christmas. I call it the "Every Other Holiday Syndrome." Wife's parents on odd years and husband's family on even years. Simple—except when unforeseen circumstances found this unsuspecting mom and pop facing a lonely Christmas for the first time. We were not looking forward to the holidays.

Okay, we can handle it, we're grown-ups and we understand, we kept reminding ourselves. Okay, that is, until our Golden Retriever collapsed under a massive seizure that forced us to say goodbye to our beloved lady. We were heartsick over the loss of our Nikki. Oh, dear God, I lamented, what a bummer just before Christmas. I cried buckets while my husband, Ken, labored to keep his macho image intact. Finally he let go and it was a dreadful scene.

Just a week later, severe arthritis and profound loneliness for Nikki rendered our fifteen-year-old Border Collie withdrawn, incontinent, and unable to walk. The excruciating trip to the veterinarian was nearly more than we old souls could handle. Ginger had been what we mountain folks call a "dump-off," and we had gladly adopted this sweet and loyal herder. Celebration of our Lord's birth took a backseat to the loss of adored family.

Christmas Eve morning, Ken popped out of bed full of vim and vigor. I, on the other hand, was still caught up in gloom and despair over the loss of our beloved dogs, and slightly miffed at his seemingly hard-nosed attitude. "I'll be back in a while, dear," he shouted on his way out the door, leaving me thinking he probably needed solitude in his grief. The house was deathly still as the rising sun's pink radiance surfaced the top of our mountain. I stood at the window pulling myself together and yearning for the holiday-charged din of impatient grandchildren around me.

At noon Ken returned through our front gate, opened the truck door, and out flew one great tri-colored mass of fur. What on earth! The ten-month-old Keeshond (Dutch barge dog) from the shelter raced through the snow into my outstretched arms. As if we had been bosom buddies forever, we fell over in a joyous heap of emotion, this medium-sized, wiggle-tailed bundle of yips and slurps and I. She had been the sorriest looking pup in the place, her brown eyes pleading, "Please Mister, take me home with you?" Ken was smitten.

Her curly tail dancing a jig atop her back, Keesha snuffled out all the interesting scents about our ranch. The sweet pup rolled and played in the snow, acquainting herself with the kitties, donkeys, ducks and geese. Gratefully, she had no desire to chase, bite, or torment. She was a keeper.

We old fools took our dog to town for a lovely Christmas Eve dinner (Keesha's was in the form of a doggy box), and then to the pet shop for all the right toys and perfect collar. She readily stuck her nose up over silly toys, her passion only to be talked to often, to sit close, to work hard, and to be loved unconditionally. Now that reminds me of just about everyone I know. The thoroughly content tousle-haired pup held down our big feather bed as we watched yuletide services between our toes. Twelve years later she still spends precious time in her place precisely between 10:00 and 11:00 PM, whether we're there or not.

Christmas morning arrived with the children's phone calls, our voices heralding joyful anticipations of the day, and sounds of excited grandchildren ringing across the miles. Instead of hanging around pretending we weren't sadly devoid of human companionship, we grabbed our new pup and headed for our Salvation Army Church headquarters. Captain Miss B welcomed all three of us as I began setting out table decorations and Ken knuckled down peeling spuds. Keesha was so frightened she might be abandoned again, she sat quiet as a mouse in the vestibule eyeing us with trepidation while Miss B's Schnauzer jumped in circles.

More volunteers arrived to help serve ham and turkey dinners to an overflowing dining room, a place where humble families and destitute homeless dined in the shadow of Jesus' house. A place where both Ken and I rose above our Christmas blues in rebirth of our faith, savoring the meaning of the day as never before. That evening we three wearily returned through our front gate to the echoes of waterfowl and heehaws lamenting their belated holiday fare. But it was such a good tired, the kind that firmly commits to memory that sharing and giving is the way of God, our most blessed Christmas ever.

~Kathe Campbell

The Wreath Makers

Strangers are just friends waiting to happen.
~Rod McKuen

My Christmas comes in October, with the first sound of migrating geese and the cooler night temperatures that sadly usher in summer's final end. I am a wreath maker, and on this particular October morning I have driven to the small local greenhouse where the remnants of hollyhocks cling to a fence. Perennials have been put back in the ground, the landscape is awash in shades of browns and grays, and the last of the brightly-colored fall leaves blow across the driveway. I have made this trip every year for eight years. There is a horse trailer parked near the workshop, where my coworkers have begun to unload forty-pound bundles of fresh balsam that have just arrived from up north. In seven weeks, we will use about eighteen tons of balsam to create more than 4,000 wreaths, the majority of which are made for the area Boy Scouts to use as a fundraiser.

We are a small and varied work force. Seasonal work coupled with changing lifestyles create yearly turnover, and with the exception of one or two regular workers, we arrive as strangers. We are not here to get rich, and this occupation would not be considered a good career move. We are, instead, homemakers, retirees, students and the currently unemployed.

We assemble in a small building that has been cleaned and converted into a workshop stocked with yards of red ribbon, pine cones and brightly-colored miniature packages. Plastic berries and poinsettias nestle next to the boxes of thin wire, and empty metal wreath rings of varying sizes are stacked near the two homemade machines that bend the ring prongs to secure the balsam.

The assorted politics, religion, social and economic standing that may define us with other groups, slowly give way to the things that bind us. For our short time working together, we become liberated from those classifications and characterizations, and we drift into a transitory relationship that does not require our adherence to be anything or anyone other than just ourselves.

There is a trick to snapping the boughs so the small bundles look like fans, and our workforce is split into two groups—those who snap boughs and those who decorate the wreaths. Amid the continuing background sound of SNAP, SNAP, SNAP, hard work and a relaxed atmosphere seem to smooth out the rough edges in our lives. It may start with a joke from the quick wit of a seventeen-year-old who, while carrying two large bundles of pine branches, declares he is having a "bough movement." More like children at play than adults at work, it is the laughter that rings most clear in my memory.

With the lack of judgment come sanctuary and an ease in which we confide to each other things which we hesitate to tell even those closest to us. We regale each other with the stories of our most embarrassing moments, we discuss our physical fears and ailments, and we merge into the comfort of camaraderie.

Thanks to a local radio station that gets the season going early, the workshop is filled with the sounds of holiday music, and by the end of the season, the barn is filled to capacity with the smell of pine and crafted greenery to add a touch of Christmas warmth to homes nearby.

Few of us will return next season, but for that brief time, our daily lives take on a slight shift in perspective. Our voices heard, our eccentricities accepted, and an awareness of basic human kindness and commonality of spirit gently fill our souls. It's a funny thing about Christmas, sometimes the gifts you need most come early.

~Pamela Underhill Altendorf

When Christmas "Fell" on a Thursday

Simplicity is the ultimate sophistication.
~Leonardo da Vinci

No, December 25th is not what the calendar read when my husband and I made a very early Thursday morning trip to our local shopping mall. But it might as well have. For weeks all the light poles and storefronts for blocks around had been adorned with festive Christmas symbols, and the papers were packed with colorful urgent ads.

But Christmas was still more than two weeks away. My birthday came first. "Now please pick out a gift for yourself," Don urged. "You know I haven't the slightest idea what to get you."

"All right, all right," I agreed. "But straight to the mall, straight home again, okay? We need to get the tree and everything out and start decorating. After all, we're going to have the grandkids here Christmas Day, and I don't want them to miss out on a single family tradition."

Entering the mall by one entrance, we rushed to the nearest store, where I picked up a gift card for myself (to shop with later). Then we rushed right out another entrance. An entrance that had just been hosed down.

Slipping on the wet concrete, down I went. And there I stayed.

"Sorry, dear," the urgent-care doctor informed me, "but you've broken your foot. A classic Jones Fracture. That means you need a splint and some crutches. Keep your broken foot up in the air and don't put any weight on it."

Easy for him to say. A splint with open toes in the wintertime? Brrr! But the crutches were even worse. Have you ever tried hopping up steps with crutches, while one foot's stuck out in front of you? Blam! Face down again, this time smashing both knees. Bye-bye, crutches.

So for my real birthday present that year I got a wheelchair and a visit to another doctor. "Classic Jones Fracture," he agreed, as he cut off my new splint. "That means you need surgery, not this. I'll set up an appointment for you this week."

But when I arrived at the surgical center, I got still another opinion. "Yes," the surgeon announced, after studying my X-rays, "you do have a classic Jones Fracture. But that means you don't need surgery; you need an orthopedic boot."

"Wrong!" I protested. "What I need is to be able to have this whole thing go away so I can be normal again! I still have all my Christmas shopping and decorating and baking and everything to do!"

He smiled, but he still gave me the "boot"—a Darth Vader-like contraption that armor-plated me from knee to toe. At this point, Christmas was now clearly impossible! I mean, even everyday life was almost impossible! The wheelchair wouldn't fit through half the doors in our home. My husband had to take over all my housekeeping chores—and his eyes began to glaze over with all the new skills he suddenly had to learn.

But it got worse. Suddenly my husband's glazed eyes took on a new meaning. "Don!" I cried. "You're burning up with fever!"

After his diagnosis of acute sinusitis and bronchitis, I decided, "All right, God, that's the last straw. Christmas is now out of the question. It's history."

But just before December 25th, Don got better. I got more used to my wheelchair. And we both agreed that, one way or another, we would celebrate Christmas that year!

This meant changes, of course. Instead of decking the entire house "with boughs of holly," we closed off all rooms except the ones I could move around in with my wheelchair. We put up no decorations except for our Christmas tree. Unable to attach our usual balls and ornaments, I flung red plastic poinsettia blossoms all over it instead. Right from my wheelchair. Guess what? It was beautiful!

More changes: Instead of rising at four to prepare my traditional turkey dinner, I ordered a ready-to-go meal from our local grocery deli. Paper plates replaced my china. Since I couldn't get back to the mall to shop, most of my presents were online orders or gift cards. And I learned that all the vacuuming, sweeping and scrubbing needed to get ready for the big day could be done from a wheelchair. It took me twice as long, but I got a real kick out of proving I could do it!

I even made it to our traditional Christmas Eve party at a beloved family member's apartment three flights up (and no elevator). After crawling up on my hands and knees, I was carried back down afterward like a prized trophy by a courageous young man—to everyone's applause.

But one thing didn't change: When our children and grandchildren finally poured in the front door on Christmas Day, it was to shouts of joy and hugs and giggles as always. Appetites were just as vigorous for my readymade meal as they had been for my homemade ones. And exclamations of "Oh, this is great!" and "You shouldn't have—but I'm glad you did" bubbled around the tree just as they always did.

Finally our troops headed home with their new treasures, leaving Don and me surrounded by half-eaten pies, used paper plates, bags of discarded Christmas wrapping—and warm-fuzzy memories.

Yes, Christmas "fell" on a Thursday. But it rose again on a Monday just as the calendar said it should—glorious and glowing and goosebumpy grand, as always. Straight from our hearts.

~Bonnie Compton Hanson

Christmas Gift From Heaven

There are things that we don't want to happen but have to accept,
things we don't want to know but have to learn,
and people we can't live without but have to let go... and go on.
~Author Unknown

This past Christmas was going to be a tough one for my family. It would be our first Christmas without our dad, who had lost his battle with cancer. I didn't even want to think about Christmas—and I sure didn't want to celebrate. I have been, and always will be, a devout Daddy's girl. And, so—when my mom called me eight days before Christmas, there was still no Christmas tree, not the first Christmas decoration, nothing. I was trying to forget that Christmastime was here at all.

My mom lives six hours away from us. Since I am the only sibling who works from home, it was my job to drive down and bring her back up for Christmas with the family. She asked if I had decorated the house yet. No. That wasn't the answer she wanted to hear—she had put up a Christmas tree and she lived alone. I had two kids—what was I doing? Get the tree put up and get ready for Christmas. I am forty-two years old and still afraid of my mom—so, I put that tree up. And, picked up my mom and brought her home for Christmas.

I refused to get in the Christmas spirit, however—not without my daddy! I wouldn't! Six months before, I had watched my dad take his last breath—and I did not want to be happy. Although I was raised in a Christian home and my dad never wavered in his faith for one minute, I didn't want any part of it now. I just wanted to be left alone to die a slow death—I didn't want anyone to speak to me, I didn't want anyone to hug me or touch me. I couldn't even hug my own children. I wanted to close the world out and just sit in front of my computer and pretend that I could feel nothing.

I never stopped to think what I was doing to my family—my mom who had lost her best friend of forty-one years, my kids who needed a mother to help them get through the pain of losing a very special granddaddy, my husband who had given up his family for three months so that I could care for my dad, my sisters and brother who had also lost their dad. I couldn't think about them—all I could think about was the pain that I was feeling—and the fact that I never wanted to feel it again.

My dad had taught me how to be a Christian. He had taught me about the wonderful place that he would be living when he said goodbye to us. The days before he died, he was in his own little world—his mind had already left and he was looking ahead. The night before he began his journey home, he "woke up" from that stupor, raised his head and sang "Peace in the Valley" in that clear, beautiful bass voice that we had all loved since childhood. He wanted us to be happy for him—he was at peace—yet here I was. I couldn't be happy for him because it hurt too much to be without him.

A couple of days before Christmas, Mom told me that she had a gift for me. She didn't want me to wait until Christmas Day to open it—she wanted me to have it now. Thinking it would be a book on how to deal with loss, I agreed to open it—another book I could hide in. (Since the age of four, when I learned to read, my gifts have always been books.) So, I sat down beside her to open my book. But, what was this? There was no book in that box! In that box was an ornament for my Christmas tree. Mom told me to read it. I did. There was a poem on the front—"Merry Christmas from Heaven" by

John Wm. Mooney, Jr. It was a beautiful poem. And on the back was inscribed, "I Love You, Daddy."

I walked outside so that my mom wouldn't see my tears—and I let go, let go of the pain, let go of the tears, I just let go. When I came back inside the house, there, waiting for me was this wonderful woman—who, amidst the greatest pain of her life, thought not of herself, but of healing her children. The most special Christmas gift I will ever receive, given to me with the love that only a mother can feel, began the healing process. And, as only a daddy can, mine reached down and filled my heart once again with love with a Christmas gift from Heaven.

~Cindy Holcomb

The Christmas Lesson

The human spirit is stronger than anything that can happen to it.
~C.C. Scott

"We'll get you to do Emma's treatment tonight," the charge nurse said to me as she was doing her workload assignment. "It's difficult and takes time, but Emma will put you at ease with it."

It was Christmas Eve, and I was looking forward to the morning, when my children would see what Santa had brought them. Christmas is a hectic time for young, working mothers, and I was no exception. I was totally fatigued. There had been so many Christmas concerts and parties, and shopping, baking, and all that we do at Christmastime.

During the holidays, to accommodate the vacation schedules of the employees, our hospital reassigned nurses to where the need was greatest. I had already worked a day shift on this particular unit, and had heard about Emma, a frail little eighty-year-old lady who suffered in silence. Advanced carcinoma was gradually destroying Emma's face, exposing blood vessels and leaving her prone to hemorrhage.

Emma was on a progressive care unit, and many of its patients would be going home the next day, Christmas, to spend time with their families. I read Emma's chart and realized that going home was not an option for her. She required too much care to be eligible for a nursing home, so she stayed where she was on the unit, the place she now thought of as home.

I went to her room and introduced myself.

"Do you like my tree, dear?" she asked.

Yes, I told her. Though she could barely see it, Emma had a wonderful tree with twinkling lights, and ornaments donated by her nurses. Her tape player quietly played Christmas music, and before I started her treatment, Emma asked me to change the music. I chose a tape, put it in the player, and "Silent Night," my favorite Christmas carol, started softly playing. I glanced out the window at the glistening snow which was reflecting the Christmas lights that were part of the hospital's effort to make it feel more like home for those who could not go home for Christmas.

I started to remove the huge bandages that covered Emma's head and face. I was ill-prepared for how disfigured she was from the carcinoma, how involved her treatment was, and tried hard not to let her see my shock and disbelief. I had never, ever, seen facial deformity so severe. I found myself sweating, and my heart racing.

Emma could barely see, and spoke in a whisper. "You're not scared, are you dear?" she asked in a whisper. I assured her I was not. Tiny, frail and ill, she endured her treatments without complaint, often reassuring me that she was okay, and not to be upset for her because it wasn't too painful if her treatment was done gently.

"You're new though, and very young. Do you have children, dear?" she queried. (To Emma everyone was "dear.") I told her about my little children and how excited they were about Santa.

Then I felt her hands on my face. Emma said she wanted to know what I looked like, and remarked that I had my hair pulled up under my nurse's cap. She asked if she could touch my long hair. I stopped the treatment, removed the gloves, took off my cap and let my hair fall loose. She ran her hands through my hair, and told me about the long hair she had as a young woman, how her husband had loved it, how he would tell her how attractive she was and how proud he was of her and their children. She told me about the Christmas traditions they kept, how she loved him, and how she was relieved that, having predeceased her years ago, he did not have to see her like this.

Emma's care took over an hour, and she talked in her whispering voice as I did her treatment with a lump in my throat, and listened to the soft sounds of the Christmas carols filling the room.

When I was through, Emma asked me to sit for a moment. The night was quiet so I sat beside her as she held my hands. She continued to talk, and give me advice, which overwhelmed me. She told me she thought I was tired, and she remembered being tired when her children were small and Christmas so demanding. From under those heavy bandages, she advised me to never take my health for granted, to be thankful I could see and hear, that I could dance around my house with my baby girl in my arms as I told her I did, that I could drive a car, read a book, laugh and sing, and do all the things that make up a life, things I had never thought about to any degree. She felt my wide wedding band, and expressed how she wished she could see it.

A tear fell from my face unto her hand from the tears I could no longer hold back.

She told me not to cry, that she had accepted her fate, and I should too. Emma made me promise to live life fully while I was able, thanked me for my tenderness with her painful treatment, and wished me a Merry Christmas. The music was still softly playing.

When I left her room that night, I knew that my experience with Emma was exceptional. A weak, elderly woman, clinging to life, understood the angst of a young nurse, wanted to touch my hair, wanted to talk, and to give advice to a young nurse and mother. She made me aware of just how much I took for granted, and reminded me to remember the reason for the season.

Because I was then off for the holidays and after that I returned to work in the operating room, I never saw Emma again. That Christmas Eve with Emma was thirty years ago, but I recall it with amazing clarity. I believe our paths crossed for a reason.

Emma reminded me that I should slow down and treasure all that I had in spite of my busy life. This is especially true at Christmas, when amidst the tumult, frenzied activity and hurried preparations, the true meaning of Christmas is often lost. It was an unforgettable lesson.

~Bonnie Jarvis-Lowe

The Goofy Monkey

Let your tears come. Let them water your soul.
~Eileen Mayhew

The Christmas season has crept up on me again. I'm feeling particularly melancholy this year, the year that marks my thirtieth Christmas without my parents. I agree to shop with a friend, hoping to find some spirit to celebrate the season. We meander through crowded kiosks in a local collectibles shop named Studebaker's. My mind wanders, taking me back to happier times. I see a red and white enameled kitchen table, jadite bowls, a bedroom set just like the one in my mother's bedroom. I know it is called waterfall because the wood grain runs over the rounded edges of the pieces, like water running over Niagara Falls. Mom had told me that she and Dad honeymooned there. It was the farthest she'd ever traveled in her whole life. The world was so much smaller then....

Thirty years ago, on Christmas Eve, my mother was dying of advanced breast cancer. I was nineteen, trying my best to make it a good Christmas for her. I'd decorated our scrawny, artificial tree with the patchwork of mismatched ornaments we'd hung together every year. I'd baked butter cookies and apple pie, in a feeble attempt to recreate the smells and tastes that might remind us of happier holidays. Dad and my younger brother Billy stayed in the background, for Mom had trained them well. These were her jobs and I was being handed the baton.

That afternoon, I'd noticed shiny, wet tracks that formed as quiet tears rolled down Mom's cheeks. My first thought was "Oh no, what am I doing wrong?" as if everything somehow centered on me.

"Mom, what's the matter?" I asked.

"I don't have anything to give you for Christmas," she said.

"That doesn't matter. Don't worry about me."

She placed twenty dollars in my hand and said, "Please go to the avenue and buy yourself something. I want you to have a gift under the tree."

I knew my mother could not be left alone for any length of time. She was terribly weak and had trouble getting up from the chair. She had fallen a few times trying to walk from room to room. I was keeping a vigil and wanted to be there to help her if she needed me.

After making sure she was comfortable, I quickly grabbed my jacket and ran the two blocks to Central Avenue. Loft's Candy Store was on the corner. They sold homemade chocolates and a small selection of gifts. Something caught my eye as I approached the entrance to the store. In the window, looking at me from its perch on a display shelf, sat the goofiest ceramic monkey I had ever seen. It had a big, pink ball attached to its mouth, as if it had been chewing Bazooka gum and was trying very hard to blow a bubble.

I bought a quarter pound of Mom's favorite chocolate-covered crackers, a box of thin mints for her to give to Dad and a box of chocolate-covered cherries, which they both enjoyed. But I still hadn't bought something she could give to me. I asked the cashier if I could buy the monkey. She grinned and said, "Everyone comes into the store smiling because of that silly monkey, but no one has offered to take it home. Of course you can buy it." The lady took great care as she blanketed my monkey in tissue, placed it in a white box and wrapped it in the same Loft's paper that was used to wrap the candy.

When I got home, Mom was sleeping. Carefully, I arranged the gifts under the tree. Later that evening, when we opened them, the Bazooka bubble-blowing monkey made us all laugh. The most important thing was, the monkey made Mom laugh.

That Christmas Eve was the last time we were happy as a family.

Mom died in January of her illness. Dad died in February of a broken heart (I was told), and life, as I knew it, was over.

For many years I was angry with Mom and Dad. I thought she had accepted her cancer without a fight. I blamed my father for giving up, checking out, not loving us enough to stick around. I couldn't look at family photographs, fearful I might weaken the wall I'd built around myself to hide my pain from the world. I took pride in the fact that I never cried. That monkey sat on a shelf in my room for a few years but eventually it disappeared. Losing it was no great misfortune to me at the time, since it, too, had become a potent reminder of my loss.

I was diagnosed with breast cancer at the age of forty-two. I opted for the most aggressive treatment that was available. Throughout my illness, especially when suffering the nausea and fatigue associated with its side effects, I wanted my mother more than anything in the world. Vulnerable, a little girl again, I wanted the coolness of her hand as she'd touch my hot forehead to diagnose a fever. I remembered the way she'd held my long hair out of the way when I threw up, and how she'd sit on my bed when I was sick, softly stroking the side of my face. The wall I had built weakened and, for the first time, I dug through boxes of photos and allowed myself to remember. Those pictures seemed as if they belonged to another life, not mine, it was all so long ago. I smiled when I discovered a snapshot of the goofy monkey. The wall crumbled and the tears I had not been able to cry for so many years began to fall.

During my illness, I became determined to learn all that I could about the disease that had stolen my family and had returned to try to destroy me. I learned that at the time of my mom's diagnosis she really didn't have many choices. My anger melted away. Instead, I felt sad. Sad, because if I'd known more about cancer when I was nineteen, maybe I'd have been better able to understand. I experienced firsthand the fear she must have felt, and realized the extent of her love for me. Throughout her illness, her primary purpose had been to protect me and to allow me to remain a "kid" for as long as she could.

So here I am in Studebaker's, killing time until the holiday season is behind me. As my friend holds up a tiny figurine of a sleeping cat, I notice, sitting on the floor, partially hidden, an exact duplicate of that goofy monkey, blowing its big, pink Bazooka-bubble-gum-bubble! I pick it up and begin to cry happy tears. I cradle the little monkey in my arms and carry it to the cashier. She gently blankets it in tissue, just like the lady in Loft's did, so many years ago, bringing my life full circle and delivering my Christmas present from heaven.

~Ann M. Sheridan

Christmas Magic

Have Yourself
a Merry Little Christmas

The Missing Stocking

*A mother is a person who seeing there are only four pieces of pie for five
people, promptly announces she never did care for pie.*
~Tenneva Jordan

uddenly I felt my cheeks turn red with embarrassment. How
could I have never noticed? Every Christmas my mother
enjoyed creating special memories and traditions for her family. Mom loved Christmas—the shopping, baking, decorating, music,
gifts... even the hustle and bustle the season brings. Her enthusiasm
was contagious and that encouraged my brother, sister, and me to
experience the joy and wonder of Christmas. Although Santa came
to our home, we were taught that the real reason for the season was
to celebrate the birth of our Messiah—Jesus Christ.

Many years have passed since I was a child. Yet I can still smell
the aroma of Mom's sugar cookies baking, as she prepared a special
treat for her family and for Santa. These delicacies were a sure sign
that Christmas Day was near.

On Christmas Eve my mother laid all our stockings under the
beautifully decorated pine tree my father had picked out and cut
down in the forest. Later, in the middle of the night, Santa filled the
stockings.

The next morning we excitedly opened our gifts, leaving our
Christmas stockings for last. Santa always stuffed our stockings full

of tiny toys, trinkets, nuts, oranges, apples, and colorful hard candies in various shapes, sizes, and flavors.

In my twenties, I went Christmas shopping with a friend. She began looking for a small gift to place in her mother's stocking.

"You fix a Christmas stocking for your mother?" I asked.

"Yes," she replied. "Every year I fill a stocking with little goodies and have it waiting for her on Christmas morning. I couldn't bear for my mother to not have a Christmas stocking, especially since she prepares one for everyone else."

That's when I felt my cheeks flush with embarrassment. I realized my mother had not had a Christmas stocking for as long as I remembered. And, even worse, no one had noticed her stocking was missing.

My sister and I determined to start a tradition of our own that year. Excited, we bought jewelry, candy, socks, and an orange. We placed them in a small, red stocking. Christmas morning we snuck it under the tree while Mom was busy preparing breakfast.

Eagerly we waited to see Mom's reaction. She passed out everyone's stockings; then noticed an extra one. She picked up the stocking and read the tag: "To Betty Ann—Love, Santa."

Amazement crossed her face. "Is this stocking really for me?"

We smiled and nodded.

Tears glistened in Mom's eyes. "It's been so long… since I've had a Christmas stocking," she said. "Thank you."

Though I don't remember the gifts I received that year, I have never forgotten how thrilled my mother was to receive a simple, red stocking. Seeing her reaction was the most precious gift of all. And once again, she taught me about the joy and wonder of Christmas… that it is indeed more blessed to give than to receive.

~Teresa Ann Maxwell

Ex's and Oh's

For the spirit of Christmas fulfils the greatest hunger of mankind.
~Loring A. Schuler

Love is a funny thing, isn't it? It comes in all shapes and sizes, and you just never know when or where you're going to find it. Sometimes you know exactly where to find it; sometimes it finds you, grabbing hold of your lapels and shaking some sense back into your ever-hardening heart. And then there are times when you find that love was right there where you left it — not lost, really — like your car keys or the husband you divorced nine years ago, a man you had one partial life and two beautiful children with.

It was Christmas Day 2008 when I unexpectedly found love again. Oh, it wasn't the romantic kind of love that can go from inferno to fizzle in sixty seconds; it was the old, familiar kind — the slow burn — that can only happen between two people who once shared a life, the kind of love that can only happen between those same two people who shared the experience of giving life to two beautiful children. That's the kind of love I'm talking about, and to be honest with you, I didn't even see it coming.

He was just walking me to my car — Billy, that is, my ex-husband of nine years. I had just dropped our two teenage boys, Billy Boy and Alec, off at his house on Christmas morning. It's been our tradition since the divorce. After powering down breakfast and rifling through stockings at my place, I pack up the car with my boys and a couple of armloads of Christmas booty and head over to their dad's house, never bothering to change out of our pajamas.

It's at his house that we exchange gifts and pleasantries and then—after a bundle of Christmas hugs and kisses from my kids—I head back home with empty arms to spend the rest of the day with my mother. Oh, I know; it's not idyllic, but it's as close as we can get, considering.

Over the past couple of years our little tradition has included the new woman in Billy's life, Lisa. And even though I like her and she is good to my boys, it's a little disturbing when you find yourself sharing your family with another woman—and on such a day as Christmas, too. But such is life when you're a broken family. You learn to deal with it. I suppose it was a little harder on me this year after having just lost my job; I guess you could say that I was already feeling a little emotional, seemingly alone and left out in the cold as it was.

"Natalie, you know that I love you, right?" Billy whispered from out of the blue as we ambled toward my Jeep. His eyes unexpectedly welled up with tears as he—the consummate tough guy from Long Island—stood barefoot on that cold sidewalk in December in his green flannel pajamas, wearing his heart on his sleeve. "I will always love you."

Apparently he was feeling a tad schmaltzy, too. I hadn't heard the words "I love you" fall from his lips in a long while and even though I was completely touched by them, it was the tears in those sentimental green eyes of his that caught me off guard, those familiar eyes that brought back so many wonderful Christmas memories.

"I know," I whispered, my heart catching in my throat, as I, too, stood outside in the early morning hours of that cold Christmas day in my red, snowman pajamas, tears welling up in my own green eyes. "I love you, too."

It's not quite the exchange one might come to expect between two ex-spouses with an ocean's worth of water under the bridge. But before I knew it, we were locked in a long embrace, both of us weeping uncontrollably. What is it about Christmas that brings people together, temporarily lowering their defenses, those protective walls we build around our hearts?

It was as if—for just a moment—we were all alone, the two of us, held together by the warmth of what was and what is now our family, either that or by the static cling from our flannel pajamas. Who could tell? In any case, we were encapsulated in a proverbial snow-globe moment and we were both a little shaken. Meanwhile, deep down inside—in places I don't like to talk about at parties—I knew that Lisa and the boys were waiting inside for him; she would be making breakfast and Christmas memories all her own with my family—my children. That's not always an easy pill to swallow, even though I know in my heart I wouldn't change a thing—even if I could.

"We have two great kids together, Nat, and I wouldn't have wanted to take this walk with anyone but you," Billy breathed, giving me that same sideways (deliberate) grin that both my boys give me when they really mean something.

"Ditto," I smiled back.

I reached up onto my tiptoes, my arms squeezing evermore tightly around his neck, hot tears streaming down my cool cheeks and into the thickness of his shoulder. His arms tightened around me, too. And with all the love and sentimentality that Christmas brings with it, as well as all of the love and sentimentality that balls up between two people over the course of eighteen years, Billy and I gave each other a warm peck on the lips and wished each other a happy Christmas.

And it was then—as he tucked me into my car, shutting the door behind me—that I realized that even though life has a way of breaking our hearts—and even breaking apart our families at times—love is never really lost. In fact it can be found in some of the simplest of places—many of them locked tight in those Christmas memories both old and new.

~Natalie June Reilly

My Special
Christmas Doll

Pleasure is the flower that passes; remembrance, the lasting perfume.
~Jean de Boufflers

A special doll named Katherine lives in my four-year-old granddaughter's room. The doll perches on the window seat, arms out and head cocked a bit. Muted red polish covers her fingernails, and a few of her fingers and toes are chipped. The doll's dark blond hair could use a bit of attention, for it looks limp and badly in need of a stylist.

"This was my mommy's doll," Jordan tells me.

I pick up the doll, smooth the flower-print flannel gown she wears. "A long time ago, she belonged to me." I give Katherine a little hug and place her on the window seat again.

Jordan grasps my hand. "I know that, Grandma. Will you tell me about her?"

I scoop Jordan into my arms. "Time for bed now, but maybe tomorrow we'll talk about Katherine." I tuck her into bed and kiss her twice.

Later that evening, I sip a cup of tea and think about the doll Santa brought me more than sixty years ago. The decades slip away and I am six years old again. My parents and little brother are asleep, still snuggled under warm comforters, but I'm tip-toeing down the hallway early on Christmas morning. It's so quiet and very dark in the hallway, but I know my destination and continue on.

When I reach the living room, the early morning light filters through the windows. I kneel in front of the decorated Christmas tree, and a little shiver runs up my spine. It's cold in our apartment, but the shiver comes from what I spy next to the gaily-wrapped packages. Santa left me a beautiful doll looking very much like Shirley Temple. She's dressed in a bridal gown made of a snowy, gossamer material. Tiny satin rosettes run from waist to hem, and lace adorns the neckline and sleeves. The matching veil, trimmed in lace, surrounds her head like a billowy cloud. A white nightgown and soft blue robe lie beside her. It's the kind seen only in the movies. So pretty! Her dark blond hair curls to perfection, and her eyes appear to glow. I inch as close as I dare, for I know I should not touch her yet, not until Mommy and Daddy wake up. For now, the anticipation of holding her seems to be enough. I name her Katherine while I wait for my family to wake up.

I played with Katherine for many years, then saved her in hopes I might pass my special doll to a daughter someday. My daughter, Karen, loved the doll too, even though she no longer had the original clothes. Once again, Katherine made a little girl happy. Karen secreted the doll away in hopes that she, too, could pass her on to her own child someday. Now, Karen's daughter, Jordan, is the keeper of the doll. Though a bit tattered, Katherine's smile is just as sweet, and her blue eyes still appear to shine. Even her wilted curls are precious to me and to Karen.

I think one day Jordan will feel the same, for she is our special family doll and always will be. I will tell my granddaughter about the Christmas I found Katherine under the tree. This one cherished doll holds generations of my family within her heart. I hope Jordan will have a daughter one day so that this chain of love might continue.

~Nancy Julien Kopp

It's the Size of Your Love

What greater thing is there for human souls than to feel that they
are joined for life — to be with each other in silent unspeakable memories.
~George Eliot

Our grown-up sons and their families have always filled our holidays with delight, but one Christmas stands out above all the others. After Christmas Eve dinner and the opening of gifts we relaxed with full tummies in front of the crackling fire. The long legs of the men in my household sprawled across the carpet.

"Mom and Dad," Lane, our youngest son, began, "it's so good to be back home. I want you to know what you mean to me. I had such a happy childhood here. Remember our cat, Old Tom, and how we all teased him?"

"Yeah," Lance added. "Remember when Mark and I got in a paint fight and got white paint all over the brick wall?"

"It's still there too," their daddy interrupts.

"Remember the tricks we did with Chow and the dish towel?" Mark replies. "And we'll never forget the miles you drove to see us play ball."

"Or all the rock hunting trips and picnics," the boys reminisced.

They set me up every time. I think they like to see me cry.

In the wee hours of the night, our house becomes strangely

quiet again. Those little boys who grew up so quickly were back in their own beds. The same familiar refrain from previous years echoed from grandchildren: "Good night, Mommy. Good night, Daddy. I love you."

The same clock chimed its soothing sounds, blessing me that everyone had come home once more. Grandchildren slept in sleeping bags on the floor. People snored all over the place.

The next morning brought the chaos of taking turns for showers, drying hair and doing laundry. The dining room held "shoulder to shoulder" chairs but hungry people didn't seem to mind.

On Sunday morning everyone flew around getting ready for church. I cooked breakfast in shifts and found myself apologizing for the lack of room to my daughter-in-law Connie. Her reply is something I will hold in my heart forever: "It isn't the size of your house. It's the size of your love."

Her statement reminded me what family is all about, especially at Christmas.

Several days later my beloved ones started packing to go home. I resolved not to cry. Who am I kidding? It's the love I have that brings the tears. I watched them drive away as far as I could see. My husband took me in his arms as we waved goodbye.

It's all about the size of your love.

My Connie taught me that families are forever, especially at Christmastime.

~Joan Clayton

The Package

Christmas is not as much about opening our presents as opening our hearts.
~Janice Maeditere

As surely as turkey and dressing followed jack-o'-lanterns, every December since I left home a package from my mother arrived signaling the official beginning of the holidays in my household. Upon its arrival, I would place the package in a prominent place and ponder the ethics of opening a parcel clearly labeled with the admonition, "DO NOT OPEN 'TIL CHRISTMAS!" In the battle of ethics versus curiosity, ethics never prevailed.

I rationalized, "What if Mom sent perishables?" I do confess that in all those years, I never opened a parcel containing tuna sandwiches and potato salad.

The packages did contain a mixture of items that were so varied and unrelated, they were worthy of inclusion in a time capsule prepared in a moment of pure whimsy. Over the years, there were jewelry caddies, address books covered in simulated zebra skin, swizzle sticks with cute sayings like "Alexander Graham Bell had hang-ups," and a gold electroplated Rudolph the Red Nosed Reindeer necklace, complete with "genuine ruby Nose."

The one constant was my mom's date and nut loaf, not to be confused with fruitcake. The date and nut loaves became legendary among my friends and work associates. The day after Thanksgiving, my friends became unusually solicitous. "How's your mom?" Or "Have you heard from your mom lately?" Finally, when subtlety failed,

"Has the package arrived yet and when will we get some of that wonderful cake?"

As my children became worldly enough to understand the package also contained things for them, they joined the post-Thanksgiving vigil. They viewed the package as a mystical link to a grandmother they rarely saw, but were utterly convinced loved them without reservation. My children were quick to differentiate between the somewhat conditional nature of Santa's gifts and their grandmother's, which were given with no expectation of scholastic achievement or moral fortitude. This phenomenon puzzled me until I had grandchildren.

The package never contained big-ticket items and we never expected any. The pleasure came from not knowing what to expect. My mom had a talent for finding mutant variations of rather ordinary things. I remember the wooden salad spoons with hula dancer handles, the Indian Head pennies, and the children's sunglasses with pink plastic ballet dancers on the frames. My daughter wore them to dance class and was a sugarplum sensation.

An item that perplexed and then delighted me with its diabolical logic, when explained, was a book bag emblazoned with the name KIM. I did not have a child named Kim. Mom explained that she had heard on *Oprah* that it was not a good idea to allow young children to carry articles with their names in plain view. Some "bad person" could trick children into believing he knew them because he called them by name. Since my daughter's name was not Kim, she could not be tricked. Flawless in its simplicity.

Mom was one of those rare people who understood completely there was more to gift giving than going to Macy's. She knew anticipation far outweighed dollar value.

Even though we knew the package never arrived earlier than December 7th, we started actively discussing it at Halloween and then seriously looking for it after Thanksgiving. By the time it arrived, we had worked ourselves into a giddy frenzy. We adopted an almost Victorian formality when accepting the package from the postman: It's here! Let the season begin.

My mom died in mid-October, too early for the package to have been mailed.

While cleaning Mom's house in preparation for sale, I found a package, wrapped in brown paper, tied with string, addressed to me. I have never opened that last package, but every Christmas, sometime around December 7th, I take the package, now somewhat tattered, and gently place it under our Christmas tree.

Let the festivities begin!

~Barbara D'Amario

Little Boxes

The only gift is a portion of thyself.
~Ralph Waldo Emerson

Mom wanted to go Christmas shopping. It was hard to understand why exactly—she was so sick at this point, and if she would just give us a list, we could take care of this for her—but no, she wanted to go Christmas shopping. One day when her pain seemed relatively under control, we put aside our "sensible" thoughts about whether Christmas shopping was an appropriate activity for someone terminally ill, and we decided to go.

Somehow, we managed to get her, the wheelchair, little Joshua, his stroller, and the rest of the gang packed into the minivan and we were off to the mall. We took the diaper bag for Joshua and a bag full of pain meds for Mom. It was December 23rd, and we felt full of mischief.

The mall was packed, obviously, and it was helpful that we had the handicapped parking permit, so that we didn't have to battle it out for parking. We took turns pushing Mom in her wheelchair and Joshua in his stroller. Most people were pretty decent about getting out of our way. Joshua smiled over at his grandma, wheeling along next to him. He actually sat in his stroller without complaint.

Soon after we arrived, after the initial giddiness of the outing wore off, it seemed as though Mom got a little overwhelmed. We started in a department store, but it was hard to wheel her through the racks of clothes and gift items. We tried to figure out what she wanted to look at, leaving her in the aisles while we brought things over to her.

Eventually she got a little upset. "I just want to go over and look at things, like everyone else." Once we understood this, we made greater efforts to wheel her through those tight spaces.

We went out into the main part of the mall and she finally told us what she was really looking for—little boxes. She wasn't looking for traditional gifts at all, and this caught me off guard. She was looking for little boxes in which she could display her most prized pieces of jewelry, to give them away to her loved ones on her final Christmas.

We found some little boxes at a watch store, and returned home soon after. Mom was exhausted from the outing.

On Christmas morning, Melissa, Mark's then fiancée, now wife, was the first to open her little box from Mom. It was one of Mom's favorites—a necklace with matching earrings, made of topaz. Melissa looked both stunned and deeply touched.

I knew what would be in my own little box, opened a bit later in the morning. It contained a marvelous diamond pendant on a spectacular gold omega chain. My dad had given Mom this piece on her 50th birthday, five years earlier. It was her most beloved piece of jewelry, and she had given it to me.

"Don't save it for special occasions," she told me. I couldn't answer. The lump in my throat made it impossible to speak.

Despite Mom's advice, most days the diamond pendant on its omega chain simply sits in its little box, tucked away in my armoire. When I do wear it, typically on special occasions, I feel as though I'm carrying around a little piece of her.

Just like Mom, it is beautiful and sparkling and never fails to attract admiration. But I am much too afraid of losing it, of losing this little piece of her, to wear it every day.

~Lisa Pawlak

Always Room in Our Inn

We should give as we would receive, cheerfully, quickly, and without hesitation; for there is no grace in a benefit that sticks to the fingers.
~Seneca

Kenny Rogers was serenading us with "I'll Be Home for Christmas" from the stereo as the aroma of cinnamon created a holiday atmosphere in the kitchen. "Mom, Jen's on the phone," Becca called excitedly from the family room.

"Really? I wonder if they had to change plans?" I answered feeling an unwelcome knot forming in my stomach. Because of the high cost, phone calls from our daughter on mission in an orphanage in Mexico were rare. Shaking flour from my hands, I took the phone. "Hi, Honey, this is a nice surprise."

"Hi, Mom, how's everything in Kansas? Have you ordered snow for Christmas?"

"Well, I'm hoping, but you know Kansas. It might be seventy degrees or it could be seven. But I'm sure you didn't call to discuss the weather."

"Well, Mom, I need a huge, Huge, HUGE favor. One of my friends back at college is pregnant, and she can't let her family know. This is reprehensible in their culture, and she is really afraid of her brothers."

"And what do you want me to do?" I asked, anticipating the answer.

"Well, could she come and stay with you guys until she has the baby? She plans to place it for adoption."

Less than a week before Christmas, how could I turn away a pregnant young woman? So, I replied, "Well, I'll have to talk to your dad, but I know it'll be okay. Don't you think you should try to get her to talk with her parents first though? I really don't like being part of a family deception."

"Her mom is still in Saudi Arabia, and she hasn't seen her dad in years. I guess you've figured out who it is."

"After what you just said, it's obviously Sim," I replied, visualizing this spirited Middle Eastern beauty. "When is she coming?"

"Her last final is Friday morning, so she should be there Friday night, not long after Pete and I arrive. When will Beth and Thomas get home from college?"

"All of my sweeties are coming in Friday. I can't wait," I answered excitedly.

"I can't wait either," Becca called over my shoulder.

"Hey, Bec! Can't wait to see you too. Would talk more, but these calls are going to kill my budget!" Jen called to her sister.

"Does your flight still arrive at noon on Friday?" I asked, trying to cut it short.

"Yes. Pete said to tell you his mouth is watering for your home-made rolls. Thank you so much, Mom. Love you."

"Tell Pete I don't know. I've got lots to do at school before end of semester. Love you lots, honey," I answered, smiling at the dough drying on my hands as I hung up. Our "inn" was going to be full for Christmas. Jen would be extra cozy, sharing a room with her two sisters while we transformed her tiny, old room for Sim to have a little more privacy.

Four days later, we were enjoying a house full of noisy fun: wrapping gifts, cooking, and making last minute preparations for Christmas. The phone rang and Thomas answered it and asked, "Hey, Mom, you wanna take a weird collect call?"

When he handed me the receiver, I heard the operator ask, "Will you accept a collect call from the Vernon County jail?" Puzzled but curious, I accepted the call.

"This is Officer Kasteel from the Vernon County Sheriff's office. Is this the residence of Thomas Garrity?" he asked, as my eyes wandered to my son now lounging on the couch.

"Yes," I answered. "What's this about?"

"Well, Ma'am, we have a Christmas release policy for prisoners for good behavior. They must have a place to go, and a responsible adult has to sign them out. Mike Preston asked us to try this name and number."

"Just a second," I replied, and quickly shared this information with Thomas. "Why doesn't Mike call his parents? What's he in jail for anyway?" I asked.

"They moved to Wyoming. Long story," came the reply, as Thomas sat up.

After a brief conversation with him and the officer, we were suddenly expecting another guest. My husband Max and Thomas left to fetch Mike as a light snow began to fall, and I went upstairs to see if we had enough blankets and towels for one more person. Glancing into Thomas's small room, I thought, "It's going to be crowded, but much cozier than a jail cell." Thomas, Mike and Pete, our future son-in-law, would just have to flip for the bed or sleeping bags. When I came back down, the girls had already added another place at the dining table and were chatting and laughing as they baked waffles.

Searching through my purse for some cash, I asked, "Will someone run to Walmart before it closes and pick up something for Mike so he can have a gift under the tree? It sounds like he could use everything from deodorant to underwear."

"Oh, Mom, those aren't gifts," Beth replied, taking the cash, and giving me a sweet peck on the cheek. "Come on everybody, get your purses. Let's go shopping for practical and FUN!"

Amid squeals and laughter, the girls and Pete emptied the house on their Good Samaritan adventure.

Dinner was much later than planned, but the house seemed

to burst with fun and joy as we sat around the table for our traditional Christmas Eve supper of sausage, waffles and strawberries. Candlelight reflected in bright, happy eyes and on the tears sneaking down Sim's cheeks. I squeezed her hand and whispered, "It will all be fine." Midnight Mass seemed especially holy that night, surrounded by my family, including a young expectant mother and a "lost" wayfarer.

The next morning, Mike slept in, or pretended to sleep, so we could have a "family" Christmas. When the living room floor was covered with wrappings and ribbons, and the girls were trying on their new gifts, Thomas plopped down next to me, and threw a muscular arm over my shoulder. "Mom, would you be hurt if we rewrapped my coat and gave it to Mike?"

"Oh honey, the girls made sure Mike got a couple of nice gifts. You need a new coat so badly. Your high school letter jacket's popping at the seams."

"We can get me one from Goodwill or someplace before I go back to school. Mike didn't even have a sweatshirt to keep himself warm when we picked him up yesterday," he replied. I gave my son a hug, and went in search of tape to rewrap the coat.

Later, I watched the snow fall outside while listening to the comforting sounds of family in the background. Max joined me, wrapping an arm around my waist and noticed my brimming eyes. "You okay?" he asked.

"Absolutely wonderful. I just feel so covered with blessings and gifts from our kids. They really know the true meaning of Christmas," I answered with glistening eyes.

~Gerri Wetta-Hilger

Pajama Day

Don't underestimate the value of Doing Nothing,
of just going along, listening to all the things you can't hear,
and not bothering.
~Pooh's Little Instruction Book, *inspired by A.A. Milne*

As wonderful as Christmas Day is, for me it takes second place to December 26th—otherwise known around our house as Pajama Day. It's a tradition that came into being entirely by accident about ten years ago during a particularly hectic holiday season.

That year, Christmas Eve found my husband Steve and me staying up until close to dawn, wrapping presents and preparing for Christmas with our four kids. Just as our heads hit the pillow, the door to our two younger children's bedroom opened and we heard them sneak out. I took a nap to the sound of their excited whispers.

Christmas Day at our home is one long and joyous celebration that includes a revolving cast of family members from both sides that arrive in shifts. We host a breakfast for eight to twelve people, with a break for clean up and showers, and then begin prepping for dinner for up to twenty-five people.

I was so exhausted I found myself dozing off, head propped in hand, while sitting at the dining room table over shrimp cocktail and artichoke dip at 3:00 in the afternoon. Luckily my chef husband was in charge of dinner because I simply couldn't do it.

The next day, while poor Steve headed to work, I slept late and then curled up on the couch with the new novel he had given me for Christmas. The kids played quietly with their toys and it was a lovely day all around. When Steve came home, I was still in my pajamas and we had leftovers for dinner. The day ended with me finishing the novel in front of a crackling fire.

Afterwards I realized it was probably the best day I had had all year and declared it a new tradition. It has grown ever since. Now, I build a big fire in the fireplace early in the day and pull out the bed in the sleeper sofa. Everyone brings his or her pillow and favorite blanket. We cuddle, snooze, watch movies, play games and read books. At some point in the middle of the day, I take a shower, but I don't get dressed. I just put clean pajamas on. Even friends and family know that if they want to stop by, they'd better be in their PJs.

The beauty of a self-created holiday is you get to make all the rules. My rules are simple, but unwavering. On Pajama Day everyone sleeps as late as they want and no one wakes anyone else. There is no cleaning and no cooking, and there are no hours spent putting together impossibly complicated toys with hundreds of pieces. The kids know that if Dad didn't put it together yesterday, it will wait until tomorrow.

Pajama Day is such a perfect pleasure that after the first few years I encouraged Steve to take the day off and join us. That was a mistake. Even though I patiently explained the rules, he just didn't get it. I awoke to the smell of coffee already brewed. When I ventured out to the kitchen, he was taking out the garbage. And he kept doing it. He spent the whole day cleaning and organizing. Even worse, his activity spurred our second daughter, who was almost seventeen at the time, to do the same.

They were like the dynamic duo, whose mission was to fight the household crime wave of Christmas chaos. I'm pretty sure I mumbled or maybe screamed, "You're ruining Pajama Day," but nothing would stop them.

It was pretty hard to relax and read a book with all that cleaning going on. I resentfully started helping them, hoping that if I helped it would be done sooner and we could all relax. It didn't happen. Our conflicting missions had set the tone and the day was ruined.

So now there's a new rule: The only people who can be home for Pajama Day are those who respect the spirit of the holiday. I'm willing to forgive and forget past transgressions only if they aren't repeated. My husband has tried to mend his ways in the years since, but the truth is he just doesn't enjoy lounging around the house all day. These days he kisses me goodbye and heads to work, happily donning his pajamas to join us as evening falls.

Even though it began as a day of rest for me, my two younger children embraced this holiday with a gusto that made it more fun for all of us. They understood that all normal rules were suspended and they built their own traditions around the day. They ate candy for breakfast and cookies for lunch. They built tent colonies with blankets in their bedrooms and could play all day without anyone asking them to clean up.

Over the years, the basic rules have stayed the same, but the cast has changed and the celebration has evolved. In the beginning, dinners were simply the bounty of leftovers that always includes shrimp, prime rib, cheesy potatoes and stuffed shells. The only exception to the cooking rule was roasting hotdogs and marshmallows in the fireplace, because that's just plain fun. At some point I decided that since I love to cook, making a real dinner wasn't actually work if I kept it simple. Now Pajama Day dinner is always beef stroganoff made with the leftover prime rib, using my mom's recipe from my childhood.

Our two oldest daughters have grown and moved to cities near and far. Both come home for Christmas and our second daughter is now happy to spend the day relaxing with her family. Best of all, we now have a granddaughter who loves Pajama Day as much as I do. This past year, she pulled me aside on Christmas and whispered in my ear, "Can I sleep over at your house tonight so I can be here for Pajama Day?"

Of course the answer was yes, and the next morning while everyone else slept until long past noon, she and I pulled out the sleeper sofa and built the fire. We snuggled under the covers and I read to her from the mountain of picture books she piled next to us. Later in the day her teenage uncle showed her how to build a fort using the cast-off couch cushions. I set aside the novel I was reading to enjoy the sound of their laughter as the fort collapsed on their heads. As I got up to put another log on the fire, I realized there was nothing better than passing on my favorite tradition to the next generation. May she do the same...

~Laurie Higgins

18

Gifts of Bloom

At whatever straws we must grasp, there is always a time for gratitude and new beginnings.
~J. Robert Moskin

I t had been a tumultuous year for my three sons: new town, new house, new schools, new friends, new life. It was a time filled with adjustment, uncertainty and pockets of deep sadness. As our first Christmas approached, I was determined to give "new" a facelift. We needed a fresh outlook. We needed a new tradition—with an old-fashioned sense of warmth, togetherness, hope and awakening. I devised a plan.

Early Christmas morning, we donned our warmest gear and headed to the beach two miles away. It was cold, but the waking sun was brilliant. We parked our car, grabbed the cooler filled with hot chocolate and sweet rolls, and headed down the beach toward the rock jetty which hugged the entrance to the harbor. My plan was a simple one: to sit together on a rock overlooking the wondrous ocean and acknowledge the stunning gifts we are given—for free—each day.

My middle son, Peter, spotted it first: "Look, Mom, a flower!" he said as he ran down the length of piled rocks. Lying on its side framed in gray speckled granite was a single white lily—the flower of purity, grace and beauty. Peter picked it up and examined it as we all converged. "Where do you think this came from?" he asked. We looked down the length of the beach but saw no one.

We sat down in a circle, placed the lily between us, and marveled at our find. We were full of questions: "Who left it? Why? Were we meant to find it?" As we sipped our hot drinks, we talked of hope and the wonder of new beginnings. When a cold wind forced our departure, we placed the lily back on the rock and headed down beach, pocketing shells and sea glass along the way.

When we got home, we opened our gifts from under the tree. The usual fervor surrounding boxes and bows was quieted, however, by talk of the lily. Late in the afternoon, we surrendered our beach treasures to the center of the kitchen table, and with ribbon and a glue gun, made ornaments for the tree. We marked the back of each creation with the date and an inscription: "Year one. The year of the lily."

Our beach excursion has become an annual Christmas tradition. Now, however, we bring our own gifts to the jetty. The day before Christmas, we head to the florist and we each pick out our own flower. When we leave the jetty on Christmas morning we find our own special rock on which to lay our blooms. As we amble back along the beach picking treasures for our new ornaments, we wonder who will find—and receive—our gifts of new beginnings.

~Susan Garrard

19

Caroling

Each day comes bearing its own gifts. Untie the ribbons.
~Ruth Ann Schabacker

Nothing warms the heart quite like Christmas caroling. The holidays can be hectic and the spirit of Christmas can easily become lost in the rush and worry of getting everything "just right." Eight of us neighbors decided to take a much-needed break and spend an evening Christmas caroling with our children. Setting out with the intention of lifting the spirits of our other neighbors, we spread Christmas cheer until we were tired, cranky and felt like popsicles.

One more house, we decided, and piling into our cars again, spotted the perfect target. The elderly man sitting alone in his kitchen window seemed like he needed us. Pulling over, we parked our cars in front of his house and argued about which songs to sing. Half of the children were either whining or crying about the cold and the Utah snow seemed to have lost its sparkle despite our good intentions.

Finally settling on four songs for the man, we rang the bell and waited for him to open his door. Already thinking about getting the kids to bed and the work I had yet to do, I automatically started in on "We Wish You a Merry Christmas" with the others. But as the man stood in the doorway, his eyes filling with tears, my sidetracked thoughts came to a screeching halt. As we sang, I could hear the tears in many of my friends' voices and my own voice caught and my singing grew softer as I fought the tears myself.

The elderly gentleman stood in his doorway, the ceiling fixture lighting his soft silver hair like a gentle halo. He clapped with delight as we finished the first song and glided right into the next. Warmth spilled from his home and out the door. He didn't seem to care, so happy he was with our visit. He seemed to personify the Spirit of Christmas and I felt a guilty twinge at my grouchiness. True joy began to fill my soul as I sang my heart out for this man. No one had greeted us with such enthusiasm and joy all night. No one had made us feel so welcome and so loved. Gratitude filled me like hot cocoa and I was so thankful we were guided to this man.

Finishing up with "Silent Night," we sang with great love for our neighbor, and I heard his own shaky voice join in with ours. Tears streamed down my cold cheeks and I knew not one of us would forget this man. Our song ended and we all stood on his porch, no one willing to break the spell of this glorious moment. The man stood grinning through his tears as we grinned right back through our own.

Thanking us profusely and wishing us a Merry Christmas, he went back inside his warm home, his big grin and the tears on his cheeks the last things we saw. We slowly and regretfully left the man, whose spirit and tears made all the difference in our night, all the difference in our Christmas. Although he had sat alone in his window, looking as if he needed us, we had no idea how much we needed him, and what a gift to our group of carolers that man would be. In him we found the true spirit of Christmas.

~Susan Farr-Fahncke

"THE Christmas Carol?"

© 2010 Jonny Hawkins

Reprinted by permission of
Jonny Hawkins ©2010.

My Little
Christmas Songbird

He who sings frightens away his ills.
~Miguel de Cervantes

"Oh, the weather outside was frightful" in our sleepy little town in Virginia. We were not accustomed to the arctic air and crystalline icing that was covering our rural community. With twenty-four inches of snow on the ground, icy conditions everywhere and temperatures in the teens, our teeth were chattering and we were already looking forward to spring. Except... Christmas was right around the corner and maybe a winter wonderland would be fun for Santa's annual trek.

Like many busy mothers, I worked full-time, had a twenty-month-old daughter, and tried to squeeze too much into every day. My husband worked long hours as a high school assistant principal so my daughter, Savannah, and I often spent the weekday evenings running errands, making supper, and keeping up with the day-to-day activities of life.

On this particularly cold December evening, we had made a quick dash through the grocery store and we raced home to get settled in for the night. Juggling groceries and a wiggly toddler, I picked my way gingerly across the ice-covered patio and in the kitchen door. Yanking off coat, hat, mittens, and winter boots, I told Savannah that I had to run out to the car to get my purse but I would be right back.

Out to the car I went. Literally a twenty-second endeavor. And then I was back. I grabbed the kitchen door handle and... LOCKED! How could this be? Our sliding glass door had a deadbolt and required a key to open or lock it.

I panicked as I watched my little one dancing around the kitchen, humming to herself, completely oblivious to our predicament. I tried two windows, which of course were locked. Gently tapping on the glass, I called Savannah to the door. As she toddled over, she smiled, got up on tiptoes proudly showing me how she was a big girl and could "Yock (lock) it." Unfortunately, she was too short and did not yet have the dexterity to rotate her wrist counter clockwise to "UNyock" it. We were stuck! And it was cold!

Since this was before the days of cell phones, I began mentally exploring how to break into the house. Savannah, however, spotted our Christmas tree in the living room. The glittering, sparkling tree was a toddler's delight! I had been fearful of Savannah tugging on the tree and pulling it over on top of her, so we had spent many evenings talking about how pretty it was and how we needed to "look with our eyes instead of our hands." Now, however, Momma was outside and the tree was there for the touching. As Savannah ambled toward the living room, I quickly began singing Christmas carols through the glass door. There is nothing like a rousing rendition of "Jingle Bells" to attract a toddler's attention. Savannah quickly ran back to the door, sat on the floor and chimed in loudly at "one horse open sleigh-HEY!" After many, many carols, Savannah peered through the glass and said, "It's cold, Momma. Come in." Little did she know that this Christmas adventure was warming my heart even as the cold wind howled around me.

My husband arrived home about thirty minutes later, finding me on the outside of the sliding glass door and Savannah tucked up against the window on the inside, loudly belting, "Santa Claus Is Coming to Town." When I finally got inside and felt the warmth of our cozy home and the hugs of my little songbird, I realized that Christmas had arrived early that year!

~Corinne "Cori" Foley Hill

Christmas Magic

Away in a Manger

What Really Matters

Truly wonderful the mind of a child is.
~Yoda

In her eight short years my daughter had attended three different schools in as many countries. We had transferred to Maryland with our government careers and she and her brother were thrilled at the prospect of putting down roots for a little while in one place. We chose a small suburban community outside of Washington, D.C. and settled in. The parish we chose for worship was warm and felt like home. Every Christmas the oldest elementary school students, the sixth graders, presented a Christmas pageant complete with angels, shepherds, wise men, the innkeeper, Mary and Joseph, and a "real" baby volunteered for stardom by one of the trusting parish families.

For three years the nun who was the parish education director promised Jessica that she would make a fine "Mary" if she took her classes seriously and tried to be a role model to younger students. In October of her sixth grade year, the parish began to prepare for the long awaited, cherished presentation that honored the meaning of Christmas. Sister Margie asked me if she might speak to me one evening after religion classes. Amid the excitement of the upcoming spectacle and the measuring of all sixth graders for some role somewhere in the pageant, I detected a note of concern and panic in her voice. I was not the only one to notice and while Sister pulled me aside in the church vestibule, any number of other teachers, parents, and students suddenly quieted in hopes of hearing what could possibly be so important. Sister spoke in her lowest whisper that she was very worried about the fact that Jessica had grown into a lovely, yet tall young girl, and in fact now towered six inches over the boy who had equally had his heart set on being Joseph.

"Mary," she whispered, "must carry the baby Jesus on one arm and take Joseph's elbow for support as they walk the length of the aisle and make their entrance accompanied by the choir of the angels. I just don't know how that will look with her being so much taller than he." With this she cast a troubled look at me. I joined in her panic and tried not to look at my daughter who was now obviously focused on us. I explained to her that I feared the heart-wrenching anguish of my daughter who might now be denied her honored debut after anticipating it for three years.

Jessica bravely approached us and swallowed hard. She had heard every word of this "secret" meeting. She addressed the dilemma head on. "Excuse me, Sister," she sweetly said. "If it didn't make any difference to Joseph if Mary was pregnant when he married her—do you think it mattered to him if she was taller than him?"

Being the wise, warm woman that she was, Sister hugged Jessica and swept the whole company of players into the church for prayers. The pageant went off without a hitch and my husband and I watched proudly as Mary carefully and gently carried her baby with her other hand softly, confidently placed on Joseph's strong shoulder.

~Julia G. Powell

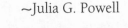

The Perfect Gift

Love is, above all, the gift of oneself.
~Jean Anouilh

Two weeks before Christmas, I left my suburban neighborhood with a small group of friends, and followed an urban minister through the streets of Los Angeles. "Silver bells, silver bells. It's Christmas time in the city...." I sang to myself as we walked busy sidewalks. Contrary to the lyrics of the classic carol by Livingston and Evans, I did not see "children laughing and people passing, meeting smile after smile."

Instead, I saw hundreds of homeless people, shattered by addiction and abuse, crowding the streets of a wealthy city. They carried plastic bags containing their meager possessions, while blocks away, busy shoppers rushed home with treasures from designer boutiques.

The contrast was sobering and did nothing to improve my holiday funk. I longed for God to provide a divine interruption and remind me of the real reason for celebration.

On the second day of our reality tour, the guide invited us to observe a mobile street ministry called Metro Kidz. We followed their lunch wagon, painted with holy graffiti, as it circled poor neighborhoods. Bright music blared from the speakers and drew hundreds of local children to a quiet cul-de-sac. Ranging in age from toddlers to teens, they raced to hug the pastor as if he were the Pied Piper. He opened his arms and braced himself for a wave of energy. Within minutes, volunteers spread plastic tarps on the asphalt and a human huddle formed on the ground.

"Who wants to play some games?" the young pastor yelled to the attentive crowd.

"I do, I do," said one young boy who popped to his feet with confidence.

"Let me, let me," a chorus of voices responded.

Their joy was contagious and I started to smile on the inside.

"Okay," the pastor said. "We'll play some games and pass out some prizes. Then I want to tell the Christmas story. How many have ever heard the story of baby Jesus?"

Almost every brown arm shot into the air.

I was seated cross-legged between wiggling, giggling children when a small boy crawled into my lap and fell asleep. His candy cane smeared sticky sweetness all over my jeans. A warm weight pressed against my side and I turned to find a pretty young lady with dark curly hair. Her braids were clipped with a rainbow of many colors and framed her large brown eyes.

"Hello, my name is Sandy. What's your name?" I asked.

"Erika," she whispered shyly and glanced down.

"How old are you?" I asked, and put my arm around her shoulder.

"Five," she told me with a smile.

"Do you want to play one of the relay games?" I queried.

She grabbed my arm, shook her head vigorously and said, "No please."

"That's okay, we can just sit here and watch together," I said and felt her relax. Experienced volunteers helped the children have silly fun. Prizes of food, toys, candy and books were given to the competitors for as many categories as the leaders could concoct. Winners snatched the rewards and raised them overhead like victory trophies.

"Look what I got!" they yelled to their peers.

Finally, it was time to hear the Christmas story and to learn a new memory verse.

"Listen up," the pastor said to hundreds of squirming kids. "We have a few more rewards to give away. Adults will watch the group and pick out eight boys and girls to receive a quiet prize for the best listening skills during the story."

A sudden hush came over the crowd, but lasted only a few seconds. The harder the kids tried to be quiet, the more they wanted to laugh. A giggle started inside of me and I had to swallow a snort before it escaped.

Seated among poor children in the streets of Los Angeles, I felt joy! I felt celebration. I listened to the story of two parents who were forced to seek shelter in a stable, because there was no room for them at the inn. I felt the sleeping boy in my lap and could picture a child, wrapped in swaddling clothes, embraced at the breast of his mother.

Erika listened carefully to the brief version of Christmas Eve and never moved an inch. She watched, and waited patiently for the memory verse competition.

"Today's memory verse is from James 1:17. I'll read the words and you repeat after me," the pastor instructed. "Every good and perfect gift comes from God the Father," he said in English and then repeated the verse in Spanish.

"Every good and perfect gift comes from God the Father," they repeated.

Moments later, an adult volunteer tapped Erika on the shoulder.

"Thank you for listening so well, for so long. You have earned one of our quiet prizes," she said and handed the little girl a gift wrapped in red and green tissue paper.

"Thank you," Erika responded and hugged the gift without another word.

I watched her face grow a big smile. Other children tore the paper off their prizes to see what treasure they had earned, but not Erika. Instead, she looked down at the child still asleep in my lap, pressed her lips close to my ear, and whispered words that took my breath away.

"Now I have something to give my brother for Christmas," she said. Without examining the contents, or knowing if there would be something else for her, Erika gave her gift away.

Tears welled in my eyes when I recognized that my own prayer for a divine interruption had just been answered. Erika's Christ-like generosity, and unselfish love for her brother, showed me the true spirit of Christmas. At five years old, Erika understood that love is the perfect gift, and that the best gift of all is the chance to give love away.

~Sandra Wood

A Basket of Hope

Hope is faith holding out its hand in the dark.
~George Iles

I had hidden the car a few blocks away and with finger-over-lips silently motioned and directed our three kids out of the station wagon and toward a softly-lit small weathered house set back from the highway. I felt like a cat burglar, with family-in-training, skulking along the bushes that warned wayward drivers they were far too close to the now snow-filled ditch.

We took a shortcut through the church lot. I could feel a soft smile forming playfully as we passed the church building, imagining our burly pastor's reaction if he could see us "applying" his message on how little ones would someday follow in our footsteps. Somehow I don't think this little snow scene was exactly what Pastor had in mind. I paused to belatedly reassure myself that we hadn't forgotten anything. Yep — the girls and I each had our assigned bags, and our little guy alternately carried and dragged a brightly painted red empty bushel basket.

Another car whizzed by and our little towheaded son was amazingly solemn when I gently pressed my flattened hand on top of his stocking-hatted head — once again repeating my silent message to scrunch down out of sight from the headlight glare passing over the yard. The girls immediately followed suit, quietly ducking until the white light rode over us, the yard, and then finally slid over the bank by the road.

It was their idea after all. Laurie had memorized Luke 2: 8-14 for the Christmas play and its story of the babe with no place to lay his head had profoundly affected her and her siblings as she shared it multiple times in preparation for the big event. Cheri, the thoughtful one, was always reaching out to others, so our eyes met in understanding when she'd climbed into the car without her mittens a few Sundays before, then shrugged her shoulders in response to her daddy's inquiry, pointing to the new visitors—a red-mittened shy little girl plowing across the snow-covered field with her mom to the same weather-beaten house that now stood before us. I think she had the idea then, but I love to read a different Christmas story each night of the entire month of December and the reading of *The Gift of the Magi* where both husband and wife gave their precious possessions to purchase a gift for the other had cemented it. All three insisted they could give up one or more of their gifts for someone who probably would not get a gift otherwise, and thus the plan was born. What parent could refuse such a selfless act that also ended up sharing a family tradition—new pajamas and hot cocoa for Christmas Eve?

Add gloves for everyone, a doll for the little girl and a truck for her brother, the makings of a simple Christmas meal and here we were, whispering and darting from one bush to the other. Quietly the children completed the plan—circling the trees that flanked the sloping porch, Kevin first placed the basket. I added the plastic bags of food and raced with him behind the big scraggly bush at the edge of the yard while the girls quietly topped the basket with the wrapped gifts. Cheri retraced her steps to me, and Laurie, as planned, knocked hard twice and raced back to join us collectively holding our breath as the door opened. It was the dad—he stood on crutches, looking around to the left—to the right—then called his wife. She stepped out and also scanned the yard, then bent to pick up the basket. Two little faces appeared stair-stepped in the lighted doorway and excited squeals sounded as eager hands helped to lift and carry the packages in as the door closed off their wondering chatter.

That was our signal and we ran like the wind, our mitten-clasped hands joining reverently this time for a dash across the field to the waiting, and by now, cold car. None of the usual clamoring for front seat, or murmuring about the car's chill occurred as we each privately recalled the faces outlined in the doorway's glow, and I knew the children's hearts were as warmed as mine had been.

It was a special Christmas and the beginning of a fun tradition to find a family and leave a surprise on their doorstep, but this one became especially meaningful a few months later when the family announced at church that the father's leg had healed, he'd gotten a new job, and they were moving.

As Cheri and I were about to exit behind our family, the mom stepped up behind me and slipped a plastic bag into my hand, which I could feel contained a frame. Don't open it until you get home," she admonished, "and," she paused and whispered, "Merry Christmas." I looked up in shocked dismay, wondering if she'd discovered our secret, but she shyly smiled and touching Cheri's hair explained, "I've been working on this since your little one gave Edna the red mittens last December, so now it seems kind of Christmasy. Hope you don't mind, but those mittens were the start of our Christmas hope."

Touched, I tearfully assured her we'd surely love whatever it was, and after Cheri and I gave last farewell hugs, we rushed to the rest of the waiting family in the car. For once dinner could wait, and the moment we were in the door everyone hovered around the package as I drew out a simple cross-stitched picture of Mary holding a contented baby Jesus, their hearts close. It seemed to remind us that there was the place of Hope—close to the heart of Jesus. We lost touch with that family, but the picture still speaks the Christmas message in our home year-round and I knew Cheri still treasured the memory years later when she told me what she'd named her first little girl—Kristin Hope.

~Delores Christian Liesner

Celebrating Christmas Away from Home

Christmas is a time when you get homesick—even when you're home.
~Carol Nelson

I stood misty-eyed on our apartment balcony, my back to my husband, trying not to cry while I stared at our sunny December view of the Mediterranean Sea. How I wished I were back in California. Gordon came and stood beside me, his hand on my shoulder. I turned to face him, then choked out the words. "It just doesn't feel like Christmas. Not here in Beirut, so far away from home."

I snuggled into his shoulder and let my tears flow. "I thought being so close to Israel would make Christmas brighter, more real. Bethlehem actually seems farther away than it did when we lived in the U.S."

We joined hands as we walked into our living room and sank onto the couch. I wasn't through talking yet. "Because we live in an Arab Christian neighborhood, I expected to enjoy our usual Christmas experience," I grumbled. "I was so wrong."

My voice rose as I began to list all the missing seasonal signs. "Families don't decorate the outside of their houses for Christmas. No Christmas tree lights shine from our neighbors' apartment windows. No Christmas carols are playing in the background as we shop. No

Christmas cantatas are advertized. No manger scenes. Plus we'll miss the family Christmas party. Buying a live Christmas tree with that pleasant, fragrant smell is out of the question here because trees are too precious to cut down. It will be impossible to decorate that skinny, artificial tree we bought to resemble last year's gorgeous fir."

I slumped lower on the couch. "It's going to be a bleak Christmas without the trimmings."

Gordon nodded as he softly rubbed my hand in his. "We're obviously going to have to generate our own Christmas mood. Since our kids are so young, they have no preconceived ideas about how to celebrate Christmas. We've got to create traditions for them to remember. Christmas customs that work for all of us no matter where we live."

He watched me closely. "What part of our traditional Christmas celebration seems most important to you?"

I looked down at the floor and allowed memories of past Christmases to flood my mind. I raised my eyes and lifted up a finger for each point. "Being with family and friends. Singing Christmas carols. Sharing a Christmas Day meal with pumpkin and pecan pies for dessert. Playing the White Elephant game with adults on Christmas Eve."

He nodded his head. "Think about it. We can initiate traditions that include sharing food and playing our favorite gift exchange game right here in Beirut." He walked over to the desk and returned to the couch with a tablet and pen.

"We don't have family here," he continued, "but we do have new friends. How many people will our living room hold?"

"Probably twenty-four."

The list-making began. Eventually, twenty-two friends received invitations to a Christmas Eve buffet. Instructions for the evening included wearing something red and bringing a wrapped white elephant present for a gift exchange game. The British and Australian couples laughed when we described that a white elephant gift meant giving away something you already owned, with no "to or from" stickers required. "It wouldn't be proper to bring a used item as a gift where we come from," they explained. Getting into the spirit, they brought "old" gifts.

Christmas music played in the background as our guests arrived on Christmas Eve.

We played a couple of "get-to-know-you" games and feasted from the buffet. After we ate I started the white elephant gift exchange game. After I initiated a two-minute-only swapping rule, the room turned into a grabbing, lurching, uproar as our guests rushed around after every gift was opened, trying to swap what they held for their preferred item.

The evening ended with us plopped down on couches, chairs, and the carpet, singing Christmas carols and listening to the Apostle Luke's Christmas story. Verse seven resounded with the essence of Christmas: "And she brought forth her firstborn son, and wrapped him in swaddling clothes, and laid him in a manger" (KJV). We felt the bond of love that Jesus gives to those who follow him.

It was close to midnight before our last guests left, prized (or maybe not) gifts in tow, many loudly vowing to plan a better strategy for next year's game. I pulled off my heels and flopped down on the couch. Gordon soon joined me, a big grin lighting up his face.

"You have to admit this room's been saturated with Christmas cheer," he commented.

"That's true," I replied with a smile.

We sat silently, reveling in the moment. "You know what?" Gordon said. "With this new Christmas party tradition established, I don't think we'll ever need to worry about how to celebrate Christmas again."

I slowly nodded my head. He was so right. We'd done it! We'd learned how to celebrate Christmas away from home.

~Pat Stockett Johnston

My First Noel

We can only be said to be alive in those moments
when our hearts are conscious of our treasures.
~Thornton Wilder

W e all know the story—how Jesus was born in a stable
after Joseph and Mary journeyed to Bethlehem and
couldn't find an inn with a vacant room. And we've
also seen it depicted on Christmas cards and in Nativity scenes—Mary
in her flowing gown, the well-kept stable, the Christ Child wrapped
in spotless white or baby blue swaddling clothes. But what was the
first Christmas really like? I've often wondered about that, and now
I think I know.

It was almost Christmas 2004, and a few of us had made the long
trip from Kampala, Uganda, to a remote mountainous region in the
north. We were taking medicine, school materials, and the Gospel to
a primitive agrarian and goat-herder people known as the Ik.

It was the furthest from modern civilization that I had ever been.
The people's dress couldn't have been simpler—colorful beads and
unfinished swaths of fabric that they draped over their shoulders
or wrapped around themselves. Their homes were mud huts. We
pitched our tents inside the stick-fence borders of their villages.

Each day we trekked along goat trails to another village, where
people gathered to meet and listen to us. I'd brought a whiteboard

and colored markers, and told them stories from the Bible as I illustrated the main events and characters.

In the third village we visited, a mother had recently given birth. I knocked on the door of the "medical center," which was no more than four mud walls.

As I stepped inside, I was met by the smell of stale air mingled with smoke. There, on the hay-strewn floor, beside a few hot coals, sat a thin woman nursing a tiny baby boy wrapped in a towel. The mother looked up at me, her eyes filled with anxiety. "My breasts are dry," she said, in her own language, gesturing to the small bundle that suckled hopelessly.

A little light streamed in through a small opening in the wall that served as the only window. As I looked around the room, trying to imagine what it would be like to give birth under such circumstances, village sounds drifted in—bleats from the goats, little children's laughter as they played, and faint, scratchy music from someone's radio that was hooked to a hand-cranked generator, the Iks' only source of electricity.

I stepped outside and called Katrina, a Czechoslovakian linguist who had come along to make a documentary about the Ik. I explained the situation, and we quickly agreed to give the mother what was left of our milk.

As Katrina went for the milk, I asked the mother if I could hold the baby. She smiled and handed him to me. His towel fell open and I could see that he was still unwashed, and the umbilical cord still hung from his navel.

A breeze swept through the tiny window. The mother shivered and pulled her wrap tightly around her shoulders. The temperature had dropped unexpectedly in the last week.

Then a thought from my childhood came back—If I could have seen the newborn Jesus, what would I have given Him? The similarity of this situation seemed to cry out to me. No, I told myself, the parallel is absurd. This is no Christ Child, and this isn't Bethlehem two thousand years ago!

But the truth rang even louder. Did it matter that this baby was no one special? Did it matter that his mother was a lowly tribes-woman who few in this world knew or cared about? Every detail of this new birth mattered to God, who at that moment was peering down from Heaven, proud and pleased with His new creation. And this was, in truth, probably a more accurate picture of the world into which Jesus was born than the idealized one depicted in most Christmas cards, Nativity scenes, and paintings.

What would I have given Him? The thought came again, followed by Jesus' own words from the Gospels, "If you have two shirts, give to him who has none."

I had two shirts. In fact, I had two on and plenty more at home. I didn't need both of these. Meanwhile, in my arms, I held a representation of that wonderful birth celebrated by billions. Suddenly, I felt an unexplainable joy. Here was my chance to give the Lord something real at Christmas!

Taking off one shirt, I gently wrapped the baby boy in it. How handsome he looked now, and how proud his mother seemed, the smile on her face reflecting the gratitude in her heart.

The music from the radio outside came through stronger now—Christmas music! "Joy to the world, the Lord has come! Let Earth receive her King!"

He had truly come. This wasn't a mere stage reenactment with actors in costume. This was real—as real and as close as I had ever come to knowing what the first Christmas might have been like.

The song on the radio finished and another began. "The first Noel the angel did say was to certain poor shepherds in fields as they lay; in fields where they lay tending their sheep, on a cold winter's night that was so deep…."

There, far away from civilization and the usual glitter of Christmas, with humble goat herders in the remote mountains of Uganda, I experienced my own First Noel.

~Nyx Martinez

A Place for Christmas

He who has not Christmas in his heart will never find it under a tree.
~Roy L. Smith

"Joy to the World," blared on the stereo, filtering through the closed door of the guest room. I sat on my borrowed bed, wiping a tear that slipped down my cheek. What was there to be joyful about?

My mom came into the room where I stayed. "We're getting ready to play *Yahtzee*. You coming?" She saw that I was upset and sat down next to me. "What's the matter, honey? Aren't you having a good Christmas?"

There wasn't a lot to celebrate that year. We'd just moved away from my hometown. My mother and stepfather were out of work and we didn't even have our own house yet. We were staying with our friends, the Allens, for the holiday season while looking for jobs and a house in a nearby town. It was the first Christmas I wouldn't be able to celebrate with my dad, stepmom, and little sisters—not to mention grandparents, aunts, uncles, and cousins.

"I just miss everyone back home, that's all. I'll be out in a while." It wasn't the whole story, but Mom hadn't had an easy time either. I didn't want to bother her with all the rest. She patted me on the shoulder and told me she'd see me later.

I thought of all the Christmases in the past when we crammed into Grandma's house in rural Wyoming. My cousins and I gleefully slept in a "tent" under the big dining room table while all of the adults slept in the beds. During mealtimes, we'd crowd around the table and devour homemade holiday favorites like turkey with all the trimmings. There was raucous laughter and singing around the piano. We all pitched in, washing and drying dishes.

That seemed worlds away from Amity, Oregon. Rain poured down constantly, and there was not a snowflake in sight. None of our decorations were on the tree—those were packed away somewhere in a box with the rest of our stuff. Mrs. Allen's tree was beautiful, but I missed the special ornaments I looked forward to every year.

I imagined all of my relatives celebrating without me while I sat here, in another place. It was a nice place, just not the place for Christmas.

I picked up my Bible, long-neglected since I'd found out about the move. As I thumbed through it, I thought I might as well read "The Christmas Story." Even though I'd heard the Bible story of Christ's birth many times before, a new understanding dawned on me. Mary and Joseph were homeless, far from home, away from the comfort of family and friends. The smelly, dirty manger was no place to celebrate the birth of any child, let alone the Christ child—and yet it turned into one of the most memorable celebrations ever—announced by a whole host of angels and attended by shepherds and even a few Kings from the Orient. The very first Christmas was celebrated far away from home, family, and comfort.

Suddenly I didn't feel so alone anymore. I shared something in common with Mary. Besides, I did still have my immediate family and even some friends with me. I washed my face and appeared in the kitchen. Soon I was caught up in a rousing game of *Yahtzee*—not exactly a teen's dream activity, but it was better than feeling sorry for myself.

Later that afternoon, preparations for the next day were well underway. "Mrs. Allen, can I help you bake the pies?" I asked.

"Sure, we've got lots of them to make." She set out the big pie plates and several individual pies. I helped roll out pie crusts and peeled apples. Soon the house smelled of cinnamon, cloves, and apples baking. We even found a lot to laugh about as we pitched in to help each other make preparations for the day ahead. When everything was ready, we pulled out the *Yahtzee* game again and played long into the night.

The next morning, as we gathered I looked around the dim living room, lit with only the lights from the tree. The tired but eager faces of the Allen children shone with expectation, awaiting their turns to open gifts. It wasn't the place I'd envisioned celebrating Christmas, but then again, a manger wasn't the place Mary and Joseph envisioned welcoming Jesus into the world either. I discovered that Christmas isn't about a place or traditions; the place where Christmas lives is simply in our hearts.

~Lynetta L. Smith

Na'aseh V'Nishma

I can understand people simply fleeing the mountainous effort Christmas
has become... but there are always saving graces
and finally they make up for all the bother and distress.
~May Sarton

Dark clouds churned low over the freeway, dropping torrents of rain. My wipers ticked steadily, but uselessly, just like my harried mind.

December 1st, I thought. How will I get it all done? The ninth-grade essays, the paper for my degree, Sean's basketball game and Cristin's history paper. Not to mention the vet, the refrigerator repairman, Mark's office party... and Christmas.

Christmas. The last thing I needed was that empty set of chores — not that I did much anymore. Every year I dropped something else. Gone were lights on the house and the banister greens. The crèche remained in storage; if only we could skip the tree. And Christmas Eve Mass: standing for two hours in an overcrowded church, listening to children sing off-key; wishing peace to total strangers on cue, greeting a wooden Holy Family. Pointless — at least to me.

I exited the freeway. The rain was letting up a bit, but the wind was wild; fir branches skated over the street. With luck, I'd reach my classroom before my students.

My students. Talk about pointless chores! As Orthodox Jews, their lives were crammed with them. Every morning they prayed and studied the Old Testament—Torah to them—for four hours before the standard high school curriculum began. They had nine classes per day, raced from classroom to classroom, every boy with a yarmulke on his head, every girl in a long skirt, each time kissing their fingers and tapping the mezuzah, a cylinder encasing a tiny prayer scroll affixed to every doorframe in the school. Kiss-tap. Kiss-tap. Kiss-tap. All day long. And Jewish holidays! There were so many: Rosh Hashanah, Yom Kippur, Sukkot, Hanukah, each requiring toilsome preparations, all between Labor Day and Christmas! How did they manage—and why?

Truth was, I envied them. How wonderful to believe so deeply in God that all those acts seemed meaningful, worth the time. When I was a teenager, I too had believed in God. I prayed every night on my knees, celebrated the holidays in awe. No more. Earthquakes, bombings, poverty, disease. I simply couldn't understand God—but my students obviously could. It never seemed to occur to them that their acts of faith were futile, a waste of time. Like Christmas.

I pulled into the school parking lot. Oh well, I thought. They're chosen. I'm not.

"Okay," I said to my freshmen later that day, "please open to chapter five. At this point in the memoir, Eliezer is in the concentration camp and has just witnessed the hanging of an innocent Jewish boy, only slightly younger than he is. How did the hanging affect him?" A hand darted up. "Amira?"

"He stopped believing in God."

"That's right," added Nitza, "because later in the chapter Eliezer refused to pray on Yom Kippur. He'd always prayed before."

"And how did he feel about that?" I asked.

"Oh, he says right here," called Riva, pointing at a page: "I was alone—terribly alone in a world without God.... I stood amid that praying congregation, observing it like a stranger." Riva looked up, her blue eyes piercing me: "Eliezer felt empty, cut off from God."

"He should have prayed anyway," suggested Avraham.

That confused me: "If he didn't believe in God," I said, "wouldn't praying have been hypocritical?"

"No," replied Suri. "The Torah tells you to follow God's rituals even when they make no sense. It's called Na'aseh V'Nishma—We will act and we will understand. First you do the acts, then you'll understand God. If Eliezer had observed the holiday, he might have recovered some faith."

I stared at her... and wondered: "Just like that?"

"Well, you also have to read the Torah to understand the symbolism of the acts, and think about it."

I pondered Suri's words on the drive home from school: Na'aseh V'Nishma.—First do the acts, then you'll understand God. Had I had everything backwards? I'd assumed that faith came first and brought meaning to the acts—but maybe meaningful acts came first and brought faith. I glanced through the windshield at the fir trees at the roadside, their branches now at rest, and an emerging ray of sunlight made me squint.

That evening I pulled out the battered cardboard crate marked "Xmas." I opened it, plunged my hand in among the wires and rummaged through the multicolored lights. I untangled a string of tiny white lights, then marched into the family room, ignoring the books and papers stacked beside my chair. Slowly, methodically, I strung the lights on the ficus tree that always stood in the corner of the room—my first Christmas act. Then I plugged in the cord, and the lights winked at me.

I searched through the adjacent bookshelves. There it was: The Family Bible—abridged, annotated and illustrated—perfect for a novice like me. I pulled the Bible out and ran my finger along its edge, dislodging a layer of dust. The spine creaked as I opened it, and for the first time in my life, I sat down to read the Old Testament: "In the beginning, God created the heavens and the earth...."

December days slipped by. Somehow, I completed my tasks, decorated a Christmas tree, set out the crèche, and came to know Abraham, Jacob, Moses, David, Solomon and Esther. They were nothing like I'd expected—not pious or perfect saints. Instead, they were flawed and floundered in their faith—just like me, yet chosen.

On Christmas Eve, I sat down in my chair to read God's final promise to the Jewish people: "See I will send my messenger, who will prepare the way before me. Then suddenly the Lord you are seeking will come to his temple: the messenger of the covenant, whom you desire will come."

And he did come—that night at Christmas Eve Mass. As the children sang like angels and the people prayed for peace, the Holy Family entered the cathedral. Living and breathing—at least to me.

My family was silent as we drove home from church. The streets were vacant, still. I gazed through the window at the dark cloudless night, the countless winking stars. Na'aseh V'Nishma. I had acted and understood.

~Jan Vallone

A Sign Unto You

*The message of Christmas is that the visible material world is bound
to the invisible spiritual world.*
~Author Unknown

A honk of the mailman's horn meant something special.
Most days Mr. Robert barely slowed as he eased the mail
into our box and disappeared around the bend. My sisters
and I were fascinated to watch the old man maneuvering his weathered hatchback from the passenger seat—left arm clamped to the
wheel, the right deftly stuffing envelopes and small packages into our
box, his eyes never leaving the road.

But a toot of his horn signaled something else entirely. It meant
a package too big to fit in the box. Since my two brothers left for
Vietnam, the packages had been exciting. One brother sent stuffed
animals with transistor radios in their bellies. Mine was a purple
poodle which I took everywhere with me. The other brother sent
eighteen inch-dolls dressed in traditional Vietnamese attire which
Mama declared "for the shelf, not the toy box."

At the sound of the horn, my sister, Michelle, and I scrambled
off the front porch and raced each other to the highway. No matter
how fast we were, the old man would be incensed at how long we'd
taken. Sure enough, by the time I made it to his car, he was handing
Michelle a box—that looked like it had been through a battle or two
itself—and was off in a huff. I wasn't old enough to read all the writing but recognized the foreign looking stamps and knew that either

Duff or Wayne had sent something mysterious from the other side of the world. With Christmas only months away, my mind reeled with possibilities.

Instead of making Mama happy the way I always expected them to, a package from one of her boys made her quieter than usual. She'd never let us see her cry or even look blue but the same boxes that elated my six sisters and me had the opposite effect on Mama. She read the letter to herself then, with a quiet smile, invited us to, "Go ahead. Open the box." She didn't have to ask twice.

The first thing we saw was strange looking newsprint. We fished around in it and pulled out figures of animals—sheep, a donkey, a large brown cow, a camel—and people—kings, shepherds, Mary, Joseph, an angel and the baby Jesus. It was the Holy Family. There was also a primitive barn complete with straw attached to the floor and roof—like the one on the lawn at church, only smaller.

And so began one of my favorite Christmas traditions—one my sisters and I continue with our own kids and grandkids to this day. That night Mama meted out the nativity figures and nestled the empty barn under the Christmas tree. Daddy—a born performer—read the story of the birth of Jesus from the Bible, making it come alive for us.

We girls sat, feet tucked beneath us, nativity figures in our laps. As the story unfolded, we took turns placing each figure in its proper place—first the animals, then Mary and Joseph, the infant King, the angel, shepherds and eventually the wise men who traveled from afar (or in our case, from the coffee table).

After the story was complete, Daddy produced a tape recorder and we took turns recording messages to our brothers which Mama would mail the next morning.

A year later, Duff and Wayne were back with us—they and their young wives and babies—as we reenacted the story again.

Over the years, we shared that tradition with cousins, neighbors and one grandchild after another. As each of us learned to read, Daddy invited us into his lap to take turns reading with him.

I'm not sure how I ended up with the old nativity set. The years (over forty) have taken their toll. The figures are chipped, glued and faded — pretty shabby looking, really. The cow is minus one horn and one sheep disappeared all together. The newspaper with the foreign writing disintegrated decades ago.

Every Christmas Eve though, the kids and I pull out those battered figures and that well-worn stable. Their daddy reads the story to us and the Holy Family makes their annual march to the nativity one more time.

~Mimi Greenwood Knight

Christmas Magic

Deck the Halls

The Griswold House

*I wish we could put up some of the Christmas spirit in jars
and open a jar of it every month.*
~Harlan Miller

Every Christmas season for the past fifteen years, my elderly neighbor Mr. Jones (around the corner and down the street) begins putting up elaborate Christmas decorations approximately three weeks before Thanksgiving. A moderate myself, I'd always thought the amount of time and labor this extensive project took was absurd. And to begin exhibiting all this "holiday cheer" so early, well, that seemed even more absurd.

I couldn't imagine why anyone would want to haul out: thousands of strands of colored lights; puffy garlanded wreaths and decorated trees for every window; an illuminated choir of carolers lined up along the driveway, actually singing a full, robust repertoire of musical seasonal favorites; a life-sized Nativity scene in the center of the yard which included several plastic animals, a heralding angel hovering beside a huge star of Bethlehem with the three wise men hunkered worshipfully near the Holy Family; and a Santa's Workshop stretched along one side of the house, complete with a motorized assembly line featuring myriad miniature elves working their cheery little hearts out to produce an immense pile of glowing packages at the end of the conveyor belt. All this seemed like major overkill to me, especially for a man obviously past his prime. And I couldn't help but groan when I thought of poor old Mr. Jones having to haul all this junk down again eventually and find a place to store it until this time next year.

Scrooge-like, I always chuckled as I passed by the elaborate array each morning on my power walk; I'd labeled the Jones' place "The Griswold House" after the movie *National Lampoon's Christmas Vacation* with Chevy Chase. "Want to find my house?" I'd say to my own holiday guests. "Turn left at The Griswold House. You can't miss it."

Yet, as festive as The Griswold House was, this year I harbored lonely, desperate feelings as I walked by each morning. The magic that came alive at night seemed depressingly drab and lifeless during daylight hours. "Just an illusion, make believe," I'd huff to myself sadly, thinking about the horrendous year I'd just spent struggling to remain a source of optimism and support to three close family members who'd been diagnosed, one right after the other, with various forms of cancer. Sometimes, on the dark days when the ravaging effects of chemotherapy took their toll and the awful doubts crept over me that my loved ones might not survive, my heart and mind would seem just as bleak and cheerless as The Griswold House did in the daytime.

One evening while driving home a couple of weeks before Christmas, I was in a gloomy frame of mind. My daughter-in-law Amy had had a particularly difficult day battling her disease, and I'd spent the long hours of her misery simply being there for her, feeling impotent and desperate that I couldn't make her pain go away. Multiply Amy's misery by three, and what did anything about Christmas matter when my mother, niece, and daughter-in-law were suffering so? Today, Amy's battle in particular seemed hopeless. Weary and depressed, I eased my car along the snowy streets, making my way toward home.

"Turn left at The Griswold House," I mumbled to myself distractedly, the left turn still several blocks away. But then, something wondrous happened. The dazzling lights and bustle that is the magical soul of Christmas fairly burst from Mr. Jones' property, lighting up the neighborhood in an explosion of splendor that robbed me of my breath. The gray tiredness that cloaked the Jones' property by day had completely disappeared. In its place stood the merry little elves fashioning their marvelous toys. Illuminated Christmas trees and wreaths stood in splendiferous array behind each bay window. What seemed like mile upon mile of tiny colorful lights flooded the roof and roared in joyous rivulets down the sides of the house. Hearing music, I slowed the car and rolled down my window. The line of carolers was performing "Silent Night," my all-time favorite Christmas carol.

My eyes fell upon the Holy Family as flakes of snow fell quietly, reverently, upon the straw-strewn crèche. My heart all of a sudden filled with such awe and reverence I could barely contain my emotion. Here before my broken heart, arrayed like a glowing crowd of answered prayers, stood the true meaning of Christmas:

"And lo, the angel of the Lord… said unto them, 'Fear not: for, behold, I bring you good tidings of great joy, which shall be to all people. For unto you is born this day in the city of David a Savior, which is Christ the Lord.'"

And Jesus said, "…The spirit of the Lord God… has anointed me to preach good tidings… he hath sent me to bind up the brokenhearted, to proclaim liberty to the captives… to comfort all that mourn… to give unto them beauty for ashes, the oil of joy for mourning, the garment of praise for the spirit of heaviness…."

I do not chuckle as I walk by The Griswold House anymore. Nor do I poke fun at Mr. Jones' yearly labors of love as he so diligently works to ready his home for the holiday season. Mr. Jones is my hero. "I do it for the kids," he told me lamely once, looking baffled that I should not readily understand his motivation.

Well, Mr. Jones, I understand now. It isn't just for the children that you labor so hard every year. You do it because you want to proclaim to hurting people like me everywhere the astonishing meaning of Jesus' birth. You do it because you understand that even in our darkest of nights, the star of Bethlehem shines bright, pointing the way to hope and healing and promise. You do it for people just like me who need to be reminded that we can all strive just a little harder to become the magic that transforms another's sorrow into joy.

God bless you, Mr. Jones. God bless The Griswold House.

~Paula L. Silici

Lights of Hope

*In the depth of winter I finally learned that there was in me
an invincible summer.*
~Albert Camus

I was diagnosed with cancer in October of 2004, which meant
my treatment lasted straight through the month of December.
Chemo for Christmas was not something I looked forward to.
I prayed every day that Christmas would not be ruined by my illness and treatment. With two small children, and a need for hope, I
wanted desperately to keep the magic alive.

The doctors were very aggressive because I was only thirty-four
years old and in an early stage. The chemo didn't knock my hair out,
but it made me sick as a dog. The radiation zapped all my energy.
At 5'9" I actually felt puny. Weight loss and exhaustion left me weak
and barely able to walk across the house. In the past, I'd carried the
Christmas tree into the house, but that year I could barely manage
the ornaments and had to delegate most of the decorating to my
mom and kids.

The outdoor Christmas lights went up around my neighborhood,
and my husband, Jeff, asked if I'd like to go out and see them.

"Not if I can't see all of them," I said. I wanted to go on our
traditional family Christmas walks at night, but how could I when
I couldn't even make it to the end of the driveway to get the mail?

I wanted to drive around the surrounding neighborhoods, but how could I when riding in the car caused motion sickness? The thought of sitting in front of the house, staring at the same blinking string of lights across the street, roused the snarly head of depression.

"I know how you can see all of them," Jeff said, and darted to the phone to call his parents. "Mom, Dad... do you still have Grandpa's wheelchair?"

Night after night, Jeff loaded me into the wheelchair, covered me in thick blankets, and pushed me—thump, thump, over the threshold—out the front door.

My two-year-old daughter, bundled in her little pink jacket, snuggled under the blankets with me, her warmth calming my shivering bones. My son, four years old and much bigger than his sister, walked next to us and held my hand or helped his daddy push.

And just like that, wrapped in the love of my husband and two kids, I rode around my neighborhood.

The Christmas lights were more amazing than they had ever been before—than any lights had ever been before! Colorful, white, twinkling and bright, they sparkled of promise and joy... hope and healing. My spirit lifted higher than I thought possible because of those lights, and because of the love that allowed me to see them all.

Chemo took away my cancer, and it didn't take away my Christmas.

~Kat Heckenbach

A Cloth Full of Memories

Hem your blessings with thankfulness so they don't unravel.
~Author Unknown

It was an old white sheet discarded and thrown in the back of the linen closet. I was a young mother with two small children and a very small budget. We didn't have a lot of money for Christmas and we definitely didn't have money for any elaborate decorations. But I wanted to make something for my family. Something that could be used year after year as a family tradition. I had already handcrafted matching Christmas stockings from red felt appliquéd with Christmas trees, teddy bears, baby dolls and tin soldiers, but I wanted something else for my family. Then I remembered the sheet. Could I possibly use that white sheet to craft a Christmas tablecloth? My sewing abilities were amateurish, but my love for family and tradition was strong. I got out my sewing machine and started hemming the material in red and green thread. I wrote the words "Merry Christmas" in the middle of the tablecloth and spread it across the dining room table. I was so proud!

My daughter was two and a half and my son was only seven months, but I wanted to include them in this tradition. I traced their little hands and feet on the cloth, wrote down their names, ages and the date and then I penned a message for my family. I told them how much I loved them, wished them a Merry Christmas and a Happy New Year. I signed my name and wrote down the date.

Now, over thirty years later that tablecloth is full of messages, greetings, small handprints from my children and grandson Layton, large handprints and food stains. Each message is precious and contains sentiments of love, cute poems, and comical sayings. Four years ago I had to add a white border to allow more room and it's already filled with words from family and friends.

As I sit down to look at each handwritten message, my eyes tear as I come across signatures from my precious mother Bonnie, my stepfather Joseph, my friend's daughter Lindsay, my aunt Olyne, my sweet cousin Karen, all gone but never forgotten. I see the small handprints of my two children and grandson and I remember the day that I traced around their little hands for the first time. I see the messages they wrote as small children, silly teenagers and young adults. I read about snowstorms, cold weather, pecan season, new bikes, new love, old friends and departed loved ones and I remember. I see how my writing has changed as I've gotten older, the scribbles of young children and the squiggly drawings they made when I wasn't looking. All the messages are important and treasured as each one signifies a part of their lives and a journey into mine.

I realized after I made the tablecloth, in fact many years later, that this tablecloth can't be divided into squares. Some of the signatures are written so close to one another that if cut apart, a word or two would be lost forever. I know this tablecloth is old, stained and ugly, but it's full of love and laughter and is a priceless heirloom to me. I look forward to digging it out each year, spreading it out on the table and sitting down to read and remember. I enjoy writing my message each year—it really never deviates. I ask for God's blessing, good health, happiness and a wonderful new year. I savor each written word from my family and friends knowing that one day most of the messages written will be from loved ones gone but never forgotten. This old white sheet has been transformed into a beautiful gift from that young mother, me, who only wanted a tradition for her family, a simple tablecloth full of memories.

~Glenda Carol Lee

The Most Expensive Bike Ever

Never do anything that you wouldn't want to explain to the paramedics.
~Author Unknown

I t all started when our family went Christmas shopping and my husband, Jerry, decided he wanted a bicycle. While he was contemplating the best model for him, my son's heart was drawn to a black freestyle bike. He begged and pleaded but I stoically ignored him and left with Jerry's bike in tow.

A few days later I had the opportunity to go Christmas shopping on my own and was able to pick up Eli's dream bike. After all, it was a good price, and that would take care of the "special" present for Eli. When I got home I left the bike in the back of the van so I could hide it after the boys went to sleep. Jerry had been up since 3 AM and was exhausted so he headed for bed. Soon after, I sent the boys on their way. When I was sure they were asleep, I brought the bike in to hide until Christmas. I thought it would fit behind the bed in the spare room but quickly saw that that idea was not going to work, so I headed for the attic.

The door going into the attic locks automatically, so my main worry was that the door would close behind me and I'd be stuck in the attic overnight. If only.

I entered the attic and looked around, finding the perfect spot to hide the bike. As I rolled the bike over to its new home, the floor gave way beneath me. I was hanging in mid-air! You see, our attic floor is covered in plywood except for one spot that has three short planks. One of the planks had been moved and wasn't situated on the rafters properly. When I stepped on it, it flipped up like a teeter-totter, whacking me in the shin and dropping me through the ceiling of the garage.

As I dangled there listening to unknown things crashing to the ground beneath me, my first thought was, "Oh no! I hope the boys don't hear that and come out and see the bike!"

No worries. Everyone—yes, everyone—slept right through it all.

I reached down and grabbed my shin, only to pull my hand away when I felt all the blood through my jeans. Of course, my hand was now covered in blood which I wiped off on my already blood-soaked jeans. After all, I didn't want to get it on the bike. Somehow I managed to extricate myself from my dangling position and find some footing in the attic.

I examined my shin and saw that most of the blood had been soaked up by my blue jeans. The rest of the blood had reached the top of my sock and had pretty much stopped there. I decided my leg could wait while I finished hiding the bike. Part of my reasoning was that the real pain might kick in and I wouldn't be able to finish the job. The other part of my reasoning was that by taking care of it now I could avoid having to climb the stairs again (I'm almost fifty and am very good at escaping anything remotely like exercise).

After hiding the bike behind empty boxes I went downstairs. Curiosity overcame pain and I headed for the garage to survey the damage. I noticed it was rather dimly lit in there. Then I realized we were missing one of the florescent lighting boxes which had always hung on the ceiling right in the general vicinity of the now gaping hole. It occurred to me that the falling box was the delayed crashing sound I'd heard after puncturing the ceiling. I'd knocked the box off, it had dangled by the wires for a moment before coming crashing down—on Jerry's car! His prized possession!

I panicked! The car was covered in glass shards so I couldn't get a good look at the damage. I knew that if I brushed the glass off the car it would scratch it, so I went inside and got the vacuum cleaner. I gingerly took the vacuum and sucked up the glass, trying to pull it off the car vertically. Once all the glass was off, I took a look at the car in the dim light and saw that the side mirror was badly scratched and there was a two-inch scratch on the door next to it. Later, in full light, I noticed the windshield had scratches all over it and there was a small dent in the door as well. The original price of the bike combined with the cost in sheetrock, lighting, and car repairs had now become astronomical.

After finishing things up in the garage I finally took a good look at my leg. After washing the blood off, I saw that I had a scratch about the size of the one on Jerry's car. It didn't seem to be very deep. Next to it, however, was a small gouge that seemed to be the source of all the blood. On examination I realized that it could probably take one stitch, but I was determined not to add an emergency room fee to the cost of this bike. I butterflied the edges of the cut together, covered it with a huge bandage and Neosporin, and got into bed.

Before falling asleep I started thinking about the big bruise I was going to have on my upper thigh in the morning. I thought, "It's probably not a good thing to just lie down while this bruise forms. Couldn't it form some clot that will migrate to my brain and kill me?" I tossed and turned most of the night from pain and worry about blood clots and telling Jerry about his car.

Around 5 AM I woke up, turned over and was startled by flashing lights around me. I thought that possibly the neighbors across the street were driving out of their driveway and shining their lights through our windows. Then I woke up enough to realize that we have room darkening curtains and nothing ever shines in that brightly. I turned over the other way and saw more flashing lights! Now I was more panicked than I was over Jerry's car. "The blood clot has reached my brain and I'm dying! This can't be! Surely this is not IT!" But every time I moved I saw flashes of light before my eyes. I stopped moving. I lay there and thought about the cost of the funeral added to the cost of the bike.

Jerry woke up and I told him, "I fell through the ceiling in the garage last night." He chuckled, stopped short and said, "What?" I repeated, "I was hiding Eli's bike in the attic and I fell through the ceiling into the garage." He quit chuckling and said, "You're not kidding!" I related the evening's events to him and to his credit he didn't even ask how damaged the car was. I ended my story with the statement of my imminent death from a brain clot that was causing blinding flashes of light. It was a mystery to both of us.

I decided to get up and let the clot do its work. As I sat up I was hit with more blinding flashes. I also noticed that my pajamas were sticking to my body. As I pulled on one of my sleeves a flash of light emanated from the static electricity in my pajamas! I leaped out of bed with the realization that I wasn't dying! I told Jerry, "Look!" and proceeded to pull my clothes away from my skin up and down my body. Sparks were flying everywhere and in the pitch-blackness of the room, they were blinding.

At least I was going to live to pay the bills.

~Barbara Nicks

Reprinted by permission of Off the Mark
and Mark Parisi ©1998.

The Green Christmas Ball

If you have much, give of your wealth;
if you have little, give of your heart.
~Arabian Proverb

By the third year of teaching I had begun to anticipate Christmas break more for the school holiday and less for the excitement of the children. I was teaching fourth grade and my students, combined with medical problems, had exhausted me. I prayed for strength enough to get me to 3:15. I just had to get through one of the hardest days of the school year.

I groaned out loud as the morning bell rang. Time to begin the circus. I trudged through the cold between my mobile classroom (nice name for a trailer) and into the overly heated school building. I sighed and turned the corner. Twenty-two smiling faces greeted me on the fourth grade bus hall. I forced myself to return their smiles and enthusiastic hugs. "Seven and a half hours to go," I thought to myself.

Back through the cold and into the room they chattered, comparing plans for the vacation. I had to remove one student from each arm and one from around my waist before I could take a seat at my desk for my morning duties. Before I could find my roll book my desk was covered with cards and gifts followed by a chorus of "Merry Christmas" wishes.

"Oh, thank you," I must have responded a million times. Each gift was truly special to me, despite my sour mood. It was kind of them to think of me.

After the tornado had calmed to hurricane levels, I heard a small voice say my name. I looked up to see Brandon standing shyly by my desk, holding a small, round gift. "This is for you."

"Thank you, Sweetheart." I hugged him and laid it on my desk with the others.

"Um, could you open it now?"

I stopped my frantic pace to give him my full attention. This was important to him. "Sure."

I gently tugged at the crumpled paper and mounds of tape. "Careful," he said, "it's breakable."

"Oh, okay," I assured him. Slowly I unwrapped a small, green Christmas tree ornament, complete with a hook already attached. It dawned on me what he had done.

"You know he just pulled that off his tree!" a nearby student commented rudely.

I swallowed some tears. "Yes, I know," I answered. "That makes it even more special."

"It's my favorite," Brandon informed me.

"It'll be my favorite, too. I don't have anything green on my tree."

He beamed.

Later that day, during a rare quiet moment, I sat turning the ornament over in my hands. Was I really so important to this child that he had searched for something to give me? His mother did not hand him a gift bag with an elegant bow as he ran for the bus. He had considered this gift himself.

Now every year as I delicately pull a green Christmas ball from my ornament box I remember the profound impact adults have on children. More importantly, I remember the impact my students have on me.

~Aletheia D. Lee

34

Wreathed in Tradition

Perhaps the best Yuletide decoration is being wreathed in smiles.
~Author Unknown

"Make sure that the wreath is centered," I instructed my husband as we finished the last of our Christmas decorating. Looking around the house, I was proud of our day's work: stockings hung by the fireplace, colorful candles sat atop our mantle, and bright lights glittered on the tree. But nothing seemed to say "Christmas" to me like our wreath. I quickly grabbed a tape measure to assure its perfect placement on our front door.

The scent of freshly cut pine filled the air as I lovingly ran my hands through the prickly green needles. I imagined my extended family—aunts, uncles, and cousins—each hanging similar wreaths on their own front doors. Though hundreds of miles apart, we were connected, bound together by our annual pre-holiday wreath-making tradition, the "gathering of the greens" on our Western Pennsylvania family farm.

More than forty relatives assembled again this year, making their annual late-November pilgrimage to our homestead, a dairy farm first settled by my ancestors some two hundred years ago. My uncle, a retired farmer who still lived in the old white farmhouse, looked forward to our visit each year. We arrived bearing pies and casseroles, weary from our travels, but comforted by the warm embrace of family. After a feast of turkey and stuffing, we pulled on warm coats and headed outside.

"Hurry, Daddy! Everyone is getting ready to leave for the woods!"

Our two young girls bolted through the muddy yard, hoping not to be left behind.

Piled onto an old wooden wagon, hitched to my uncle's green John Deere tractor, we made quite the sight—a load of chatty Scotch-Irish relatives, ranging in age from three to seventy-something.

Stones flew up along the uneven gravel road as we bumped along the rural countryside for about a mile before turning into the woods. A canopy of pine trees welcomed us as we made our way across a muddy trail, ducking to avoid wayward branches.

"This is it," my uncle announced, turning off the engine. Jumping down from the wagon, we scrambled to collect nature's bounty—fragrant evergreens that beckoned to be cut and collected for Christmas wreaths. The youngest children, quickly disinterested with the task at hand, found a little stream that seemed just right for splashing and rock-skipping.

"They can go right in," my uncle reassured me. "When we were kids we used to play in that creek all the time."

Keeping one eye on the children, we searched for pine and spruce branches, cutting only the most wreath-worthy. I walked along and picked up a few sprigs, but mostly I looked around in wonder at the scene before me. I was walking on the grounds of my ancestors. My great aunts picnicked under the shade of these very trees. I imagined my mom and her sisters, splashing in the stream where my own girls now played. This place, with its babbling creek and towering trees, seemed almost sacred. I tried to take it all in—the giggles of the girls, the crisp, strangely invigorating air—but all too soon the setting sun signaled that it was time to hop aboard the wagon and head back home.

An old barn shed, our wreath-making headquarters, soon became a hubbub of activity. An assembly line formed as we carefully wove evergreens through metal wreath forms. Like busy elves, we hummed along in our workshop, swapping family gossip as our Christmas masterpieces took shape. The bow committee, headed by those with artistic flair, added ribbons, bells, and crimson berries to our festive creations. One by one, completed wreaths hung on the wall for inspection. Which one would we choose to take home this year? What wreath would we take to the cemetery in memory of my dad, a man who never missed a farm holiday?

Nightfall signaled a bittersweet end to a day steeped in tradition. Wreaths packed into minivans and SUVs, we said our goodbyes, then headed our separate ways. Though we lived far apart—from Ohio to New York to the mountains of West Virginia—we would carry a piece of family with us as we went home and prepared for Christmas.

"There. Now it looks perfectly centered." Back at home in Ohio, I hung my wreath on the front door. So much more than a mere Christmas decoration, it is a constant reminder of family. Like the intertwining pine branches, we are connected—forever woven together by history and tradition.

~Stefanie Wass

35

The Post Office

A wise lover values not so much the gift of the lover as the love of the giver.
~Thomas à Kempis

It had been a roller coaster year and I wasn't feeling very merry that Christmas.

There had been highs, but the dips, wild curves and downward plummets left me battered. My husband's chronic illness, which had been stable for several years, began to spiral. Hospital stays led to bad news and more time in the hospital. It seemed like every week brought a new crisis. I lived with hope and hopes dashed, culminating with my husband of thirty years dying of heart disease.

He died in mid-October, and in December I had no energy to be merry. Perversely, I craved company, and filled my time and my house with activity. I didn't take vacation from work when others did, and I entertained family and friends during the season. I found baking to be good therapy. My life was turned upside down, and so many parts of it I didn't understand, but I knew how to make shortbreads and sugar cookies. The familiarity of the task brought me comfort.

It felt good to have the house full and noisy, and my family close. My sister-in-law and I took turns with Christmas, and that year was her turn, but I asked if I could have the celebration at my house. I couldn't face being idle on Christmas Day.

All of this activity helped me get through that difficult first Christmas. Inevitably, however, when the meal is over and the gifts are unwrapped, people begin to pack up. At the end of the day, when things got quieter and slower, I missed Bill.

He was never much of a shopper, but he always put enormous thought and effort into finding the perfect present for me. The year I'd asked for a hand-knit sweater with pictures on it, he had gone from store to store for weeks, looking for just the right one. Another time, he carefully researched which would be the best digital camera for me. The time he spent was his love language.

We were cleaning up when I spied the box. Unwrapped, it sat alone by a wall in the living room. No one claimed it or knew who it came from. No one had seen when it arrived. As I held it, a strange *Twilight Zone* feeling overtook me. It contained a ceramic post office for the Dickens village that covered the top of my piano. Bill had given me most of the other buildings for Christmas several years ago in unpainted form, and painting them throughout the next year was great fun. A train ran through the center of the village, and I created hills and farms, a schoolyard and an ice rink. It never looked the same twice. Every Christmas, I anticipated putting it together and looking into what seemed like another world.

The year before, I didn't put it up. I was overwhelmed with the stress of Bill's illness, and I did only the minimum to make Christmas for the family. The village was for me, and I decided I could live without the work it took to put it together. I missed it, though. There was something in that village that met a need inside of me during the busy season. What hurt even more than not having it up, was the fact that no one seemed to notice its absence. To me, it was a glaring message that things were not as they should be — perhaps even a cry for help. Even my husband didn't say a word about it. I wondered if he even noticed. Christmas passed, and the village stayed in its bin in the garage.

This year, when it was obvious that nothing was as it should be, I had put up the village. As I had unwrapped each building, I remembered. I loved the barn, the church, the toy shop and the train station. I added lamp posts, benches and characters scurrying around in Victorian splendor. The skating rink in the center had skaters who would dance at the push of a button.

I stared at the ceramic building in my hands. My village had been missing a post office and here it was. It was painted and ready to sit among the other buildings on the street. I moved the candy store and created a spot for it, and then stood back to reflect in wonder at what had just happened.

Maybe Bill had noticed after all.

~Ann Peachman

36

A New Tradition

Christmas, children, is not a date. It is a state of mind.
~Mary Ellen Chase

The stoplight turned yellow—then red. I waited. People scurried everywhere, their arms filled with packages. Snowflakes floated gently in the air, melting as they touched the windshield. Christmas lights blinked along the streets and sidewalks and from each shop window. Suddenly, tears filled my eyes: Christmas already?

The light turned green. Alone and feeling lonely, I headed home. Glimpses of decorated trees and flickering lights inside homes along the way brought a flood of tears and heartaches—I couldn't take Christmas this year. Single again after thirty years of marriage, everything seemed gone: family and home. There would be no holiday meals to prepare, gifts to wrap, stockings to fill, or squeals of delight from happy faces of grandchildren on Christmas Eve. Our family had disintegrated—dissolved—nothing left but shattered pieces.

My oldest grandchild, age six, had been asking, "Grandma, when are you going to put up your Christmas tree?"

"Not this year, honey," had been my reply.

Finally one day she stated, "Grandma, you can't not have a Christmas tree. It just wouldn't be right." The disappointment on her face caused me more pain than my sorrow and emotions—many things were not "right" this year.

"Okay," I agreed, "but under one condition—you ALL will help

Grandma put up the tree. You find a time when everyone can come… and I'll get everything else together. We'll have a big party to trim the tree. We'll call it Grandma's Tree-Decorating Party."

"Yes, yes, yes," she said jumping and clapping her hands in glee. She made the phone calls and called me back a couple days later with the day and time all arranged. She had been a busy little girl.

The family that I thought had been fragmented came together on the appointed afternoon. My sons laughed and joked together as they hacked and sawed the tree, getting it into its stand, and untangling themselves from the strings of lights as they circled the tree in the living room.

Seated at the table in the kitchen, the children—Stephanie, Jason, Erica, and Rachel (ages six to two)—made strings of popcorn and cranberries as they sipped and snacked on food. Parents and Grandma already had agreed, "You may have anything you want to eat at this party."

The aroma of hot fruit punch made from dried and frozen fruit, spices, and cinnamon sticks filled the air. In holiday array beside the fruit punch sat the eggnog, hot chocolate with marshmallows, homemade fudge, popcorn balls, apples, dishes of nuts, and trays of Christmas cookies. This kept everybody hilariously eating as we worked and chatted together. Adult hands lifted the little ones high enough to place their popcorn strings on the tree and hang the bulbs just a bit higher.

After the tree was decorated we gathered around the organ to sing carols. Then we read *The Christmas Story* by the lights on the tree. Soon the little ones were asleep in dreamland. Our new "tradition" had begun.

As the children became older, they assumed more of the tasks, including the Christmas background music. During their teenage years, cookie baking and decorating became a pre-party morning fun time with Grandma in Grandma's kitchen. Several times a friend or two joined us on that special day. Then the dates had to be arranged according to college schedules, and Grandma's Christmas-tree-decorating-party became the "new tradition" everyone fondly remembers.

Thirty-three years have passed since that first party. Our family now includes seven great-grandchildren and we are scattered over several states. In honor of "tradition," Grandma joyfully puts up her tree, saying a big "thank you" to her very persistent granddaughter for changing that first painful Christmas into many years of happy memories.

~Josephine Overhulser

37

The Wooden Soldier

We don't see things as they are, we see them as we are.
~Anaïs Nin

Each year it seems to take me longer to put away the Christmas tree decorations. My hands tend to linger on those ornaments that have come to have special meaning for me. Today, it's a small, painted balsa wood toy soldier that my fingers close around.

There's not anything special about it: it's just a piece from a Christmas craft kit which included easy-to-follow instructions, designed for those of us with limited artistic abilities. No, nothing special except... I am transported back in time to the winter of 1974, as my husband Roger and I, along with our two-year-old daughter, Anne and our miniature Dachshund, Muttley, arrived in Wichita Falls, Texas. It was Thanksgiving Day, and I felt far, far away from friends and family.

My husband had been accepted into the Air Force Flight Engineer program at Sheppard AFB, with orders to report for duty the day after Thanksgiving. It was officially an "unaccompanied tour"—meaning no provisions are made for families. But even though we knew it would strain our modest budget, it was unthinkable that we wouldn't all go. The year before, Roger had been in Korea for the entire holiday season, and we were determined to be together for this one.

After a long, tiring journey starting out in Washington, D.C., with side trips to Ohio and Pennsylvania to visit our respective parents, we were happy to have reached the end.

Almost magically, an inviting-looking motel appeared. Even better, a Denny's was just across the street! We were cheered by the colorful sign in the window beckoning us with the promise of "turkey dinner with all the trimmings." Spirits rising, we pried our grouchy toddler out of her car seat and into the dark, chilly night.

"We'll all have the turkey dinner," we chirped moments later to the bored-looking waitress. "All out," she responded. There was a moment of silence as this information sunk in. "Spaghetti for three," I said in a small voice.

After our untraditional Thanksgiving dinner, we checked into the motel and fell immediately into our beds.

All night long, the cold winds howled across the Texas plains, and in the morning there was a fine dusting of snow on the carpet near the door.

Roger dressed quickly and headed to the base, while the rest of us—dog included—snuggled deeper under the covers. But he was back in an amazingly short time.

"They said I didn't have to be there until Monday morning," he said, not looking directly at me.

"You mean..."

"...that we could have spent Thanksgiving with our families," he finished.

We just looked at one another.

As least I wouldn't have to look for a place to live on my own. Feeling cautiously optimistic, we set out to find something to rent for a month or two. What we were looking for was a cheap, furnished place that accepted children and dogs. Finally, we came upon a marginally adequate trailer that featured all of the above, plus, we found out later, a healthy crop of fleas.

We settled in, and soon Roger was immersed in class during the day, and intensive studying at night. The rest of us tried to keep busy, so as not to distract him. We took endless walks around the trailer park, watched TV and read countless books.

In the meantime, Christmas was growing closer. While I watched the glittery holiday specials on our small, rented black-and-white TV, I couldn't help noticing the stark difference between the festive scenes portrayed on the screen, and the depressing decor of our temporary quarters.

It is difficult for people who have never experienced it to understand how much household possessions mean to us military wives. Being aware we might find ourselves living in many different places, we tend to find comfort in the familiar things that make a house a home.

I thought about all my treasured Christmas things packed safely away in a storage unit. The only thing I had with me was the set of painted wooden ornaments I had grabbed at the last minute. There had been no room in the car to take anything else, and certainly no money to buy anything new.

Still, all of this would have been bearable if I could have looked forward to being in my own home on December 25th, surrounded by, if not family, at least friends. But I knew this would be impossible.

Christmas shopping was simple: only a few small gifts for my husband and me; more for Anne. I had bought some material and stuffing at the fabric store, and every day during her nap, with the dog curled up at my side, I worked on hand-stitching a pink elephant pillow for her.

A week before the big day, we bought a live Christmas tree that almost touched the living room ceiling. We set about making popcorn and cranberry garlands, stringing them on sturdy pieces of thread. Then, we hung the ornaments and stepped back to see the fruits of our labors. Our little girl was delighted, and even I had to admit the tree looked nice.

On Christmas morning, we watched as Anne emerged sleepily from her bedroom. We saw her eyes become suddenly full of wonder as she gazed at the splendor under the tree. She went immediately to the elephant pillow, and held it tight against her small chest. Stealing a glance at my husband, I could tell how special it was for him to see her joy.

Later, we bundled up and ventured out into the cold, equipped with a cup of quarters for the phone booth at the entrance to the trailer park. Huddled inside, we wished our families Merry Christmas and they did the same, all of us talking at the same time.

By mid-afternoon, a few of Roger's classmates arrived. Since none of these men were fortunate enough to have their families along, we wanted to include them in our modest celebration. They seemed to care little that the food was served on paper plates and eaten with plastic cutlery. Warm conversation and laughter filled the dingy living room well into the evening. Finally, reluctantly it seemed, they headed back to their lonely barracks.

Then it was over, this strange Christmas on the plains.

Many holiday seasons have passed since then—joyous times of wonderful gifts, beautifully decorated houses and glorious trees. They meld together in my mind. But the year of the tacky trailer and humble tree remains crystal clear.

Anne is a grown woman now, mother of four. She held on to her elephant pillow until the material simply wore out. Then she put it in a pillowcase and kept it even longer.

The wooden ornaments still grace our tree every year, hanging proudly among their more prestigious store-bought neighbors. They have earned their place.

If someone were to ask me why I so value the simple wooden soldier I hold in my hand, I would simply say it's because it is a priceless reminder of the Christmas I learned what really mattered.

~Susan H. Miller

Christmas Magic

There's No Place Like Home for the Holidays

38

Just Enough for Christmas

Brothers are the crab grass in the lawn of life.
~Charles M. Schulz

My brother came home for Christmas again this year. It's not him that I mind so much. It's the fuss that occurs when he arrives. He rarely calls, he never writes, he's a three-time college dropout and he's never stayed with a job for more than six months. He only sees my parents at Christmas and they have to send him airfare to get home. Sorry if this sounds harsh, but when Gerald shows up for Christmas my parents act as if Christ himself has come back to celebrate his birthday.

We can't decorate the tree until Gerald gets home; then Uncle Jim and Aunt Liz come over and Dad videotapes the evening, completely out of focus. My mother gets weepy and calls the neighbors to talk about how good it is to have the family all together at this special time.

I'm surprised my parents haven't taken the baby Jesus out of the Nativity set and replaced it with a plastic replica of my brother.

On Christmas morning, after my brother's favorite breakfast of chocolate chip pancakes, hash browns and apple juice, we experience the torture known as "gift time."

My mother always thinks she knows just what I need. She usually gets ideas when she makes unannounced visits to my apartment.

Then she drops unsubtle hints about what I should expect under the tree.

"David, you could use a coffeemaker," my mother said, when she visited one evening after doing some Christmas shopping.

"But, Mom, I don't drink coffee."

"What about when company comes over?" she replied. "Your brother drinks coffee."

"Gerald lives seven hundred miles away," I said. "He's never been to my apartment. If he happens to stop by, I'll take him out to the Starbucks around the corner."

My mother nodded. "Still, a coffeemaker is a nice thing to have."

So, on Christmas morning when we opened gifts, I got a coffeemaker, a dictionary and four packs of socks.

You know what Gerald got? A subscription to *Entertainment Weekly* magazine and a card full of cash.

Cash!

I get socks, he gets cash.

"We weren't sure what you needed," my mother said to Gerald. "We figured you could find a way to have some fun with the money."

"Hey, if you want fun," I said, holding up my dictionary. "Maybe we can look up the definitions to words. How about "irritate" or "animosity?"

But no one heard me since they were too busy watching Gerald count out his cash.

After our meal I cleared off the table and my mother sang "Rudolph the Red-Nosed Reindeer" off-key while she loaded the dishwasher. Dad and Gerald sat in the living room watching football.

I wasn't interested in the game, so I wandered upstairs, on the premise that I was going to use the bathroom.

At the top of the stairs I passed my parents' bedroom and looked into Gerald's old room.

I secretly called it "The Wonder Boy Shrine" since my mother hadn't moved a thing in the six years since Gerald had left. His bed, desk and lamp were there. His school yearbooks were on the shelf;

his posters were on the wall. For all I knew there could still be a pair of his dirty underwear stuck under the bed.

Crossing the hall, I walked into my old room, now referred to as "the guest room." The room had been stripped the weekend after I moved out: new curtains, new paint, new carpeting, new bedspread. My old things were stored in the attic.

Cold, heavy raindrops splattered against the window. I looked out at the plastic illuminated snowman my father set up in the front yard. He'd been putting that thing out there every year for as long as I could remember. Glowing brightly, the snowman was leaning to one side. His red top hat was faded and a thick wad of duct tape held the back of his head together. I knew how he felt. Christmas around this house had the same effect on me.

Why did this have to be so difficult? I probably would have been happy to see Gerald if my parents showed a bit more appreciation towards me for all that I did around here.

I was the one who was here all year long. I helped plant their Impatiens and Geraniums in the spring and never forgot their birthdays and always took them out to dinner on Mother's Day and Father's Day. I even came over at Easter and watched the entire *Ten Commandments* with them every year! I was here whenever they needed me.

But they couldn't get enough of Gerald.

"David, what are you doing up here?" My mother startled me from my mental tirade. "I thought you were downstairs watching TV."

I shrugged my shoulders and looked back out the window.

"You must have lots of memories in this room," she said, sitting down on the bed. "It's good having you both back home. But, you know something?" She took a deep breath and then sighed.

I gritted my teeth. I knew what was coming next—another ode to Gerald. Perhaps she could sing it to the tune of a Christmas carol. Would it be "Gerald We Have Heard On High" or "Joy to the Gerald?"

"I wish your brother could be more like you."

I turned to look at her. I couldn't believe it. "What?"

"Don't get me wrong," said my mother. "I love Gerald dearly, but I wish he was more responsible, more mature, more hard-working, like you are. Then I wouldn't have to worry about him so much. I hate to even touch his bedroom because I'm always worried he'll need to move back home. He's not like you at all."

I shook my head. "But I always thought…" I shook my head again. "You wish Gerald was more like me?"

"Of course I do." My mother stood up and gave me a hug. "You're a good son, David. And a wonderful person. I don't know what your father and I would do without you."

I hugged her back. "Thanks, Mom."

"I'm going downstairs," she said. "I'm going to try to get your father to turn the channel so I can watch *It's a Wonderful Life*."

Talk about a Christmas miracle. This year she had actually given me a gift that I wanted; her approval.

She liked me.

She appreciated what I did.

She thought I was as good as Gerald.

That night when I got back to my apartment, I made a pot of coffee and looked up the word "family" in my dictionary.

The definition read: "A group of related things."

With my family, that might be as close as we'd ever get. But as strange as it seemed, I was actually looking forward to next Christmas and hoping my brother would be able to make it home.

I guess knowing that my parents really did appreciate me was just enough for Christmas.

~David J. Hull

Our Own Tiny Family

There is no such cozy combination as man and wife.
~Menander

"Y ou're not going to be with family?" The question was whispered across delectable cups of hot chocolate, almost carried away in the faint wisps of steam curling up from the mugs. But it couldn't evaporate completely, weighed down as it was by a rather heavy dollop of disbelief, and it reached my ears loud and clear.

"I'm going to be with my husband," I answered gamely, not yet aware that this could possibly be the worst answer I could give.

Three pairs of eyes looked back at me, full of confusion and questions. Friends I had known for years suddenly began evaluating me in an entirely new light.

"But that's just your husband," one of them ventured. "What about your family?"

"Or his family?" another put in, glancing at the others for confirmation.

They all nodded in unison. Family, it seemed to be agreed upon by everyone, was crucial for Christmas morning.

"Well," I said slowly, suddenly feeling as if I was walking on the ice that coated the canal outside the coffee shop's window, "my husband is my family. As long as we're together we're happy."

They all exchanged a look.

"What am I missing?" I asked, slightly miffed that they all seemed to share a secret knowledge from which I never even knew I was excluded.

"It's just, well, won't it be a little... quiet on Christmas morning?"

I considered this. Compared to being around my husband's two parents, four siblings, three nephews and niece it might be a little quiet. Compared to being around my grandfather, two parents, three siblings and one almost brother-in-law it might be a little quiet. But in order to get to any of this festive commotion we'd have to travel several hours either by plane or train. And after a year of very bad health, major surgery, working overtime and paying the healthcare bills, my husband and I had very little time, energy, budget or inclination to travel.

So for the first time ever, we planned to spend the entire stretch of holidays, from Christmas Eve right through New Year's Day, in our own home. I thought what we were doing was best for us as our own little family, but maybe I'd thought wrong? Maybe Christmas wouldn't really be Christmas without a big family meal and lots of noise and wrapping paper and bad sing-alongs and fights for the bathroom?

I turned these questions over in my mind as I walked home that afternoon, and again as I planned our holiday menus. Was I making too much food? Would we feel pathetic, just the two of us, trying to get through a turkey and several sides? How many Christmas cookies were too many Christmas cookies? Should I just make restaurant reservations instead, to spare us the potential embarrassment of a table full of food and no one to eat it?

As I shopped for my husband's presents more questions crept into my mind. How many presents would be needed to keep the tree from looking bare? How could we prolong present opening so that it didn't feel pitifully short? Should I buy fancy wrapping paper and bows and ribbons so that there would be enough spread around the room as we tore through the gifts? Should I practice shrieking and jumping up and down in case we needed that little edge of Christmas clamor? (I discarded that last idea pretty quickly.)

It wasn't until Christmas Eve afternoon, while my husband wrapped gifts and I set out platters of snacks, that the doubts began to disappear. We had a Christmas movie marathon ready to be watched, candy canes ready to swirl in our hot chocolate and cinnamon-scented candles ready to be lit. That evening we ate ourselves silly and worked through our own private film festival. We also tracked Santa on the NORAD website and even watched him pay a quick visit to the International Space Station. We bantered back and forth with our siblings using e-mail, instant messenger, text messages and digital photos. At midnight we wished each other a Merry Christmas and then slept for ten long, luxurious hours.

The next day we put on Christmas carols, cooked up a storm and opened our presents with lots of love and laughter. That is, until my husband surprised me with the little leather wallet I'd been lusting after. I cried then, but from happiness rather than sadness.

"Is it okay?" he asked anxiously. "Is everything okay?"

I leaned over to kiss his cheek and wiped away my tears.

"It's perfect. Everything's perfect. I wouldn't change a thing."

As the wind whipped outside and beautiful voices sang about the holy night my husband put his arm around me.

"Neither would I," he said.

We may not have had a noisy Christmas, or a Christmas packed with relatives or a Christmas that would be remembered for convivial confusion or cheerful chaos but we had our Christmas. We celebrated as our own tiny family, and that was more than either of us needed.

~Beth Morrissey

I'll Be Home for Christmas

It takes hands to build a house, but only hearts can build a home.
~Author Unknown

I drove back toward our rental, our temporary location, listening to the radio. While I usually reserved Christmas music for the day after Thanksgiving, I needed the kind of joy only Jewel singing "Winter Wonderland" can bring.

"I'm dreaming of a place I love" came through the speakers of my white 2001 RX300. Tears started to fall as I kept my eyes on the road. It was a road I had driven nearly every day for the past three years. It was on this road three months ago that I had seen smoke coming from our neighborhood, making my heart quicken and my foot hit the accelerator pedal. We had left our dog, Shade, inside that night.

My husband, Dan, tried to reassure me that the fire wasn't near our house and that everything was fine. I was not easily persuaded.

"See, it's in the field below the house," Dan said as we drove past our neighborhood trying to find the fastest way back home.

"Are you sure?" I asked. "Okay."

I looked again.

"Are you sure?"

As we pulled into our neighborhood I nearly hit a fire engine with my car because the smoke was so thick. I sent Dan into the fire to get the animals and the photos, which he did.

Hours later we learned that was all we had left.

Our three-bedroom suburban house had been redone in custom tile and it had a kitchen that was made to feel like a diner. It had a pass-through bar and cabinets that seemed to float in the air, with several feet between them and the top of the vaulted ceiling. The previous owners had left plastic tube lighting, which seemed corny, but they gave the room a unique ambience, and so I kept them.

Dan and I had redone parts of the house, updating light fixtures, repainting walls, and building a custom 750-square foot deck in 100-degree heat. I had just finished our son Kellen's nursery, as he was due a month after the fire.

In the months since, I dreamed of that house. It was the only way to get back to the place I loved.

I had imagined our first Christmas with our new baby even before he was conceived. Even though Kellen would only be a couple of months old at Christmas, I knew he would have new pajamas under the tree and would play with the boxes. He would sit on my lap as we tore through the wrapping paper and uncovered Christmas treasures. The weekend prior to losing our house, I had finished making Dan's stocking while watching the closing ceremonies of the Beijing games. It was a crazy quilted rugged stocking and I was just starting on Kellen's which I had hoped he would keep his entire life the way that I had mine. I imagined that Kellen's stocking that first Christmas would have pacifiers, rattles, and a Christmas ornament in it. I had collected ornaments, one each year since I had been in elementary school and I had looked forward to starting the tradition with my son.

Christmas for me had always brought immense joy. I loved the smell of fresh pine. I loved the emotions of the music, which even in the sadness of songs like "Christmas Shoes" could bring joy in believing in the goodness of humanity. That, for me, was the true spirit of the season. I loved the ornaments, especially those that had been handmade by my mom and grandmother and great-grandmother. I loved wrapping gifts, maybe even more than giving them. I loved the feel of crisp paper and straight lines. I loved the whooshing sound of scissors shearing the colored paper into rectangles. I loved folding the paper down and creating edges that showed I had put effort into the beauty of the present. I made bows and tags. It was my holiday. And I loved it.

Instead of joy, however, this year brought sadness. I would have no tree in my living room, no generational ornaments, no scraps of wrapping paper from years past. Our stockings were gone. Our first house, the one I envisioned spending my first Christmas in as a family of three, was in ashes. And all I had now were floorboards and the outline of a new home.

"I'll be home for Christmas" continued over the car's speakers. Only in my dreams.

I knew that the house wouldn't be finished. Even though Dan was working as the general contractor and pushing sub-contractors through at a nearly record-setting pace, construction was expected to last until at least January. I had cried to them about this date, but I knew it was the most realistic. I didn't want to be home only in my dreams though. It wasn't enough.

When I got back to the rental, a place I refused to call my house much less home, I told Dan my plan.

"I want to spend Christmas at the new house," I said.

We talked about the logistics, like heat, and decided we could make it happen.

I started making plans for our Christmas at home. We bought a tree in the middle of December. They were being offered free to the ten families who lost their homes in our neighborhood's fire. While I had thought about not getting one, knowing that I could put it in my new, unfinished house made it okay. Boxes of gifts from friends, family, and strangers continued to arrive. Old family ornaments were graciously given to me by my mom and sister even though we had already divided them a few years ago. My mom's book club in Virginia shipped ornaments across the country. Though simple, one of my favorites said "Joy" in white, covered lightly with glitter. I may not have felt it fully in my heart yet, but I knew that joy would come.

I prepared stuffed French toast Christmas Eve to take to the house in the morning. We bought a hot pot for coffee and a few other snack items. We had invited friends, family, and some of the community to the house Christmas morning. We packed up the gifts and stockings and drove up the hill from our rental to our house.

There was heat and there were walls but not much else. We hung garland from the unfinished banister on the stairs. We set up a folding table where the kitchen would soon be, and I unfolded my reindeer table cloth from Pottery Barn. We placed folding chairs in the living room which had no carpet or paint.

Friends and family came through the house throughout the day, and we showed them around, pointing out where I envisioned our Christmas tree would go in subsequent years. We listened to Christmas songs and found solace in the sound of laughter throughout our house.

It wasn't the Christmas at home I had expected but we were home. And there was peace and joy that Christmas day.

~Brooke Linville

Christmas Eve Chili

Things may change us, but we start and end with the family.
~Anthony Brandt

"Don't push it," my mother said to me that afternoon. Her voice crackled on the phone with the static of the storm that was icing and blowing and snowing somewhere west of New England. "Wait for the storm to pass and then come home. You'll be here on Christmas. That's what's important."

Maybe, I said to myself, as I hung up the phone and looked out the window of my Boston apartment, up at the gathering clouds. It wasn't snowing. And if I left now—right now—I might beat the storm to New York and be home in time for the chili, cornbread and tree decorating that had become my family's tradition for Christmas Eve. Besides, my mother was a weather worrier, calling us in from the snow before the first flake hit the grass and handing us umbrellas when clouds were tinted any shade of gray.

What I didn't tell her, she wouldn't worry about. And when I walked in the house she'd see that I was an adult who could make decisions for myself.

And so, minutes later I was in the front seat of my 1974 Oldsmobile Omega that had been given to me by my grandmother "Ging Ging" the year before she died. It was an armored tank of a car with doors that closed with a decisive thunk and an engine that roared with power, plus a muffler that probably needed replacement.

I worried less about cars than I did about the weather. A pig-headed certainty was another of Ging Ging's legacies.

So that's how I came to be on the Massachusetts Turnpike at dusk with snow and ice hammering at my windows, the heater flashing on and off and an ominous pause whenever my wipers hit the top of their arc.

I fed the car some extra gas, trying in my pig-headed certainty to outrun the storm, and turned the radio up to drown out the thunking, thudding and roaring of the storm.

The storm, though, was having none of that.

And so that's how I came to be on the side of the Massachusetts Turnpike at dusk with a car that was slightly chilly on the inside and so frozen on the outside that the windshield wipers simply stopped working.

I sat there in the dark. In the silence. In the chill. I sat there thinking about the chili and church and my father announcing somewhere around 8 PM that it was time to haul the tree down from the attic, put it together and decorate it. One sister was in charge of the lights, another in charge of finding the colored nibs at the base of the branches to match the colored holes on the tree trunk. The twins would hang the ornaments on the lower branches. We'd toss handfuls of tinsel on the tree, and Mom and Dad would admonish, "one strand at a time."

I'd be hanging ornaments on the upper branches, taking photos and singing loudly and somewhat off-key to the *Sing Along with Mitch* Christmas album. Only I was sitting on the side of the Massachusetts Turnpike slowly becoming a drift of snow.

I got out of my car and surveyed the wipers. I took off my mittens and mopped the wipers clean and blew some hot air on them. They didn't move. Not a centimeter. I wrapped my mittens around the bases and waited a minute or two before trying again.

Nothing.

I was going to not only celebrate Christmas Eve in the breakdown lane, but quite possibly Christmas Day. In fact, I was—at that moment—pretty convinced that I'd be sitting here in this exact spot until the spring thaw. Which in Massachusetts happens sometime around May.

Why didn't I listen to my mother?

Ging Ging, of course. Ging Ging, for the entire time I'd known her, had done exactly as she pleased, when she pleased. And it was clear that I possessed that act first, think later mentality.

So as my car got whiter on the outside and colder on the inside, I had a little chat with Ging Ging. We talked about why I was here on the Massachusetts Turnpike in the middle of a blizzard and how I was so pig-headed that I thought I could control Mother Nature and that no one really was to blame except for me.

But, I argued back, I really just wanted to be home with my family for Christmas. I wanted the chili and the artificial tree and the arguments about clumps of tinsel versus strands of tinsel.

I had ventured out in the snow, it turned out, not because I was proving to my mother that I was old enough to make up my own mind, but rather because I missed my parents, and my sisters and my brother and the chili and cornbread and the Yule Log burning on the television deep into the night.

The snow might keep me away, but my mother was right. Christmas was Christmas, whether I was there or whether I was celebrating with them in my heart and in my memory.

And with that realization the windshield wipers miraculously moved back and forth and back and forth as I held my breath watching my own personal Christmas miracle. They cleared the snow from the front of the car while I went out and cleared it from the other windows.

I thought about my family the whole way home. Now they'd be complaining that Mom made them go to church an hour early to get seats, and then make them give up their seats for elderly latecomers. Now they'd be stirring the bubbling chili in the pot. Now they'd be slathering the cornbread with butter. Now they'd be getting the tree from the attic.

Each mile I slid closer to home I thought of all the things about Christmas that I loved and that would always be a part of me. The windshield wipers kept rhythm with my memories as the wind pushed the car onward.

Two and a half hours later I walked in the door, shaking snow from my hair, and announcing my arrival.

"I'm sorry I came out in the snow," I said, hugging my mother who stood in the kitchen pouring eggnog and arranging rum balls and spritz cookies on a Christmas tree tray.

"We saved you some chili," she said.

~Tracy G. Rasmussen

Back to Basics

*To give and then not feel that one has given
is the very best of all ways of giving.*
~Max Beerbohm

I've rarely been home for Christmas. In my family, the winter holiday traditionally has been an excuse to get away. Far away. So rather than hanging sparkling ornaments and baking sugar cookies, we would be riding Space Mountain at Disney World or sailing on a cruise to Mexico or viewing the once-sunken artifacts at the Titanic exhibit in Las Vegas. But for this particular year—despite a minority vote to return to Las Vegas—we decided to take it back to the basics and have Christmas at home.

It was a scary thought. What do you do when you celebrate Christmas at home? And how could it possibly compare to the exotic excursions of years gone by?

The questions hung in the air like those sparkling ornaments as my mother organized the "Christmas by the Bay" itinerary. But since we lived in the San Francisco Bay area, all wasn't lost. We had hope. Surely, there had to be something to do, some activities or tours that we hadn't yet tried that would make a local celebration worthwhile.

But it wasn't as easy as we thought. We all had various schedules and lived cities apart so the struggle was to get everyone synchronized. Each part of the family had a designated day to pitch an idea for an activity. Since the point of staying home for the holiday was to get back to basics, I came up with the idea to go caroling. I had seen it done in the movies, but I had never seen real live carolers before. And besides, many of my family members were good singers so I thought it might be fun.

I knew we weren't ready to hit the streets. You just didn't do that type of thing where we lived anyway. So I started by brainstorming locations and my grandmother suggested a senior citizens home where her church choir once sang. I called the director and she liked the idea so I set the date, e-mailed a list of ten holiday songs with lyrics and told everyone to meet at the home by 3 PM and to wear black and red.

I arrived first with my mother and three brothers. I went inside to look around. It was a dimly lit home with seniors scattered in different areas. Some were in their rooms with the doors open and others shuffled through the hallways waiting for dinner. There wasn't really a place for us to stand and sing to an audience so after speaking with the director, we just decided we would do a walk-by singing, moving through the hallways and lifting our voices at the same time.

"Everybody ready?" I asked the family once we had gathered at the far end of the hallway. Despite the rehearsal I had us do the night before at my grandmother's house, I was still anxious.

They nodded, clutching papers with the printed song lyrics.

"All right," I said, "Let's do 'Joy to the World.'"

They took their cue from me and we started to sing. Then we sang "Jingle Bells" and "Deck the Halls" and had a men-only rendition of "We Three Kings." We even sang the "The Twelve Days of Christmas" in parts. With each song, our voices grew stronger, more assured and less self-conscious. But all around us, the residents acted as if we didn't exist. Some stopped and watched, but most of them stayed in their rooms; some even closed their doors.

By the end, the family agreed it was fun, but I felt like I had failed. I didn't feel like I lifted anyone's spirits or spread the Christmas cheer. I didn't feel like I made a difference. But what was it that I needed? Did I need someone coming up to me and saying "this has been the best gift ever?" Maybe I had been self-centered in my giving. Maybe I had watched too many holiday movies.

The following day we went to a homeless shelter in Oakland. It was my aunt's idea for the itinerary. At the shelter, we would be serving meals in the multi-purpose room. The chef came out and gave us some instructions and pointed us to the plastic gloves as he began bringing out trays of steaming food. My family stood behind the buffet table and, as the residents lined up, we began filling their plates with turkey slices, mashed potatoes and macaroni and cheese.

"Why don't we sing?" my aunt suggested, once the last resident received his plate of food. It wasn't part of the plan, but a good idea nonetheless. The family had so much fun before and we already knew the songs. Why not?

"Joy to the World?" I asked.

And so we did. We sang all the songs we had memorized, sounding more alive than ever. The residents were clapping and singing along and even asked for an encore after our closing number "The Twelve Days of Christmas."

"Wow. Are you guys a singing group?" one man asked.

As I stood there, the Christmas cliché about the spirit of giving suddenly made more sense. I realized that this season has nothing to do with what you get. It's all about what's in your heart to give without looking for praise or applause. I still have a lot to learn.

At first, I had no idea how to celebrate the holiday at home. But being there, celebrating with people who had no home, I had all the holiday I needed.

~Russell Nichols

A Humble Christmas

Too many people miss the silver lining because they're expecting gold.
~Maurice Setter

"Our house is on fire!" I screamed into the phone. "Send a fire truck, quickly!" I was only fifteen at the time and made the mistake of calling 911 from inside my family's smoky home.

It was December 21, 1986, and we were making last-minute preparations for Christmas when I heard my mom's screams echoing from the basement. From the decibel and tone of her shriek, I could tell it was an emergency. Running into the hall, I saw smoke escaping from a vent. As I made that emergency call, the bedroom filled with smoke, and I realized my dreadful mistake of not calling from a neighbor's house. Deep down, I thought the fire would be isolated to one place. I soon realized my family and our home were in grave danger.

The clarity that comes with crisis is amazing. We were in the middle of a season in which material gifts abound, but in a split second my mind was cutting through the smoke and focusing on, not the wrappings under the tree, but the exact presence of loved ones in our home. I called to my beloved fat tabby Muffin trying to coax her out from under the bed, her large fright-filled eyes peering out from under the bedspread. I picked her up, her large underbelly flopping over my arm, grabbed the arm of my seven-year-old sister, Kristi, and ran out the front door of the house with my mother on our heels. My father ran our Irish Setter, Rusty, out the basement door into the backyard. My older brother was working his weekend job and was away from home.

After what seemed like an eternity, a city fire truck screeched to a halt outside our home. The firefighters sprang into action and began battling the blaze, unfurling hoses and chopping a hole in the roof. Suddenly, I realized my feet were wet and cold. I looked down at my shoeless blue socks, soaking up water from the snow that covered the ground. Coatless, my sister and I went to our next door neighbor's house to stay warm.

Later we learned that the fire, which started in the electrical wiring in the duct work, had spread and leapt up through the vents, causing damage throughout the whole house. Burnt to a charcoal black, the guest bathroom in the hall was on the verge of crumbling. Though it was in working order, my family had never heard the smoke detector's beep. Its casing had melted and it was a misshapen disaster. One of the firefighters told us that if the fire had occurred at night, our family most likely would have perished. That night we checked into a Best Western, presuming it would be our holiday haven, thankful for the gift of one another. We knew that Christmas would be drastically different than Christmas celebrations of the past.

Since my childhood years my family had gathered around the living room's brick hearth on December nights after the lighting of the Advent wreath. The tree's ornaments would be carefully coordinated to match bows, wrapping paper, and other holiday trimmings. Real pine boughs graced the hearth and burning logs filled the air with the aroma of pine. There was hot chocolate and, if the weather permitted, snow cream. One year we savored *A Christmas Carol* by the fire in the weeks leading up to December 25th. We watched sappy made-for-TV movies, plotted last-minute gift ideas, and whispered delicious gift-giving secrets, forbidding one another to browse through closets. But in only a few minutes on that cold day in 1986, black smoke seeped into every warm crevice and gift-hiding place, invading our holiday den, changing our Christmas celebration and our lives.

As it turned out, the Best Western wasn't our fate after all; a man at our church owned a rental home that was vacant. He graciously offered to let us stay there during the months it would take to repair our home. Two days before Christmas we settled in, but our trials continued. Since our live Christmas tree and the ornaments had been scorched in the fire, we had to settle for a Charlie Brown discount tree. Not accustomed to the rental house and a hole that gaped in the wall over the bathtub, we lamented when Muffin disappeared through it. Then someone stole a box of my childhood dolls and stuffed animals from the backseat of my mom's car while she deposited canned goods inside our local needs center. The toy memories, including a hand-made Raggedy Ann doll, were on their way to the cleaner to have the stench of smoke removed when they were heisted.

That Christmas could easily have been labeled the worst Christmas in our family's history, but now, unbelievably, I can see it as one of the best Christmases. There were silver linings, the most obvious one being that no one was harmed in the fire. And we still managed to make memories, grateful when Muffin came out of the hole, hungry but in one piece. We finished our Christmas shopping, turned up the heat since we had no fireplace, and watched old movies. I cried at *Gone With the Wind* for the millionth time. We relished the kindness of friends and neighbors who brought us groceries, assistance and kind words. Some of them we hadn't seen in years. I have even come to terms with my stolen childhood playthings, and I can honestly say there is no bitterness or remorse in my heart. My prayer is that they brightened the life of another child who otherwise would not have received anything for Christmas.

That Christmas we kept our tradition of going to the Christmas Eve service at our church, and I rejoiced at the birth of the Lord. I thought about how, even though He was born a king, He came to Earth in a most lowly and unexpected way. Now I understood from experience that everything can change in a few seconds. If my expectations were focused on material things, or even traditions, I might miss the blessings in what actually unfolds, however humbly Christmas comes. Even if we had spent our Christmas in that

Best Western, we would have made memories just because we were together and had Christmas in our hearts. Now at Christmastime I warm myself by our hearth with my family and wait to see what unexpected events will delight, amuse, or strengthen me.

And I am humbled by the awe and meaning of the season, no matter how it comes to me.

~Janeen Lewis

Never Alone

If you don't like something change it;
if you can't change it, change the way you think about it.
~Mary Engelbreit

My husband Lawrence and I were celebrating our fourth Christmas together and we were working to establish our own holiday traditions. I had never had children and each of the past few years we had enjoyed the holiday season with his three precious kids, whom I now felt privileged to call my own. I expected this Christmas would be much the same and the thought of each of us being alone and apart on Christmas Day had never crossed my mind.

Lawrence and I decided to spend Christmas at our cabin in the mountains in New Mexico, which was our usual practice, and we hoped our kids would join us; however, the older two had different ideas. Our older daughter chose to stay in California, where she was attending college; our son opted to stay in Mississippi to work through his college break and save money for his spring semester abroad in Europe. The visitation period with our twelve-year-old wasn't scheduled to start until noon on December 26th, but there were no flights available that day to pick her up in time, so we agreed that Lawrence would leave on Christmas to fly to Houston and bring her to our cabin in the mountains. Our family would all be in different locations and apart on Christmas Day!

I pondered this reality and remembered a conversation a few

weeks earlier during which my friend complained that she would be alone on Christmas Day. She elaborated in great detail about her long-standing tradition of having the entire family at her house to celebrate the birth of Christ, open presents, swap cookie recipes, exchange hugs and kisses, and feast happily on an oversized turkey and enough fixings to feed a small army. This year she agonized over being unable to orchestrate her historic family tradition. She also wept over the idea of being alone, and my heart ached for her.

Remembering that conversation made me wonder if I, too, would find myself terribly alone and missing my family, and that's when I realized I could make a choice about my attitude toward Christmas. It was then I decided that I would not allow whatever happened (or didn't happen) on Christmas Day to negatively impact my spiritual condition or my heart's content. I would not entertain thoughts of disappointment or resentment, nor be captive to preconceived ideas about what the perfect Christmas should be. Come what may, I resolved that I would not be depressed about being alone!

Instead, I would rejoice in the gift of my husband and family and love them from afar. I would appreciate the blessed day for what it is and celebrate the birth of our King and God's presence in my life. I would imagine the angels proclaiming from the Heavens, "Glory to God in the highest, and on earth peace to men!" I would be content in my aloneness, trusting that this too would pass and that soon I would be reunited with my husband and our youngest child.

Christmas morning came, and my husband and I awoke in our cabin in the mountains, just as planned. We called our kids and other family members to tell them all how much we loved and missed them. I later took my husband to the airport and kissed him goodbye, after which I dined with friends, appreciative for the invitation. Finally, I went home to our empty cabin.

Christmas day became Christmas night and I walked out onto the front deck. I was alone as I inhaled the crisp mountain air and admired the glistening blanket of snow. I was alone as I lovingly thought of and prayed for protection and safety for my family. I was alone as I whispered to the stars my thanksgiving for the birth of our heavenly King. And I was alone as I humbly and graciously received God's precious gift—His divine peace about the fact that I may be alone this Christmas, but with Him I will never be truly lonely.

~Kristen Clark

A Garbage Can
Christmas

Could we change our attitude, we should not only see life differently,
but life itself would come to be different.
~Katherine Mansfield

From the very beginning Matt didn't want a divorce. "What about the children?" My husband reasoned. "They need us both."

For me however, there was no reasoning. I definitely wanted out. We'd already given Matt's construction business over a year and he still wasn't making any money. I knew it wasn't his fault but it seemed as if every dime he made went for tools or costly repairs on our dilapidated pick-up truck. So it was my job as a waitress at Steve's Bakery that was keeping us going.

Resentful and tired, I found myself growing bitter and critical toward Matt. Soon arguments with no apologies became commonplace between us and I, in particular, said some very unkind things to my husband of eleven years. However it was my last cruel and cutting display that sent Matt to sleep in a makeshift bedroom in our basement, and shortly after that was when I made up my mind to file for divorce. However since Christmas was less than six weeks away, I decided it would be best for our children if I waited until after the Christmas holidays to officially file.

The next few weeks were hard. Matt and I seldom saw one

another and barely spoke when we did. The children soon picked up on our tension and it wasn't long until we were all sniping and grousing at each other. Our entire family was under stress and perhaps that's why I came down with the flu the very day my mother-in-law was to come for a Christmas visit.

"What am I going to do?" I wailed from my sickbed to Matt. "We don't even have the tree up yet and what if I get fired? This is the bakery's busiest week."

"Don't worry. I'll take care of everything," my husband reassured me. "I'll call Steve and explain. He'll understand." He looked at me lying exhausted in our bed and somehow found his boyish smile. "You just try to get all the sleep you can."

Too sick to snarl or be sarcastic, I did sleep. In fact, I was in bed for three days. In the meantime, my mother-in-law arrived and while Matt went to work, she and the children went about decorating the Christmas tree, cooking, cleaning and working on a surprise gift for Matt and me. In fact, it was Tara who let the cat out of the bag when she poked her little towhead in the bedroom door and quietly giggled, "We made a surprise for you and Daddy but I can't tell, 'cause I promised!"

By late afternoon Christmas Eve I had begun to feel human again as I awoke to the comforting smells of dinner cooking. So as not to wake me, I could hear the children attempting to muffle their squeals of excitement. Lying there in our darkened bedroom and feeling so much better, I couldn't help but enjoy my temporary contentment. Only Christmas could weave such special magic into our household right now, I thought.

We had a family favorite that evening, pot roast, and while huddling around our thrift shop dining room table that Matt had recently refinished, the children announced they had a special gift for us but they didn't want to wait until Christmas morning for us to open it. Bursting with excitement, they begged for us to "open it now."

Of course we agreed and my mother-in-law quickly ushered both Matt and me into the living room "to wait a bit." We heard the back door slam and there were a series of thuds and giggles, and then more thuds and some whispers, and more thuds until one by one our children trooped in. Their smiles could not have been wider and their excitement could not have been greater. It was my mother-in-law who explained that our special gift had arrived; however, we had to close our eyes because some very special angels were delivering it. I guess the excitement was contagious because Matt and I began giggling too.

It was Travis who insisted, "Keep your eyes closed."

The children were now all talking at once.

Another thud, the sound of something sliding, a chorus of more giggles, then the announcement, "You can open your eyes now!"

For a second there were no sounds. In front of us stood a large bulky "thing" covered in a torn sheet from my ragbag.

"You can open it when we say," said Tara with great anticipation.

"Should we all count to three before Mom and I pull the sheet off?" Matt suggested.

"Yes. Yes." We were all squealing with excitement by now. "Everybody. One, two, three!"

So the two of us pulled together which was something we hadn't done in a long time.

And there it was. Dazzling in the soft twinkling lights of the Christmas tree: our gift... a chair; and no ordinary chair either.

"Mommy," it was Tara. "It's a Christmas chair! We made it! We found it in the garbage."

"It is beautiful, honey," was all I could manage to choke out.

My mother-in-law confessed they'd spied it in the neighbor's trash along the street. So they dragged it home. Since Matt was at work and I was sick, they were able to paint it, with her artistic direction, in the garage without either of us knowing. Using old paint stashed on the shelf and paintbrushes from their paint boxes, they created a work of pure love. Different colors adorned each leg and various rungs and turns. They painted polka dots and squiggles, hearts and flowers. And there were three painted faces looking up from the seat. "Your three angels" was written in script beneath them along with each of the children's names.

There was a hushed, near sacred silence that followed this explanation.

It's strange, I know, but in that moment I was reminded of another gift of love someone gave two thousand years ago and how it changed the world. Life wasn't so perfect for that little family either, I'll bet, but they still honored their commitments to one another. I gulped hard once again.

I looked at Matt, my hard-working, devoted husband, eyes brimming with tears, moved by love and appreciation for his family, and doing the very best he could for us. I saw our three beautiful children loving us both and my mental list of gratitude exploded as I realized how much I loved my husband and family.

Maybe we didn't live the life I'd secretly dreamed, but by shifting my attitude and outlook even just a little bit I instantly began to see what we had, instead of what we didn't have. And what we needed and what we didn't need. And we sure didn't need a divorce. Why? Well, I'm not totally certain but I think it had to do with the magic of three "little angels" and the love they poured into a garbage can Christmas chair.

~Sue Smith as told to Linda LaRocque

46

Love Fills My Shopping Cart

Oh, my friend, it's not what they take away from you that counts.
It's what you do with what you have left.
~Hubert Humphrey

My friend's excitement blasted through the phone line. "I'm going to the mall. There's a fifty percent off sale, just in time for Christmas. You want to come with me?"

That chance to get a bargain would usually spark in me a quick "yes." Before she'd have finished the sentence, I would have been grabbing my purse, but not anymore. Not now. Shopping was erased from the list of things I enjoyed. So much I missed, so much I needed to do, to accomplish, to live for. All vanished. All wiped away by the retinal disease that had robbed me of my remaining eyesight just a few months before.

Tears flowed with each step of my painful adjustment.

"Mommy, can I have a peanut butter and jelly sandwich?" my five-year-old asked.

A simple task, but now, groping to find the pantry and the items in it wasn't that easy. Trying to distinguish jars or cans from one another increased my frustration. Anxiety cramped my stomach as I feared I couldn't be a "normal" mommy to my three-, five-, and seven-year old sons.

It was the Christmas season now, and my tasks multiplied. I

had to try harder to squelch my fear. While following my routine, I fumbled with apparent resignation, but inside I still longed to have even a tiny bit of eyesight.

I would have been satisfied even with the miniscule amount of sight I'd had just the Christmas before. It had allowed me to distinguish the boys' facial expressions and the sparkle in their eyes when they opened their gifts.

But this Christmas season, I saw a gray nothing—no red or green, no colors, no shadows; nothing.

Although reluctant, I accompanied my husband, Gene, on shopping trips. I held onto the shopping cart and he pulled it through crowded aisles.

"Look at that," he said. "Jeff would love that."

I smiled and looked in his direction.

"Honey, I'm sorry," he said.

I shrugged my shoulders. "Hey, I forget too."

But I never forgot. The truth was that time and time again, out of habit, I glanced in the direction of the object, but with no retina function, my brain didn't register anything. That part of my life was painfully empty… as empty as the shopping cart seemed to me.

Then, one cold morning in December, I inhaled a long breath and vowed that this upcoming Christmas season would be the one where I would conquer my emotions and follow through with the usual holiday tasks. I lined up all the boxes holding decorations against the wall.

"Okay, guys, who wants to watch a movie?" Gene rounded up our sons, giving me the time to arrange the decorations.

"You go with Daddy," I said, "and maybe I'll have some cookies for you later."

Months of practice made baking easier, the burning episodes less frequent, and mistakes like using flour for powdered sugar were also a thing of the past. I navigated through the kitchen with relative ease. Even doing laundry and cleaning became simpler each time I did them. Barefoot, I could tell which spots I'd missed while sweeping the kitchen floor.

I reached into the storage boxes filled with Christmas treasures, and the moment my fingers touched an item, the shape and texture told me what it was. Since I'd seen it while sighted, memories of its color painted the item in my mind. I decorated each area of the house, leaving the tree decoration as a task for our sons and leaving Gene the job of placing the star atop the Christmas tree.

I raised the volume of "Silent Night" on the stereo and relaxed on the sofa. My darkness suddenly had a soothing melody.

Christmas morning came quickly, and I heard the high-pitched voices of our sons outside our bedroom door. They came in and rushed to our bed. "Guys, get up, we want to open presents."

Each voice had a distinct sound and I could tell their mood by the inflection and tone. They jumped, giggled, and teased each other as we wiped the sleep from our eyes.

I reached for my robe and held out my hand, "C'mon, let's see what Santa brought."

Leading me by the hand was normal for them. But this time, they rushed out the door and headed toward the Christmas tree in our family room.

I followed the familiar path to the couch. A fresh pine scent wafted through, and bells on the tree chimed as they lifted packages to find theirs.

"Let's take turns," their daddy said. "And don't forget to tell Mommy what you got."

I sighed inwardly. My husband's thoughtfulness warmed my heart, but following that instruction would be difficult in the midst of their excitement.

"Look what I got." Joe ripped wrapping paper and placed it on my lap.

I reached out my hand. "Show your mommy."

It wasn't really the gift I wanted to see, but the expressions of delight that matched their words. I longed to see the sparkle in their eyes when they opened what they had asked for all year long.

That's when I realized that dwelling on what I couldn't see threatened to erase the Christmas joy. I fought the temptation to sink into self-pity, and swallowed hard to keep the tears inside.

My husband appeared behind me on the couch and whispered in my ear, "Are you okay?"

I nodded. "I'll be back."

I rose from the couch and groped my way to the bedroom. I sat on the bed and chided myself for being unable to handle this time with my family.

I had been so strong, had faced tough moments with courage, but now… why the sadness, the anguish and impatience?

I couldn't understand. With a tissue, I pressed my eyes and sobs poured out.

My husband slid beside me on the bed. "What can I do for you?"

His sweetness and warmth further emphasized my sorrow. I was disappointing him, causing an added burden for him. With emotional distress, I'd failed in my role as a wife to him and a mom to my sons.

And when anguish nearly overwhelmed me, I suppressed one last sob and looked up. "God, help me to have the courage and strength I need."

"This is the best present yet!" one of our sons cried out.

I held my breath and paused for a few moments. My son's words brought a sobering truth that opened the eyes of my heart. His gift delighted him. But I had missed mine, overlooking and disregarding my greatest present—the one that filled the emptiness of my dark world. It was in the family room—it sang to me with little voices, with little arms that hugged me, and with the sweetest melody of each "I love you, Mommy."

I stuffed the wrinkled tissue in my pocket and reached for Gene's hand. "Let's go. I don't want to miss a minute of this."

I had asked God to help me cope. But rather than just coping, He taught me to enjoy what lies beyond physical sight, what the warmth of love offers and what truly holds meaning and purpose.

Years have passed, and I now do a better kind of shopping.

Walking through the aisles of life, I find the bargains of a lifetime. I put in my cart a large package of appreciation for what I still have, followed by boxes of creativity to tackle all the tasks of being a mom and wife, a good supply of courage to defeat thoughts of gloom, and even add a few jars labeled "sense of humor."

Equipped to care for my family, I wait with anticipation for each Christmas, when the gift of their love delights the eyes of my heart.

~Janet Perez Eckles

Christmas Magic

Joy to the World

47

Love Squared

It's such a grand thing to be a father of a father —
that's why the world calls him grandfather.
~Author Unknown

We had our own miracle last Christmas Eve. Like the first Christmas miracle, ours was a miracle of birth. Only our miracle didn't take place in a stable; it happened in a modern, state-of-the-art hospital. Instead of a manger filled with straw, our Christmas baby lay down her sweet head in a comfortably warm, carefully sterilized bassinet. And while there were no cattle or shepherds to attend the birth of our precious little one, there were plenty of nurses, grandparents, aunts, uncles and cousins.

Not to mention the wise man/doctor occasionally poking his head in. From the east, as I recall.

Now, I know there are tens of thousands of births every day on this planet, and there was nothing that made our experience any more "miraculous" than any other. But for me, it was a magical moment of transformation. Before my very eyes, my son became a father, my wife became a grandmother, my daughters became aunts, my youngest son became an uncle and that basketball in my daughter-in-law's tummy became The World's Most Adorable Granddaughter.

Miraculously.

There were some extraordinary moments during that long and...

well, almost sacred Christmas Eve. No, we didn't have herald angels harking in the heavens, or a new star overhead to light the way to baby Becky. But we did have eight-year-old Jon, excitedly telling everyone, "I'm an uncle! I'm an uncle!" We had two grandmothers—one a veteran, one a first-timer—taking turns monitoring the hospital staff to make sure they were taking proper care of "their" granddaughter. And we had two families coming together at the nursery window to "ooh" and "ahh" at the little dark-haired bundle who represented their confluence.

For me, however, the most profound moments involved my son: the joy in his eyes as he held up his daughter for all the family to see; the tender concern etched on his face as he oversaw the poking and probing and assorted testing of little Becky; and the peaceful contentment that emanated from him as he sat in a hospital rocking chair holding his sweet, slumbering child.

I had gone to get him some food—hey, a guy's gotta eat, even on Christmas Eve—and I took it to the hospital room where the new little family was headquartered. New Mama Jenny was resting comfortably after her ordeal, and Joe was holding Becky. For a moment, I stood silently and watched my son gently cradle his baby in his long, powerful arms. At first, all I could see was the top of Joe's head, as he bent to her, examining her, studying her, kissing her little hands and cheeks. Then he looked up at me, and I could see the tears that were streaming down his face.

"You were right," he said as a tear dripped off his cheek and fell softly on Becky's hand.

I hesitated. I had lectured Joe about so many things through the years; I wasn't exactly sure which thing I had been right about. "I was?" I asked.

He glanced down at Becky, then back at me. "This... this... feeling," he said. "It's overwhelming. I've never felt anything like it. It's like... love... squared. To the Nth degree."

I understood. I was feeling that same feeling for my child—and my grandchild. And it made me think that perhaps that is truly the essence of Christmas. It's not just about a child, and it's not just about parents — heavenly or otherwise. It's about love.

Squared.

Miraculously.

~Joseph Walker

48

My New Friend

How wonderful it is that nobody need wait a single moment
before starting to improve the world.
~Anne Frank

When I used to think of Christmas, I thought of presents, cookies, decorations, and a huge tree. Now I think of Christmas as a time to spend with your family and appreciate what you have. My vision of this holiday changed one remarkable night.

My parents had told my brother and me that we were working at the homeless shelter on Christmas Eve to help with the dinner. Honestly, I could not believe what my parents wanted to do and I threw a fit. I was only nine years old, but still, looking back on that behavior shocks me. As I walked into the homeless shelter and saw about thirty homeless men and women gathered around their tables singing holiday carols with smiles spread across their cheerful faces, my heart melted. Just this sight changed my whole attitude about not being home on Christmas Eve.

I headed to the kitchen and started making plates of turkey and mashed potatoes. As I piled the mashed potatoes on each plate I looked outside the window to see each and every person's eyes sparkle and their mouths move to the words of "Jingle Bells." I remember just wanting to go out there and sing along with them. I looked past all the differences I had with them and just felt like they were family. As the carols died down, we started to bring out the food that was on plastic plates with a Santa in the middle. Every single person would smile and thank me once I put their food down and wish me a Merry Christmas.

One specific man really touched me. As I set down his plate he said, "Thank you sweetie." Now this was not unusual — basically everyone there said it, but then he said to me, "You know, this is very kind what you are doing for us. Not many people would help us out, or even want to get close to us. You're a real angel for doing this. I remember when I was your age I would keep my distance from homeless people, but it's reassuring for me to see a young girl like you help us out. Thank you and Merry Christmas."

I was at a loss for words but I managed to say, "Thank you very much. Merry Christmas to you too."

When we left to go home I turned back to look for that nice man. I saw him in the corner bundled up with one thin blanket and a two-inch pillow. Tears blurred my vision; all I wanted to do was stay with him, bring him my big comforter I sleep with at night that I usually push to the side of my bed, and give him someone to talk to. But I had to keep walking out to our car. Now I never wanted to leave, and I couldn't believe I had complained that I didn't want to come.

I got home and as I sat down to eat a pizza with my family for Christmas Eve dinner I started crying my eyes out just thinking about the night I had, the smiles on the people's faces, and most of all the friend I had made. The man who I will never forget, who said the words I will carry with me forever.

I snuck downstairs that night, not to check for Santa, but to take away the letter I wrote him and write a new one. It said:

Dear Santa,

I wrote you a letter earlier, but I am writing a new one now. Please take care of the man I met earlier and give him some of my gifts that you were bringing me. Please keep him safe from the outdoors and make sure he is happy. That's all I want this year. You can still bring me presents, but the one thing I want is for you to look out for my new friend.

Love,

Erin

My vision of everything had changed that night. Christmas is now the time I think about my friend, and how lucky I am to have what I have. It's not the time to worry about the new bike I want anymore; it's time to worry about how my friend is and if he realizes how he changed my life.

~Erin McCormack, age 13

The Christmas Tree Sale

You can't live a perfect day without doing something for someone who will never be able to repay you.

~John Wooden

When my son was in Cub Scouts a few years ago, I volunteered to be in charge of the annual Cub Scout Christmas tree sale here in our small town of Woodstock, Connecticut. I was able to find a supplier who agreed to sell me sixty trees at a good price, which the Cub Scouts could then sell at a nice profit. The day before the sale, the trees were delivered and locked just inside the gates of the fairgrounds. The plan was to open the gates the next morning and sell the trees. I had carefully scheduled each Cub Scout in the pack for a two-hour shift in which they would sell the Christmas trees (with a parent, of course). I had even stood up at the pack meeting and given the Scouts a pep talk about doing a good job selling the trees and about having Christmas spirit. (I think the scouts had more spirit than the parents did, as they grudgingly signed up for their shifts.)

The problem occurred when there was a heavy snowfall that night; about one foot of snow fell, and the snowplows had plowed the snow up high right against the gates as they were clearing off the road in front of the fairgrounds entrance. I arrived there early that morning with my young son and daughter and two snow shovels. My husband was at work, so he was unable to help. As we tried to shovel away the huge mountain of snow, I realized it was hopeless, and it would take two days to shovel the snow away from the gates in order to get the Christmas trees out.

I thought of all the time I had spent organizing the sale, and how disappointed the Cub Scouts would be if they couldn't sell the trees. I also thought of all the money they would lose. As we continued our futile attempt to shovel away the mountain, I thought about my options. I could not afford to call a snowplow company to clear away the snow. I was also sure that all of the snowplows were busy anyway, clearing off parking lots and driveways. If the Cub Scouts had to pay for plowing, their profit on this fundraiser would be gone. I thought of calling parents to help me shovel, but I knew that would take hours, even if I could get any of them to agree to help, and the booth was scheduled to open in one hour!

Just then, a man with a large snowplow pulled up and offered to plow the entire area for free. I watched in awe as he quickly did the job. He also took the time to clear off another large area, so that cars could pull up and park.

I was so overcome with gratitude that I forgot to ask the gentleman his name. But he had white hair, a long white beard, and as he drove away he said "Merry Christmas." I remember my son asking "Mommy, why do you have a tear on your cheek?" I looked down at him, with his little Scout uniform on under his coat and said "I'm just happy it's Christmas." The Christmas tree sale was a big success, and we sold all the trees that day.

~Teri Stohlberg

The Fifty-Dollar Christmas

Kindness, like a boomerang, always returns.
~Author Unknown

I quit my job in September believing I had a better one lined up. The better one fell through. It was a week before Christmas and I was still unemployed. I was a single mother. A series of temporary jobs had enabled me to keep the rent current and put groceries on the table, but not much else.

My daughter Leslie was in junior high so one morning, at breakfast, I was a bit taken aback when she blurted out, "Mom, I know money is really tight because you don't have a job. So it's okay if you can't get me anything for Christmas. Maybe you'll have a job by my birthday and we can plan something really special for that."

"Thank you, honey, that's a great idea," I said as I hugged her. Then I quickly gathered up dishes to take over to the sink so she would not see the tears welling up in my eyes. I regained my composure adequately enough to get her off to school, but the minute she was out the door a flood of tears overwhelmed me.

"Any kid with that good an attitude deserves a nice Christmas!" I shouted, banging the arm of the sofa with my fist. "Oh Lord, if I just had fifty extra dollars I could get her a few presents," I squeaked as my tears began to subside.

That evening Leslie and I drove to church. She ran off to her youth group meeting, while I went into the chapel where the adult service was being held. Halfway across the foyer I decided I was not in the mood for any "isn't it all so joyful" messages. I reversed my direction and headed back outside. My friend Jodie was entering through the same doorway. Grabbing my arm, she said, "Hey, where are you going?"

"Home" I curtly responded.

"Why?" She asked, naturally enough.

"Because I don't feel like hearing how wonderful Christmas is," I replied.

"I know what you mean," she sympathized. "I'm not sure I do either, but that probably suggests that we both need to be here. Tell you what, why don't you stay and sit with me? We can hide in the back of the balcony and hate Christmas together without anybody seeing us." Putting it that way made the prospect of staying sound kind of fun. Like two little girls conspiring to do something naughty in Sunday school. Linking arms we headed up the stairs.

As I listened to Bible verses that told the story of our Savior's birth my anger and resentment began to slip away. Focusing on the message of good news announced by angels on that long ago night comforted me. It reminded me that with or without packages under the tree, Christmas is a joyful, hopeful time, full of promise. I was glad Jodie had talked me into staying.

As I reached for my jacket, Jodie took my arm. "I want you to have this," she said as she handed me a folded piece of paper. "But you can't use it to pay bills. You have to spend it on gifts for your daughter."

I unfolded a fifty-dollar check. The significance of the amount humbled me. I felt tears begin to well up again. I had not told Jodie anything about my angry prayer that morning. I was amazed by the way God was answering that prayer, awestruck that the silly desires of my heart mattered to Him.

"I don't know when I will be able to pay you back," I stammered.

"I don't expect you to pay me back," she responded. "When you get on your feet, do the same thing for someone else, that's all."

"I can do that!" I exclaimed. "Thank you so much," I choked out.

Jodie put her arm around me as we silently exited the balcony. I hugged her when we got outside and thanked her again as we parted. The uplifting service and Jodie's timely generosity had removed a heavy burden from my heart. I had a renewed sense of joyful expectation.

On Christmas Eve a cardboard box was left on my doorstep. It contained a large turkey and all the trimmings for a lavish dinner, with the fixings for breakfast, lunch, and dessert thrown in. Leslie and I gasped in amazement as we pulled item after item from the carton. When it was empty the entire surface of our dining table was covered with food.

"Where are we going to put it all?" Leslie questioned.

"These perishable items will go bad before we can possibly finish them," I said.

"I don't think this turkey will fit in our freezer," she exclaimed.

As I looked into her distressed face, our eyes met. In that brief exchange we both knew what to do. Simultaneously and in almost the same voice we said, "Let's give it away!"

We knew of a larger family that was also struggling with the hardship of an unemployed parent. So we repacked the carton. We added a few things from our own pantry and a parcel of candy that had been given to us the day before.

"I have an idea," Leslie said over her shoulder as she dashed off to her bedroom. She came back with a couple of stuffed animals, some action figures, and a game.

"For the kids," she said, placing them on top of the groceries.

We covered the bulging package with Saran Wrap and taped multicolored bows all over it. Then balancing it precariously between us, we loaded it into the car and deposited it on another doorstep.

"Drive down the street a little way and wait for me," Leslie pleaded.

A few minutes later she jumped in beside me, gasping for breath. "It was great! I rang the doorbell and ran like crazy."

We laughed all the way home as we rehashed "the great food basket caper." When our laughter was spent, we made some hot cocoa. As we drank it, we talked about how rich we felt giving all that food away. Eventually Leslie went off to bed.

I arranged my meager stash of colorful packages under the artificial tree that had seemed so bedraggled the week before. How lovely it looked to me now! Then I filled Leslie's stocking with the "goodies" my parents had given me a few days earlier for that purpose. Mom had neatly wrapped each trinket, refusing to give me even a tiny hint of what they contained. "Because," she explained, "Christmas should be a time of wonder, even for grown-ups!"

How right you are, Mom! How very right you are!

~Bridget Colern

51

Chicken Soup for the Soul

Holy Night

A bit of fragrance always clings to the hand that gives roses.
~Chinese Proverb

Sometimes the magic and miracles of Christmas come to us in ways we don't expect. A number of years ago, when my husband, Larry, and I were newly married, we took off for a two-year adventure in Asia. We left behind family, friends and jobs to work for a charity in Hong Kong.

Two months after we arrived in our new home, it was Christmastime. But there were no frosted windowpanes or sleigh rides or holly branches in Hong Kong. I had never spent a Christmas away from home before, and I found myself desperately homesick for my family and for our traditions—Christmas Eve with friends, singing carols at the piano, crowds of people coming and going, and a big tree loaded with gifts.

Instead, we found ourselves living in a tiny flat on the thirtieth floor of a high rise. We did our best to decorate. Our tree was a pathetic thing that we had inherited: green plastic, about eighteen inches tall with little white presents glued onto its branches. We didn't have two cents to rub together for anything better, so we strung popcorn and wound it around. And under the tree went a few small presents.

As Christmas got closer, I felt ready to throw in the towel on this whole idea of working for a charity. All the warm fuzzies about spending two years to help change the world didn't seem all that glamorous anymore.

When a British family invited us to share the day in their lovely home, I thought we had hit the jackpot. But my excitement soon dissipated when Larry suggested we decline the invitation.

"We've met so many people here who don't have anywhere to go for Christmas," he said. "I think we need to cook a turkey and open our door to whoever wants to come."

So we declined the invitation, and got the word out to our new friends: "We're cooking a turkey. If you need a place to spend Christmas, come and join us."

Of course, now we know all about the rules of Christmas entertaining. If you're going to have people in, the tree should be beautiful, the table should be set with candles and good china, there should be a fire blazing in the hearth and a big wreath on the door.

But then, we didn't know any better. We didn't know that paper plates were not enough, that a plastic tree didn't make a good focal point, that a living room the size of a sandbox wasn't big enough for a crowd.

In the days leading up to Christmas, our guest list started growing. Even on Christmas morning, the phone rang several times—new acquaintances, people we had met in passing—"I heard you were having Christmas dinner today. Is there room for a few more?"

When they arrived, they introduced themselves to us and to one another, loaded their plates with food and found a place on the floor. The room buzzed as twenty people shared their stories—some were traveling through Asia, some were volunteers in China or Hong Kong, some were just lonely and had no one else to spend the day with.

When the meal was finished, we sat around the living room, enjoying the conversation. In a quiet moment, someone started singing: "Silent night, holy night, all is calm, all is bright...." And everyone joined in. When the song ended, it was quiet. And then someone started to sing again: "Away in a manger, no crib for a bed, the little Lord Jesus lay down his sweet head...."

And there we were—like Mary and Joseph and Jesus, we were all uprooted from our families and friends. Like them, we were vagabonds a long way from home. They were being asked to do something big to change the world. We were all trying to do our small part to change the world too.

And in that tiny living room on the thirtieth floor of a high rise in the bustling city of Hong Kong, we found a Christmas that none of us had planned. It was simply a gift to us all. For the vagabonds and volunteers around that little tree, it was a holy night.

~Marla Stewart Konrad

52

A Box at Midnight

Wherever there is a human being, there is an opportunity for a kindness.
~Seneca

s I unpacked the boxes of new coats in the back room of Atkinson's Department Store, I saw it. My dream coat. I'd been poring over catalogs for ages in search of the stunning style that I'd first glimpsed in a magazine. Nothing had been exactly right. Until now.

The fur collar, the princess line, the smell of the rich gold suede—everything was as I'd imagined. I tried it on. It fit perfectly. I wrapped the luxurious softness around myself like a model on a runway, preening in the tri-fold mirror. I looked much more sophisticated than my sixteen years. I picked up the price tag, then dropped it as though it had burned my hand. Wow! I never knew we sold merchandise this expensive. Even with my employee discount, this one coat would use up all the money I'd worked so hard to save.

I knew that I shouldn't buy myself a present at Christmastime, but I'd purchased the gifts for my family long before. Mom and I had discussed me buying a coat at Atkinson's months ago. Besides, I earned this, toiling all last summer and every weekend this fall for this one prize. I couldn't help it that my ideal coat waited until this moment to appear.

Still, I felt just a little selfish. I couldn't get that Bible verse out of my mind that we'd talked about at youth group the week before. "It is more blessed to give than to receive." Those words haunted me all day. I had only been a follower of Christ for a couple of years, but I was learning and growing all the time. I wanted to live my life in a way that reflected my savior to those around me. But I also wanted my dream coat.

The next morning, on the school bus, I noticed my friend, Letisha Robinson, with fresh eyes. She climbed aboard with her brother, Jerome, who played on the varsity football team with my brother. Two more sisters got on while four other siblings, much younger, waved from their dilapidated stoop. It looked as though a good wind could easily topple their wooden house. Not one of them wore a winter coat, and a chill hung in the air. As a matter of fact, I recognized Letisha's dress as the same one she'd worn yesterday and the day before. Come to think of it, I couldn't remember ever seeing her in anything else.

At dinner, I asked my parents about Letisha's family.

"I hear that her mother worked at the factory. You know, the one that just closed down," Mom said.

"What does her father do?" I asked.

"Not much, honey." Dad looked me in the eyes. "He's an alcoholic. Been in and out of jail. He probably drank up all the money his wife was able to pull together."

"I wonder what Christmas will be like at their house, if they'll even get any Christmas presents at all." My brother, Gary, was much nicer than me. As I plotted buying my dream coat, he thought about others.

I excused myself to do my homework, but really I wanted to exit because I felt uncomfortable—convicted, even. I didn't want to entertain the idea that was tugging at my mind so I tried to divert myself with geometry. It didn't work.

That night I dreamed about Letisha's family sitting around a barren tree on Christmas morning. I saw the little kids traipsing through the snow, looking forlornly in our windows and shivering, while we opened gift after gift. When I awoke, I was certain of what I had to do, of what Jesus would want for me.

At breakfast, I took a deep breath and announced my plan to my family. It turned out I wasn't the only one who was thinking that way. It almost seemed as though they were waiting for me to come around. We mapped out our strategy.

Gary and I were to observe every kid in Letisha and Jerome's family, noting their ages, gender, and approximate size. Christmas Eve was only two days away, so we had no time to waste. After school, we pooled our information and counted out our savings. My brother and I wanted to buy these gifts with our own money.

Gary went shopping on Saturday for a football for Jerome and toys for the younger Robinson kids. I bought a basic but warm outfit for each of the eight kids with my discount at Atkinson's. Eight outfits for the price of one coat. That took some of the sting out of giving up my dream coat. Mom and Dad added mittens and scarves to our stash, enough for the children and their parents, too.

I wrapped the gifts and made them shine, adding tags that read "To Letisha" or "To Toddler Boy." Each tag was signed "Someone who loves you." Gary stuffed the gifts into a huge box and loaded it into our station wagon.

On Christmas Eve, we went to our church as usual, lighting our white candles and singing about the "wondrous gift that's given." I thought about the precious gift of the baby born so long ago, and I felt that warm and wonderful peace wash over me. Our gift was puny in comparison, but somehow it seemed holy on this most blessed of nights.

We went home to have hot chocolate in front of the twinkling tree lights, and wait. This time we weren't waiting for Santa. It wouldn't do to go to Letisha's until we were certain everyone would be in bed. At midnight we donned our warmest coats and all four of us piled into our station wagon. Dad turned the car lights off as we approached their house, soundlessly, listening for any noise coming from their direction.

It was safe. Gary, the fastest of us, grabbed the box and took off across the yard to deposit it on the stoop. I couldn't see him in the pitch blackness, but I could hear. A dog's sharp bark pierced the air. A big German Shepherd started rounding the corner of the house and

Gary's footsteps quickened their pace. I held the car door open for him and he slid in just in front of the dog's bared teeth.

The first day back to school after Christmas break, Gary winked at me from his seat on the bus, willing me to keep my poker face as we neared the house of our midnight run. Jerome, Letisha, and the other six kids were all dressed in the clothes we'd given them. Every outfit seemed to fit as though it had been designed with that particular child in mind.

It's been many years now since that Christmas Eve, and I have not forgotten it. I hope I never will. After months of pining over my dream coat, I never missed it after all. Looking back, I can't even remember exactly how it looked. But Letisha Robinson's beautiful smile as she proudly wore her new sweater is permanently etched in my memory. I learned the joy of giving that Christmas.

~Taryn R. Hutchison

Just Tell Us You Love Us

Silent gratitude isn't much use to anyone.
~G.B. Stern

Most of my life I've been the type of person who listened to the opinion of others and if they said something couldn't be done, I accepted their decision and went about what I needed to get done that day. That was before an event that happened last year just before Christmas. At the time I was standing at the counter in a gift shop signing a copy of my latest book, *Christmas in the Maritimes*, when I overheard a lady say, "I'm sending this to my nephew in Afghanistan and I know he'll love it. When he's finished, he'll pass it around to the other Maritimers in his unit."

"Other Maritimers in his unit," her words kept repeating themselves over and over in my mind. Gradually an idea began to take shape. I shared my idea with a friend but she said, "You'd have to raise the money. You'd have to know where to ship the books. You'd... forget it, there's no way!" But this time I wasn't about to take "no" for an answer. The news last year was full of stories about the conditions our troops were serving under and I thought if this little book would mean something to the members serving our country, then I was going to at least try to find a way to send some copies to them.

My first step was to write to Roger Cyr, a friend who had been in the air force before his retirement. I asked him if he thought the book would be welcomed. He wrote back right away encouraging me to pursue this idea. He also said, "I spent four years in Europe during the Cold War serving with our NATO troops plus a tour as a peacekeeper in Africa (Congo). One of the things we treasured the most was a Canadian newspaper or a word from home."

The more I thought on it, the more I was convinced stories from home would be such a morale booster. I began investigating the possibilities and started by making phone calls, doing web searches and writing e-mails. However, the results from my inquiries only served to add to my earlier doubts. It was fast becoming evident that it wasn't a workable project. My major stumbling block was the fact that I'd never done anything like this before, so I was unfamiliar with all the rules and considerations involved in sending something to our troops. I discovered parcels could only be sent if you knew the specific name and address of the unit and the name and number of the person receiving the gift. My friend was right. This idea might have been a good idea but it was fast becoming a dream that would never be fulfilled.

Somewhere along the way I read an article about another Elaine who was able to help the troops through her project "Operation Wish." She didn't listen to the "no's" and her story encouraged me to press on.

Finally, on a Wednesday, November 15th I made contact with Margaret Reid, Coordinator of Deployment Services of 14 Wing Greenwood. Her response was immediate. She wrote, "Great idea! Definitely possible from my perspective anyway. We're doing our packages to the troops on Nov 21st. I guess the question now for you is if you can make the Christmas miracles happen by next Tuesday?"

I called Nimbus, my publisher. "Do you have 140 books in stock?" (They were waiting for more books from the printers and I wasn't sure if they had enough to fill their immediate orders.) The managing editor assured me they could fill my order if I could raise the funds needed to purchase the books by Friday at 3:00 PM. I needed to meet that deadline in order to leave enough time for the books to be delivered from Nimbus' warehouse to Greenwood in time to be packed with the parcels on Tuesday.

I wrote back, "Dear Ms. Reid, I believe this Christmas miracle will happen!"

My idea was to ask the community (through contacts with the media) to get involved and sponsor the books as a way of showing the men and women serving our country they were being remembered. Two reporters agreed to help, but before the afternoon was over I ran into another snag. I didn't have a business address where people could drop off the money and my telephone inquiries to this point suggested setting up an account for this purpose would take some time. The deadline for getting the story out in Thursday's papers was fast approaching. Around four o'clock I remember thinking that Ms. Reid said I needed a Christmas miracle, so why not ask God? I did. Within minutes I had an unexpected phone call from someone I'd talked to earlier in the day.

"Elaine, I was touched by what you want to do. You're going to get your Christmas miracle. I'll cover the cost!"

Two days later the books arrived in Greenwood in time to be packed in the Christmas parcels being made up for 140 troop members of 14 Wing Greenwood who were serving our great country, Canada, in various places throughout the world.

As I wrote my Christmas letters last year I thought of a poem I'd received from a friend. In the poem, the author asked a young soldier who had left a wife and child at home to serve his country, what he could give him for Christmas—money or a feast? The young soldier's answer was, "Just tell us you love us." When I sent the books it was my prayer that the small gift of stories and memories from home would do just that—tell 140 soldiers who were serving their country that I loved them.

~Elaine Ingalls Hogg

Angel in a Chocolate Shop

Anyone can be an angel.
~Author Unknown

As I hustled and bustled into each and every store, trying to find last-minute Christmas gifts for friends and family, I could feel the stress of the holidays upon me. Life would change after I walked into a high-end chocolate shop where not even the fancy silk bows around the boxes could have prepared me for the day's unraveling.

What struck me was an older African American woman, who gently caressed the glass with her finger. She looked as if she was dressed in her Sunday best, with coiffed hair and shoes that matched her purse. There was something about her that made me hover closely. I went behind her and made motions with my hands to the salesperson—signing that she looked as if she was going to cry. As if I gave a director's signal, the actress behind the counter asked on cue, "Can I help you with anything?"

"Oh," the lady sighed. "This was what my husband bought me each and every Christmas," pointing to the caramel-filled milk chocolates. "This is my first year without him. We were married for forty-nine years. My husband was a good man and he bought me caramels every Christmas, knowing how much I loved them." Her voice was soft, her finger shook a little, but her words floated on air. "At first, it was just a couple, one for him, one for me — 'cause we didn't have much money. But at the end, he'd have them wrapped in those fancy boxes. And then he'd give me a certain number and make it special, like when we added our first baby, I got three that year and then oh, it was up to quite a bit with my own children, grandchildren and grandbabies." She chuckled.

"We would have been married fifty years this Christmas." My heart sank. It was as if she turned the faucet on in her soul and all the love and memories came pouring out. It was difficult for me to hold back my own tears as her story touched me deeply.

She turned and looked at me with a smile and looked back at the glass and quietly said, "I still remember my first Christmas when he gave me two. It was just as special the first time as it has been all these years." She looked down and said in a whisper, "I'd give any-thing to just have him again." She wiped a tear from her face with a handkerchief she kept tucked in her sleeve. She gently put the cloth back into her purse and walked out of the store.

The saleslady just looked at me and said, "Wow."

I told the saleslady that I wanted to buy the lady a bag of choco-lates with caramel in them and asked if she would be willing to run down the mall to give them to her if I kept an eye on the store, know-ing I could sneak out the other direction and the lady would never see me. She loved the idea and charged me only 50% for the bag (which was very expensive, mind you).

"What do you want me to say?" she asked.

"Tell her an angel sent them."

She ran away with the bag with so much glee in her step and returned, face wet from crying.

"That was such a sweet thing you did for her," she said to me. "What a gift of love from a stranger."

"No," I said, matter-of-factly. "The truth is, her story of devoted love was a gift to me." I had been rushing around to buy meaningless gifts for a holiday that had become more commercial than heartfelt. That lady had made me slow down and think about the people I loved and the ways I could show them how I felt through thoughtful gifts and gestures.

The true Christmas angel that day in the mall was not me, but a beautiful woman who passed through my life at just the right time—in a chocolate shop, in the middle of the mall.

~Cheri Eplin

A Christmas Prayer Answered

I can no other answer make, but, thanks, and thanks.
~William Shakespeare

My husband, Chris, joined the Marine Corps in April of 2007. Shortly after, we were stationed at Camp Lejeune, North Carolina—seven hours from our home in Virginia. Our first Christmas in the United States Marine Corps was bittersweet, knowing that Chris would be deploying less than a year later and we'd be separated during the holidays. So we stretched our last few dollars to the limit to make the trip home.

Unfortunately, we realized once we were there we would be about a tank of gas short of making it home and he would have to either suck up his pride and ask someone in his family for money, which he refused to do, or try to make it home with what we had.

On Christmas night, after spending the day with his family, we stopped at a gas station to top off the tank and began to pray this would carry us home. My husband was in uniform and he began to fill the tank. My car, as is the case with many Marine wives' cars, is decorated heavily with United States Marine stickers and quotes.

To our surprise, a middle-aged lady at the next pump over came up to Chris. "Are you a Marine?" the lady asked him. With his head held high and his shoulders back, "Yes Ma'am," was his reply. She proceeded to thank him for his service to his country and to ask him questions about where he was stationed and if he was from around this area originally.

At the conclusion of their conversation, she thanked him again and insisted on paying for his gas. She handed my husband forty dollars. Although he asked, the kind woman would not give her name or any information to contact her.

She walked away toward the front of the store where my mother-in-law was coming out from paying for her gas. "Is that your boy?" was her question to Chris's mom.

Smiling, she answered, "Yes, that's my son."

"I want to thank you also for allowing and supporting your son to serve in the military," she said. God smiled on us for our first Christmas in the Marine Corps and sent an angel to answer our prayers. I only wish that woman knew how much she affected my husband and me with her selfless gift.

~Carrie Morris

Christmas Magic

Holly Jolly Christmas

It's the Thought that Counts

*A person without a sense of humor is like a wagon without springs—
jolted by every pebble in the road.*
~Henry Ward Beecher

By 11:30, a second UPS driver sprinted to our porch clutching yet another box. It was looking like UPS had relocated their local distribution facility to my driveway. With just a few days left until Christmas, I began to sense Barbara's and my "no-gift agreement" was off.

Back in November, my fiancée and I had decided that new granite kitchen countertops and appliances would be our Christmas gifts to one another. I went along with the plan. After all, lugging fifteen-pound granite samples into our house for several days was considerably less painful than strolling zombie-like through the women's department at Macy's in search of the girlie things she would delight in receiving for Christmas. I was off the hook.

How could she be so incredibly thoughtful every Christmas? How could I be so predictably clueless when it came to buying a few nice gifts for the woman I love? How naive was I to think I could avoid perfume counters and jewelry cases this year? I hoped these daily deliveries were for Barbara's kids or grandchildren, but somehow, I knew some of those boxes would be for me.

At 3:35, a FedEx truck delivered yet another reminder that I was probably getting more than a slab of gold-flecked granite and a dual-fuel oven in my stocking. The stark realization that I might be the only one opening presents on Christmas morning caused a sudden rush of blood to my face. At fifty-eight, I hadn't experienced a hot flash. Until now.

The pressure was on and I needed to produce a couple of tasteful gifts with about ninety-six hours to get it done. I immediately thought of the online pajama company I had heard about on the radio earlier that morning.

"Guaranteed Christmas delivery," echoed through my brain. These ads were directed at men like me. I was familiar with their line of PJs and knew I could find just the right set for Barbara to slip into while I opened the gifts that now lined the front hallway of our home.

I browsed and browsed. Then I pointed and clicked some more. "Sugarplum flannel." Nice, but flannel isn't too sexy. "Sweet snowflake thermal pajamas." Even I know this is not the best choice for a menopausal woman. "Red Seduction Chemise." Nice! But would Barb question my motivation for such a selection? The search continued.

Then they caught my eye. "Oh-So-Soft Lavender Pin Dot Nursing Pajamas." Barbara is a Registered Nurse and loves all things lavender. How clever was I? I'd managed to find a personal gift with time to spare. All I needed was a couple of stocking stuffers and I'd be golden.

Christmas morning arrived with all the festive touches. Lighted tree, fireplace aglow. Warm cinnamon buns rested on a glistening new granite kitchen countertop. And a set of pajamas just waiting to be opened sat under the Christmas tree.

Without ever acknowledging that both parties broke the no-gift rule, we began to unwrap our presents. Baking supplies for me. Lindt chocolates and a final unwrapped gift for her. "TO: Barbie, FROM: Mikey," the tag read.

"Oh! I love the color," she exclaimed with joyful enthusiasm. "And so soft." It looked like the PJs were a hit. Barb pulled them from the tissue-lined box and held them up to be sure they would fit. "Perfect fit," she assured me.

Barbara's twenty-eight-year-old daughter Shannon was visiting and seemed to approve as well.

"Are those buttons on the shoulders?" she asked her mom. Even though I hadn't recalled seeing shoulder buttons from the Internet pictures, I thought they added a nice touch.

"What kind of pajamas did you say these were?" Shannon asked me. "Nurse's pajamas," I replied. "See? The top looks like hospital scrubs. They're pajamas for a nurse."

As if on cue, both Barbara and Shannon laughed about as loudly as I'd ever heard. Before they explained, it dawned on me why they were so amused.

"See? The buttons allow these flaps to…" Yes, I got it. Those weren't hospital scrubs. I bought nursing pajamas for a woman who, as far as I knew, would never need them again.

But Barbara loved them and wore them to bed later that Christmas night. And not once did she question my motivation for giving her a shoulder-buttoned pajama top for nursing mothers!

~Mike Morin

Reprinted by permission of Off the Mark
and Mark Parisi ©2004.

How I Spent My Christmas Vacation

By and large, mothers are the only workers who do not have regular time off.
They are the great vacationless class.
~Anne Morrow Lindbergh

Day One: Here's a parenting tip for the New Year; never ground your children from the Nintendo and the Xbox the day before Christmas vacation begins! However, I managed to keep four boys busy decorating cookies. The over-use of cinnamon dots left our snowmen looking rather bloody, but the boys seemed to enjoy that.

Day Two: I thought it would be fun to spend the afternoon singing Christmas carols, but if I hear "Jingle Bells, Santa Smells" one more time, I'm going to scream! I took our oldest son out to buy presents for his brothers. He is really thoughtful. Too thoughtful. Two hours too thoughtful. I've never spent two hours in the Dollar Store before today. I never will again.

Day Three: My husband isn't speaking to me. He took our seven-year-old Christmas shopping. Many hours later they're back. Having bested his brother's shopping time, our younger son was quite pleased with himself. My husband, however, was not. "Have you ever spent THREE hours at the Dollar Store, trying to get a kid to spend his allowance on his brothers?" All I said was, "Why do you think I sent you?" Now it's colder in here than it is outside.

Day Four: Since the current temperature is a whopping five degrees, it would be nice if there was snow on the ground. All we have is ice. Unable to bear the whining about the Nintendo, I bundled up the children and sent them out to play on the ice. They played happily for ten minutes. Unfortunately they discovered the painful difference between ice balls and snowballs. Hot cocoa soothed fragile nerves—until we ran out of marshmallows.

Day Five: It's Christmas Eve. Eight hours with the in-laws, sixteen people for dinner and children who've discovered Grandma's ceramic reindeer holds M&M's. Around midnight, snow began to fall and silence descended as well. I filled the stockings to the soft strains of "Silent Night" and enjoyed the fragile peace.

Day Six: Christmas morning, 4 AM. "Mom! Mom! It's Christmas! Santa came, he came!" Through the dim glow of the clock, I gaze blearily into the big, blue eyes of a wide-awake boy. "If you don't get back in bed this instant, Santa is going to make a return trip to give you a lump of coal," I growled. "It is NOT Christmas morning when you can see the moon and the street lights are on." I kept the stocking and the child trudged back to bed. At this point I wasn't even sure he was mine.

Day Six officially: Christmas morning, 6 AM. Ho Ho Ho! The blue-eyed boy came back. He really does belong to me.

Day Seven: The kids played happily. The Nintendo/Xbox ban has been lifted. Now I am the one that is whining. My pleas to the grandparents for restraint had once again fallen on deaf ears. Now, it's been left to me to figure out where to put all this stuff. I waded through colorful debris and stepped on G.I. Joe's pistol. I think it's permanently embedded between my toes.

Day Eight: We are out of batteries already! Fights broke out over whose turn it is to play Nintendo. You'd think a forty-three-year-old man would be better at sharing.

Day Nine: The rain fell, the ice melted, the children whined and I cried.

Day Ten: I called the daycare on the corner to ask about their rates. "Oh are you going back to work?" the owner asked. "No," I replied, "I'm going crazy." She hung up on me.

Day 11: I staggered home from the mall where I exchanged one remote control car, which never "remotely" worked, one set of jammies labeled too lame to be worn by a twelve-year-old and one set of dishes so hideous that they prove beyond all doubt, I am NOT my grandmother's favorite. My husband greeted me at the door, waving the Visa bill. I turned to run, but could still hear him bellow, "Can you explain this one-way ticket to Hawaii?"

Day 12: When I was a child, Christmas vacation seemed to last a couple of seconds, but now I understand why Mom would cross each day of vacation off the calendar in bright red marker. Four lunches are packed and ready to go. Four backpacks wait by the front door. I realized I might have been rushing things when my oldest child refused to get out of bed. I checked the clock. It was 5 AM. The streetlights still shone and the moon was faintly visible in the dusky sky. I sat down in the living room and smiled as I sipped my coffee. I'll let the children sleep a little bit longer while I enjoy the first day of MY Christmas vacation.

~Cindy Hval

Yeah, and I'm the Easter Bunny!

Mirth is God's medicine. Everybody ought to bathe in it.
~Henry Ward Beecher

Christmas was inching closer and closer. At least it seemed that way to we kids who were anxious to hear the last blissful school bell that would herald our holiday vacation. Dad was out of town, Mom was at the grocery store, and my sister and oldest brother were off visiting friends. At the impressionable young age of thirteen, I was in charge.

Being entrusted with the care of my little brothers wasn't a typical thing at that tender age. My mom was in a babysitter's club where the mothers took turns watching each other's kids but the urgent need to run to the store arose unexpectedly without time to arrange for another sitter.

Taking my grown-up position of responsibility with the utmost sobriety, I was diligently watching my brothers who were four and six. With the boys engrossed in a TV show, my job had been easy so far. I sure never expected anything else.

When heavy footsteps clomped onto the front porch and a big fist banged on the door, adrenalin shot through my young frame. Mother's instructions had been strict: don't open the door to anyone! I planned to follow them to the letter. Summoning courage, I asked who was there, fully expecting a reply from a well-known neighbor or friend.

"Santa Claus!" A deep, booming voice cried to my surprise.

Right. Certain the fellow on the porch was not who he claimed, I ran to the bathroom and peeked out the small, high window that looked onto the porch. Whoever had knocked stood just out of view. Unfortunately, our front window looked out to the yard and street but not the driveway. Seeing no car, or sleigh with reindeer for that matter, I sprinted back to the door.

"I'm sorry, you'll have to come back later." My words were firm.

"It's Santa, let him in!" clamored the boys as I whispered that it was not the real Kris Kringle.

"Ho, Ho, Ho!" our mysterious caller bellowed. "I've come to see the Sullivans. Can you ask your mother to come to the door?" Yikes! Now what to do? If I told him Mom wasn't home, we'd be sitting ducks. This guy could be some crazed yuletide killer like the ones dreamed up for that spooky Alfred Hitchcock show.

"Who are you really?" I asked with more courage than I felt.

"It's Santa Claus." The voice boomed again.

"Yeah, and I'm the Easter Bunny!" I sniped defiantly. "You can't come in. Go away!" I waited breathlessly for him to leave as the boys raced back to the window in hopes of catching a glimpse. Muttering something I couldn't make out, the pseudo-Santa finally plodded down the steps.

Unnerved by the encounter, I shooed the boys back into the den to watch TV and wait for Mom's return. Before my poor mother was even through the door, the saga of our Santa stalker came gushing out.

"I didn't let him in, Mom!" I beamed with pride.

"Oh, no!" Mom slapped a hand to her forehead. "I forgot."

"Forgot what?" I was confused.

"Mr. Simons." After assuring me I had done the right thing, she made a beeline for the phone. Within moments, Mom was apologizing profusely to the husband of one of the babysitter club members who had kindly agreed to play Santa for the kids in the club. In the craziness of preparations for the holidays, dealing with a houseful of kids, and the unexpected trip to the store, she had forgotten the big guy was scheduled to visit.

Looking back, I know she was pleased we were all safe and sound. But it's more than likely my ever proper and polite mother was as mortified by my smart aleck "And I'm the Easter Bunny" retort as she was by forgetting the appointment. The tale soon grew to legendary proportions and remains a favorite chapter in our family's colorful repertoire.

~Nancy Sullivan

Reprinted by permission of Off the Mark
and Mark Parisi ©1998.

The Secret's Out

I am extraordinarily patient, provided I get my own way in the end.
~Margaret Thatcher

"Mommy! What's that?" three-year-old Avery peered into the cart.

Pretending I didn't hear, I scanned the holiday merchandise with studied concentration and tried to ignore her. Earlier, when I thought she wasn't looking, I had slipped a fairy-themed coloring book between the mounds of groceries, knowing it would make the perfect stocking stuffer for my bright little sprite who adored all things girly.

Avery persisted. "Mommy! I see something. What is it?"

I tried to distract her. "Avery, look at this Care Bear. Do you think baby Gavin would like it?"

She refused to be distracted. Her gamine face focused only on the glimpse of tiny fairy wings teasing her from the cart. "Mommy! What is that? Can I see it? Please?" Her head full of blond curls bounced in her excitement. "It looks like something I would like."

With a deep sigh, I moved the boxes of Cheerios aside, pulled the coloring book from its useless hiding place, and handed it over to her. Avery's blazing blue eyes widened with excitement.

"I was going to give you this as a Christmas present," I explained, a tad peeved. "It was supposed to be a secret."

Her expression froze. I knew how terrible she always felt when a surprise was spoiled, and I worried that she would start crying right there in the Super Walmart. Already, a small frown creased her pixie brow. Yet when I started to console her, she interrupted.

"But, Mommy—I already have lots of presents under the tree. And I got to open the new nightie Grammy made me. And the book Pops sent." She peered earnestly into my eyes. "I don't really need this for Christmas, Mommy."

Her sweet selflessness melted my heart. When had she matured? I beamed with pride at her generous attitude.

"I don't need this for Christmas, Mommy," my wee enchantress insisted with a charitable bob of her head. Avery hugged the coveted coloring book closer to her chest and announced pointedly, "I need it right NOW!"

~Kayla Rehme Crockett as told to Carol McAdoo Rehme

I've Got a Secret

If there is any larceny in a man, golf will bring it out.
~Paul Gallico

In November, my stepdaughter Christy came up with a new plan for Christmas. "This year, we all put our names in a hat and everyone picks just one person to buy for," she announced excitedly.

"But what if someone who doesn't know what I like draws my name?" I asked.

"Dude, all you ever want is golf stuff. How hard is that?"

"What about Leila and Charlie?"

"Everyone gets them gifts."

"What? No fair!"

"They're kids...."

I stomped my foot and stuck out my lower lip.

"... little kids."

So even though I was still worried about not getting all the stuff I so richly deserved, I warmed to the plan. For one thing I hate to shop, and for another, my gifts aren't always appreciated.

"What is this?" my wife asked last year.

"It's a cap cleaner. You put it on your baseball caps and they keep their shape when you wash them."

That's when she reminded me she didn't wear caps and I realized I'd totally wasted three bucks.

"Okay, I'm in," I said.

So, Carl, Christy, Jon, Patrick, Shane, Ashley, my wife and I all put our names in a hat and we drew.

Five minutes after we drew Christy asked: "So, who'd you get?"

"I thought this was supposed to be a secret Santa."

"Well, yeah, just tell me… not everyone."

"You know," I said. "Years ago I worked at this company in New Hampshire. Every day it seemed like someone would come up to me and say, 'Don't tell anyone, but…' The thing was I never told anyone, so I became known as a dead link and pretty soon people stopped telling me secrets because I kept them to myself."

"Yeah, yeah," Christy said. "That's a great story. Now who do you have?"

I smiled and did the old zipper lip thing.

"You know I'll figure it out." She tried to pry the paper from my hand but I crumpled it up and shoved it deep into my pocket.

"Freak," Christy said, then stomped away.

And that was that — until I suddenly realized it was December and remembered that I had to actually buy a gift, so I raced off to the mall. That's when I called Christy.

"What's the spending limit?" I asked.

"No real limit. Why?"

"Well, I was looking at games that come in a frame. You hang them up like art when you're not playing."

"Ah ha! Games. You must have Shane or Ashley. They love games."

"Nope. Not Shane or Ashley," I said and hung up.

Ten minutes later I called again. "They've got these incredible photo tiles in a frame — scenes of Santa Barbara and Catalina Island. Way cool."

"Tiles! Mom loves tiles. Ha-ha, youuu'vvvve got Mmmommmmm."

"No, it's not your mother," I said, then hung up. I now realized this was the most fun I'd ever had shopping.

The next call I placed to my wife, perhaps the second worst secret keeper in the family. "They've got this engraving cart set up down here at the mall. Do you think a silver flask is a good gift?"

"No," she said.

Two minutes later Christy called. "Ha. Mom called. Only Jon would ever want an engraved silver flask. Gotcha."

"I think you're right," I said. "So now I'm in the calendar store. Wow, there's a great surf calendar."

"You've got Carl!" she yelled in triumph.

"Oh wait, here's the great chefs of the world calendar complete with recipes."

"Patrick," she yelled so loud I had to hold the phone away from my ear.

"Nope," I said.

"Well that only leaves... ME!"

"Gotta go," I said.

"Clothes!" she yelled. "Jewelry! No spending limit...."

I hung up. Then I left the mall and went to another shop.

"Don't suppose you gift wrap?" I asked as I laid my purchase on the counter.

"Sorry, we don't wrap," he said. "But if this is a gift, then someone sure got lucky this year. This is a real beauty."

I beamed with pride, grabbed my purchase and headed for the door.

"Ernie?" the guy said, just as I got to the door.

"Yes?"

"You dropped this." He held out a crumpled piece of paper.

"Oh. Just throw that away, will ya? It's supposed to be a surprise."

Then I went home to wrap up my brand new three-wood.

~Ernie Witham

Ho Ho Ho, Ouch!

If you carry your childhood with you, you never become older.
~Tom Stoppard

As Christmas was approaching, my husband and I decided that a perfect gift for our then three-year-old son would be a battery-operated motorcycle similar to the real one my husband rode in his free time. We knew our son would love it. After searching in what seemed like every store in our area for just the right replica, we finally found it. The purchase was made and it was stored in our bedroom closet.

We talked about our purchase during the weeks leading up to Christmas, anticipating the joy it would bring to our son. But, being parents new to this toy assembly job, we never anticipated the amount of time that it would require to put the motorcycle together. We thought that Christmas Eve would be the perfect time to start the job. We always go to a family Christmas Eve celebration so this meant that it was already 9 PM, after our son was fast asleep, before we could even get the box out of the closet and begin the assembly. Big mistake!

Once the box was opened, it was apparent that this "simple vehicle" was not so simple. It came with multiple screws, plastic pieces, stickers, pages and pages of vague instructions and a miniature Allen wrench... all of the things needed to put the motorcycle together. Both my husband and I worked on it, and it took almost three hours.

After careful inspection of a job well done I decided that the best way to test the new vehicle was to take a ride on it. The instructions indicated that it would hold up to one hundred pounds. The thought never crossed my mind that they actually meant it. I mean look at all of the other things the instructions mentioned that were not necessary—like the four extra screws! I hopped on. It was a great ride. I drove through the living room and around the dining table. I was having a ball until, well until we heard the sound... the sound of plastic cracking! I jumped off only to find that I had cracked the entire frame. My husband was furious and had that "what have you done" look on his face. I was hurt, offended and then panicked. It was 11:45 PM on Christmas Eve and I had just broken my son's main gift. What was I going to do?

I immediately called the store where we bought the motorcycle. They always stayed open until midnight on Christmas Eve, thank goodness for us, and they had another motorcycle in stock. They said I'd have to hurry as they were closing in fifteen minutes. My husband, who was not speaking to me by this time, drove to the store and got the new motorcycle. By the time he returned home he was a little calmer but still thought I was a crazy woman and couldn't understand why I had to try riding the thing in the first place.

We began again. Unfortunately, it didn't go any faster the second time around, but we did manage to use more of the screws this time. At 3:00 AM the new motorcycle was built. Much to my husband's relief, this time I decided that I would not try and ride it. I would let my son test it out in the morning. I got into bed tired, relieved and depressed. Depressed to learn the truth... I was too big for children's toys and motorcycles.

Christmas morning came in less than four hours. My son was so excited about his new motorcycle—it was just like his dad's. And Dad was pretty pleased too.

My son is now thirteen and his real motorcycle is in our garage... right next to Dad's. I can't say the child in me has gone away but I have learned that there are some things better left for the boys.

Now my husband and son go for their long motorcycle rides

together. My son tries to talk me into going with them. I make eye contact with my husband and remember why this is "their" thing. I had my day on the bike in the living room and that was all I needed.

~D'ette Corona

The Gingerbread House

*May the roof above us never fall in
and may we good companions beneath it never fall out.*
~Irish Blessing

A few years ago at Christmastime, a decision was made that would change things forever in my family. It was the year that the traditional family Christmas cookie baking extravaganza was done away with. It was not an easy decision to make. As we all know, there are certain traditions that, if not continued, create disappointment for your children. The tree must be just so big and decorated just so, the house, both inside and out, must have that certain festive glow, we must all sing "Grandma Got Run Over by a Reindeer" much to the disgust of my mother-in-law, and cookies, lots of cookies, must be baked. But my three sons were all adults now so I thought it would be acceptable to them if we deviated a little from the norm. Rather than the traditional cookies, this year would be the year of... the gingerbread house.

I will say, up front, that I am not a baker. I do not enjoy baking, I never have and I never will. I love to cook but baking just doesn't do anything for me. But my daughter-in-law, Crescent, is an excellent baker. She loves baking and is very creative. She is the one who suggested that she and I make a gingerbread house together. She was so excited about the idea and wanted to start a new tradition in our family. I suggested that we make Christmas meatballs and decorate them but she just didn't go for that. Oh well, I tried. Not wanting to disappoint her, I agreed that she and I would make a gingerbread house. Mike, who is my middle son and her husband, would also be there to help. Since he is a licensed general contractor and electrician, his help could be very valuable during the construction... or not.

This was going to be fun. I kept coming up with the most spectacular plans for our house. I thought we could make a three-story Victorian mansion. No. We would make a castle complete with a turret, alligators and a moat. No, no. We would make a replica of the Empire State Building... all 102 stories of it. "Hold on, Mom." Crescent reasoned with me and kind of insisted that for our first try in the construction business, we should settle for a plain one-story ranch house. Boring, boring... but I finally agreed.

Crescent and I went to the market and bought the ingredients for the dough, the icing and all of the decorations we thought we could possibly need for our masterpiece. We bought gumdrops, chocolate chips, peppermints, candy swirl sticks, licorice, M&M's, Red Hots, silver balls and sprinkles... lots and lots of different colored sprinkles. We were ready to start.

Mixing the dough for the walls and roof went really well. Making the dough for regular Christmas cookies had never gone this well; I was excited. Next step: we were supposed to roll the dough evenly to a thickness of 3/8". Really? Were they kidding? Remember, I am the woman who is not a baker. I couldn't roll anything to the same thickness, ever. But Crescent could do it and she was in charge. She took over, rolled the dough to the required thickness and then we got it in the oven. When it was ready, we cut out the pieces for the walls and the roof. After it cooled we were ready to build our spectacular house.

Before we could start to assemble our house, we had to make the icing—the "glue" that would hold our magnificent structure together. During the mixing, some of the powdered sugar got loose and went flying all over us and the kitchen counters and floor, but for the most part the making of the glue went well. The recipe said to put icing on the edges of the pieces of the walls, stand them up and hold them together for a few minutes while they dried. We did as we were instructed to do. We held the walls together with our hands, waited… waited… waited… and then slowly let go. Wow, how exciting! The sides of our house were standing up. The walls really held together — for all of about ten seconds. Then, down they came. Crash! We tried again and again. Same results… the walls came tumbling down. And please, don't even ask about the roof. Was this really supposed to be fun? And where was Mike, the contractor, during this? He was standing way over there — laughing and laughing. Big help!

But by this time Crescent and I — and even Mike — were all covered in that special icing and the kitchen was unrecognizable. Icing was absolutely everywhere. I was going to have to call in the Hazmat team to spray us off. I do know now why they call the icing "glue." In reality I think "cement" might even be a better description. Everything it touches sticks together… except of course, the pieces of our gingerbread house. Nothing could make those pieces hold together. Mike finally got out the trusty glue gun and glued everything together with real glue. That worked. And we also used toothpicks to help prop the walls up and keep the roof pieces from crashing down. Finally our house stood.

Actually once we did get the house standing, decorating it was fun. More of the decorations went into our mouths than went onto the house, but when all was said and done it looked… well, it looked… hmmm… really, really awful. Lopsided. Crooked. Cracked. Dripping in icing glop. The decorations that stood out the most were the toothpicks that helped hold the darn thing together. The chimney was at a ninety-degree angle to the roof so Santa would have a really hard time getting down it to deliver presents. The front door ended up on the roof and there were no windows. But Crescent, Mike and I were really happy. There were smiles, love and lots of laughter in the kitchen that day.

Did this become a new Christmas tradition for us? Did we make fabulous and intricate gingerbread houses each year for the next hundred years? Are you crazy?! No way! Our construction business folded after one try. The new tradition we did start was going to the store right after Thanksgiving and buying a Christmas gingerbread house. It's so much easier that way and there is nothing to clean up. The house would start out being part of our Christmas decorations and then, on Christmas morning, we would eat it and laugh about the year we tried to build our own house. And now, I have turned the Christmas cookie baking over to Crescent. She does a wonderful, delicious and beautiful job and creates new treats for our family each year. I think that, of all the people in our family, I enjoy those cookies the most because… I don't have to bake them. All I have to do is eat!

~Barbara LoMonaco

Ho-Hoing in Hawaii

The sun lay like a friendly arm across her shoulder.
~Marjorie Kinnan Rawlings

"The snowman's so cold we had to put a jacket on him," I whined to my husband as I unzipped our youngest from his parka. "Hon," I continued, "I've had it with snow; I want sun—hot sun. And palm trees, not pine trees. And beautiful, white beaches. And exotic fruit."

Visions of pineapple began to dance in my head.

My husband, Rick, and I are a study in contrast. He likes cold; I like heat. He was quite content in the minus-thirty-degree weather and two feet of snow that engulfed our rural northeastern British Columbia community. We mud-wrestled (without the mud), and I won.

"Oh good, we're going to Hawaii," I gushed. "Let's take the kids."

This would be the first time my pale, sun-deprived body would bask on a tropical island, and I was tickled pink.

En route, our family—which included eight-year-old-twins and a two-year-old—discarded our mass of winter clothing: parkas, mukluks, sealskin mitts and hats. As soon as we landed in Honolulu I jumped out of the plane.

Swaying to the sound of exotic Hawaiian music, grass-skirted, lei-draped hula girls reached out with welcoming arms. I kissed the ground. Rick teetered along, feet barely showing under our ton of winter wear.

Our Honolulu apartment was spacious (a troop of Boy Scouts could have lived there), cool (Rick and I arm-wrestled over the air conditioning; he won and it stayed on), and best of all, it was only minutes from the beach and a shopping mall—Yes! Everything at our condo was sooo inviting: the exotic gardens, the game room, the swimming pool.

At the beach I almost expected our three sons to stare blankly at the sea. After all, they had never been on a beach where the water was so warm one could actually swim in it. Instinctively though, they knew what to do—charge!

Rick and I watched them dutifully from shore. I, the I-don't-know-how-to-swim type, gingerly dipped my newly thawed toes into that wonderfully warm Pacific Ocean.

Ahhh... yes... warm sand we could dig our feet into, sun that actually heated our bodies, and malls, awash with familiar Christmas decorations and traditional Christmas songs.

And of course, there was Santa—the perfectly suited Santa.

He sauntered in—outside a beach-fronting mall, where a large crowd, including our family, awaited him. (No sign of any cumbersome reindeer). Santa was dressed in full regalia... almost. He had the customary pom-pommed red hat, fake white beard, red jacket with white trim... and beach sandals... and bright red shorts!

Our kids didn't care what Santa wore; he was handing out presents: candy canes, balloons, trinkets of various kinds... and leis.

The kids took their turns sitting on Santa's knees. There was the usual "Have you been a good boy?" question that garnered the usual "Yes, I've been very good!" answer. Santa blew up some ever-so-long balloons, which he shaped into animals—giraffes, elephants, fish—and handed one to each child.

"Merry Christmas, Merry Christmas," Santa boomed.

After the merriment, it was time for breakfast—with Santa. At patio tables shaded by multicoloured umbrellas, to the gentle sounds of Christmas carols floating in the background, our family noshed on fresh croissants and exotic fruit. Before I could say, "Kids, leave that last piece of pineapple for me," Santa and the kids—stacks of kids, including our own trio—skipped down to the beach, pied-piper style. There, Santa played beach ball with the kids, all of them appropriately clad in shorts or swim wear.

Rick and I, likewise attired, parked ourselves on lawn chairs and watched our kids get sand in their trunks. I wish I'd taken photos of Santa, but that would have meant eating less pineapple, a sacrifice I wasn't prepared to make.

Two weeks later Rick dragged me back into the plane. As we neared our destination, muffled in sub-zero gear, I stared bleakly at the reappearing frozen landscape. "Don't worry, dear," Rick piped. "Your body and bleached hair will return to their natural colours in no time."

I liked being red. I was going to flaunt that everywhere.

As the parents of four children (one more came along after that trip… not because of it) we've seen oodles of Santas over the years since then. But the most memorable Santa by far is the one who Ho-Hoed with our children under swaying palm trees in his flaming red shorts.

Visions of that Christmas still dance in my head, and that field-fresh pineapple still lingers on my palate.

~Chantal Meijer

Nothing Under the Tree

The best things in life are unexpected—because there were no expectations.
~Eli Khamarov, *Surviving on Planet Reebok*

"Don't get me anything for Christmas!" my husband's voice broke into my thoughts, which were full of all the Christmas preparations I planned to complete in the next few weeks. I looked at him and nodded, "You say that every year."

"This year I'm serious. There won't be anything for you under the tree or in your stocking, at least not from me. So don't get me any gifts either. Put the extra money to more things for the kids," he repeated.

I didn't bother replying. We went through this every year. Most years I'd listen and get him a few little gifts so the children could enjoy watching him empty his stocking. Every year he'd have a gift under the tree for me and my stocking would have lots of surprises in it, sometimes costly surprises. Every year I wished I hadn't listened to his instructions. This year I wouldn't.

Days passed in a whirlwind of activities including baking, shopping, decorating and sending out Christmas cards and letters. My husband repeated his nothing-for-me message frequently. Each time I would look deeply into his eyes for the teasing glint that was sure to be there, yet he seemed more serious than in the past.

Finally, the gifts were all wrapped and under the tree, the items for stockings well hidden from prying eyes, and the children's Christmas programs were done. Christmas Eve had arrived. I tucked the children in. Sleep would be delayed by their excitement so I curled up on the couch and settled in for a long wait.

"You know there's no gift under the tree for you, right?" my husband asked.

"Yup! I checked."

"Don't have anything for your stocking either. So don't be disappointed. I warned you. You listened and didn't get me anything either—right?" he said.

I looked at him and smiled. I'd wait and see. Maybe this year he listened to his own rules and I'd be one up on him. Then I tried to shake those thoughts right out of my head. Since when had giving gifts become such a competition? That shouldn't be what Christmas was all about.

I felt like I had barely laid my head on the pillow when I heard the children's voices attempting to break into my sleep-fogged brain. "Get up. It's Christmas! Get up!"

They pulled at our arms, urging us to hurry. They needed to see what Santa had put in their stockings. I pulled on my robe and followed them to the living room where I watched them eagerly empty all the treasures from the stockings. I loved to see their smiling faces. Then I turned to watch Brian empty his stocking. He leaned over and whispered for my ears alone, "I wasn't supposed to get anything."

I pulled a few chocolate candies and an orange from my stocking. He had been serious. There was no gift under the tree and nothing in my stocking. I tried to hide my disappointment.

Later that morning, we headed the few blocks to my parents' house to celebrate with the rest of the family. As we entered their house the fragrant aroma of roasting turkey and pies filled our nostrils. Christmas dinner always provided a bountiful supply of scrumptious food. I quickly pitched in to help put the food on the table while the children ran off to play with their cousins.

Following the meal the children clamored for present exchange but first all of us women took on the mundane chore of kitchen cleanup while the men headed out to check the trucks and warehouse. With impeccable timing they returned just as we completed the last of the dishes and I looked forward to a relaxing afternoon of visiting. Brian looked at me and said, "Before we open the presents why don't you take some of these leftovers to our fridge and bring back a couple of games for later."

"Sounds good to me, but why don't you go?" I replied.

"Nope, I'll stay here. You go. Hurry back," he countered.

I looked around but no one took my side. Frustration began building inside me when I asked him once more to do the errand and he again refused. I could not win this argument, so rather than creating an unpleasant scene, I grabbed my coat and jammed my arms into it. I pulled on my boots, grabbed some containers of leftovers from my mom and headed out the door, barely refraining from slamming it behind me. I mumbled and grumbled to myself all the way home and by the time I arrived in my own kitchen the frustration had turned to full-blown anger.

I yanked open the refrigerator door, shoved in the containers and slammed the door shut. I wheeled around, almost colliding with a huge dishwasher standing in the middle of the kitchen floor.

"A dishwasher? I don't have a dishwasher!" I yelled into the empty room. My anger drained out as tears began to run down my face. I ran my hands over the brand new appliance. My present didn't fit under the tree or in my stocking. I had been sent home to find it. Checking the warehouse had been an excuse to sneak in the dishwasher. I wiped my tears before heading back into the cold. My anger dissipated, only to be replaced by shame at my attitude. I slowly walked back into my folks' house and sheepishly faced my family. Their faces were wreathed in smiles as they waited expectantly for my reactions.

I directed my comments to my husband, "You didn't keep your word. You got me a present!"

"What present?" he said as he tried to keep a straight face. The twinkle in his eyes betrayed the losing battle he fought.

"The dishwasher in our kitchen!" I replied.

Laughter filled the room while everyone began talking at once. The laughter drove the last vestiges of frustration, anger and shame from me. That Christmas I learned a lesson or two. First, things aren't always as they seem. Second, frustration and anger should never have first place in my life at anytime but especially at Christmas.

~Carol Harrison

Christmas Magic

O' Christmas Tree

Construction Paper Stars

Those who bring sunshine to the lives of others cannot keep it from themselves.
~James Matthew Barrie

I tugged a heavy box of Christmas ornaments into the living room. The fresh, green scent of pine filled the house. Cards with whimsical reindeer and serene manger scenes nestled in a basket by the door. Even the snow cooperated, a light dusting covering the yard and front walk. It was Christmastime. But something wasn't right.

For the first time, our whole family wouldn't be together for the holidays.

Getting the house ready for Christmas used to be so much fun when the kids were little. But now our oldest, Kate, was newly married and lived out of state, and our son, Andy was away at college, unable to return for winter break. Our nest was empty, and I was the lonely mama bird.

Unpacking the ornaments, I hung them one by one on the branches of the tree. My husband Mike helped reach the high places. Many of the decorations marked something special in the kids' lives. Baby's First Christmas. Kindergarten. Getting an A on a report card. I dangled a tiny basketball before me.

"Remember how we used to love sitting in the bleachers, cheering on Andy and his team?" I asked.

"He was a great point guard," Mike recalled.

Then there was the adorable, stuffed Winnie the Pooh. "Kate's favorite book," I said.

"I used to read that to her nearly every night, until she was old enough to read it aloud to us," Mike added. Hanging those ornaments filled us with warm, happy memories.

I took another ornament out of the box, a handmade construction paper star with Kate and Andy's wobbly names printed across the top. I held onto it, not wanting to let it go. But as I clutched it, I bent a little of the corner. This is what happens when you hold things too tight, I thought. I smoothed it gently and hung it in a special spot in the center of the tree.

Although I loved Christmas, I remained sad as I baked, shopped and wrapped. I felt like I was going through the motions. Even at church. One Sunday after service, I caught sight of a little decorated tree in the corner. Twinkling white lights illuminated simple star-shaped ornaments. They were made of colored construction paper, just like the ones my kids had made when they were little. I moved closer and held one in my hand. Each one contained the name of a child in need, and a particular Christmas wish they had this year. The object was to take a tag, purchase the wished-for gift, wrap it and return it under the tree. I couldn't seem to pull myself away from the ornaments, reading each name carefully, thinking about the children who were making the Christmas wishes and the gifts they were hoping for. The moment I selected two tags, my heart instantly felt lighter.

"What's that?" asked Mike, eyeing the stars.

"Just some holiday cheer for some kids," I answered, grinning broadly.

At home, I baked cookies with red and green sprinkles, the warm sugar smell filling the kitchen. I took time to read and appreciate the cards we received. I even shopped more merrily, taking time to find just the right gifts on my list. Two gifts especially filled me with a sense of comfort and joy. In the evenings, Mike and I sipped cocoa while wrapping gifts and adorning them with big, bright bows.

The following Sunday I was anxious to get to church, carrying the special gifts into the lobby. I imagined the delighted faces on the children as they tore off the paper to reveal something special, just for them. I couldn't help smiling.

Doing something nice for others was definitely one way of taking the focus off my own problems and turning it into something positive. But it was even more than that. It was a way for me to feel connected to little Kate and Andy, who were now all grown up.

I placed the special Christmas gifts under the tree, the gifts that were just what each child had asked for on their star ornaments: A basketball, and a Winnie the Pooh book.

~Peggy Frezon

Tannenbaum Tumbleweed

To be upset over what you don't have is to waste what you do have.

~Ken S. Keyes

t was a cold, depressing day in more ways than one. Christmas was looming, and as a single mom of three living on sporadic child support payments, I was not looking forward to trying to make what little money I had stretch in several different directions.

My mom and dad, along with other caring relatives, would see to it that the boys had gifts, and the big Christmas feast would be held at my brother's home, so the basics would be taken care of.

The annual Christmas Pageant given at the school had done little to lift my sagging spirits, and on the way home, the gray, blustery wind pushing my poor, little pick-up all over the road, only made things worse.

That night the question would be asked, as it was every night, by one or all of the boys: when were we getting our Christmas tree? I was informed in no uncertain terms that Santa wouldn't have any-where to put the presents if we didn't have a tree. Unfortunately, I had discovered that even the tiniest trees for sale at the Boy Scout lot were far beyond my budget.

Huge tumbleweeds were blowing around from all directions, making driving even more challenging. They seemed to be pushing each other out of the way as though they were having a race to see which one could jump out in front of us first. Some were round and bushy, rolling very straight and fast, while others were pointed and lurched unsteadily, as if deciding which way they wanted to go. Some of them even looked a little like a Christmas tree.

In an "Aha!" moment, I pulled to the side of the road, got out of the car, and waited for one of the tumbleweeds to come my way. The first one I grabbed was medium in size, about two feet high, and three feet wide. I tied it down in the back of the truck, and started walking through the field, looking for smaller, better shaped bushes.

I wasn't sure what I was going to do with them, but I got home with four and took them into the living room. When the kids came in, they inquired about the pile of brown, dead bushes.

"That's going to be our Christmas tree," I said, knowing I was really in for a lot of work trying to sell it. "I'm tired of the same old kind of Christmas tree we have every year. This will be a tree like no other. None of your friends will have a tree like ours! I will be surprised if a photographer doesn't come to take a picture of it to put in a magazine."

They listened politely, staring all the while at the four blobs of former foliage. The look of disbelief on their faces was the same one they have when I tell them carrots are good for their eyes and spinach will make them strong.

The next day, I had to come up with something before they came home from school. I walked around the tumbleweeds several times, studying their individual shape and size. The smallest was pointed on top, and with a fine, white string I hung it from the ceiling in front of the living room window with the rounded bottom facing the floor. The three round ones were hung around the bottom of the pointed one, giving the illusion of a suspended tree with plenty of room underneath for Santa's delivery.

But it didn't yet look like a Christmas tree. I found a spray can of white paint and some multicolored glitter left over from a school project. I hung a sheet over the window to protect it from the paint spray, sprayed the "tree" and then carefully sprinkled the glitter on the wet paint.

The tumbleweeds were too fragile for heavy lights, so I cautiously threaded tiny white lights around the perimeter of each one. The glitter reflected the lights, giving a shimmering effect. I added only the smallest of my ornaments, and our traditional angel, who had seen better days, fit perfectly on the point of the highest tumbleweed. It was beautiful.

The kids saw it in the window before they came into the house, and rushed in to see my creation. "It looks like a good dream," the youngest said approvingly. Every kid in the neighborhood came over that night and "ooohed and aaahed" over our Christmas tree.

Fortunately, that was the last year we would be on a tight budget. Our family situation changed, and after that there was always plenty of money for a big Christmas tree in our new, big house, and we are thankful. But hard times demanded creativity we wouldn't have discovered otherwise.

My boys are now men and have their own families, but each year at Christmas someone tells the story of our "free" Christmas tree. How Mom wanted something different so she chased tumbleweeds for miles through the open fields during a windstorm trying to catch the perfect ones. She was tired of the same old green trees. We smile knowingly at each other and we all agree that it was the most beautiful Christmas tree any of us has ever seen.

~Jackie Fleming

The Mermaid Tree

For those who are willing to make an effort,
great miracles and wonderful treasures are in store.
~Isaac Bashevis Singer

Interfaith families can understand the minefield the holiday season represents. My husband is Jewish; I was raised Catholic. We have decided to give equal representation to both Christmas and Hanukah in our home. The holidays give us a perfect opportunity to share with our children the traditions we had been brought up with and to create traditions of our own. We had a designated corner for a menorah, dreidels and Star of David and another corner for a small tree, lights and nativity. The kids learned the story of Hanukah, the prayer as candles were lit on each of the eight nights, and how to spin the dreidel and play for gelt (chocolate candy coins). Our tiny tree was weighed down with innumerable preschool-produced ornaments. Wrapped presents were tucked beneath. We set up our nativity and the kids learned about the birth of Christ. We stood in line every year so the kids could tell Santa how good they had been and about the presents they hoped to receive.

This year, shortly before Thanksgiving, the kids decided they wanted a "real Christmas tree." Our little Charlie Brown tabletop tree was no longer adequate? Would this disrupt the delicate balance of religious equality we had created in our home? Baffled by the kids' insistence on a "real" tree and convinced they were simply brainwashed by the rampant commercialism of the approaching holiday, we packed the kids, dog and turkey into the car and headed to Carova Beach.

We discovered Carova Beach by accident. This quiet, off-road community is located nine miles off the asphalt of Highway 12 in the Outer Banks of North Carolina and is only accessible by four-wheel drive vehicles or boats. Carova is home to wild horses that are believed to date back to the time of the Spaniards. At the time, our Jeep's four-wheel drive was broken and friends suggested we contact a realtor for a free ride up the beach to look for the horses. Carova consisted, in the mid-1990s, of 300 homes and seventy-five year-round residents. The volunteer fire department and a row of post office boxes constituted downtown Carova. We were captivated, and by year's end we had purchased a lot on a canal and began building a small cottage. This became our family retreat, wild horses running through the dunes and wandering in small herds onto the long stretch of beach. A quiet place, where more often than not, we'd be the only people walking the beach, looking for sea glass and other beach treasures. We hoped to find peace there this year as well.

The kids quickly became distracted with Thanksgiving and Marc and I decided to address the "tree dilemma" later. Thanksgiving weekend flew by. We took long walks, visited our beach neighbors, and read in the sun. Soon it was time to go, and I began the routine of packing up and closing the house. My husband and daughter took Mojo (our Golden Retriever) for a last walk on the beach.

My daughter returned, and with eyes shining announced "Mom! We found the coolest thing on the beach!"

"Where is it?" I asked, imagining a myriad of beach treasures already scattered throughout our home. Seashells, sand dollars, dried seahorses and hundreds of pieces of sea glass. "It was too big to bring back to the house! Hurry!" Now I envisioned less common treasures: a barnacle-encrusted tree branch, washed-up sharks, stingrays and turtles... and only hoped that whatever it was did not smell too bad as we still had a long ride home. My husband threw a rope and tarp into the back of the car and the three (Mojo too) led her brother and me over the dune.

There on the dune lay a beautiful six-foot Christmas tree, fresh cut, its boughs pushed upward as if still wrapped in protective netting. "We found it at the tide line being tossed by the waves. We dragged it to the dune and waited to see if anyone came for it." The beach remained deserted. "Is this okay?" I asked him over the kids' heads. "I guess we were meant to have a tree this year. How else can you explain this?" he said.

The tree (plus forty pounds of sand) was unceremoniously tied to the roof of our car for the trip home. We dubbed it "The Mermaid Tree." A stand was purchased, and unexpectedly we had more than enough of the kids' handmade ornaments to fully decorate the stunning fir. This brought to mind the parable of the loaves and fishes or the scant amount of oil that brought forth light for eight incredible days. We tied yarn on sand dollars and toasted mini bagels. We had to put those high before Mojo ate them all! Our daughter made a Star of David from aluminum foil and we placed this at the top of our tree. Lights twinkling, the house filled with the smells of Christmas. The tree became a representation of all of the things that made us unique and bound us together as a family. It was a balance long ago achieved in our hearts. We have always been unconventional. We do believe in Miracles. The Miracle of Hanukah, the Miracle of Christmas and The Mermaid Tree.

~Carol Clarke Slamowitz

Tree Trunk Traditions

Memory is a way of holding onto the things you love,
the things you are, the things you never want to lose.
~From the television show The Wonder Years

As a little girl, the worst part of the Christmas season was helping my mom pack up the tree ornaments and taking down the tree at the end of the season. One by one, we would carefully wrap up each special piece until the next year and then I would watch as Dad picked up the tree and hauled it out to the backyard where it would sit discarded, until it finally made its way to the garbage dump.

I hated that our beautiful tree, the centerpiece of our Christmas celebrations only days earlier, was deemed useless after only a few short weeks. It seemed like such a waste, and it never failed to bring me to tears.

I was about ten years old when my dad came up with a fantastic idea that changed the way that we would look at Christmas trees. Why throw out the tree that gave us so much joy, when we would keep it forever to enjoy every Christmas? Because my dad was a talented hobbyist woodworker, he had the great idea to create tree ornaments from the lumber of the previous year's tree.

That year, after Mom and I had packed up all of the decorations, Dad and I took the tree to the snow-covered backyard and cut off all the branches until only the tree trunk was left. Then I watched as Dad took the tree trunk down to his woodshop in the basement and sliced it into boards. The boards would have to dry for most of the year until the lumber would be ready.

The following December, Dad and I began brainstorming different ideas for ornaments that we could make out of last year's tree. Dad was in charge of the construction aspect, and he would build as many tiny ornaments as he could out of the limited lumber. And I was in charge of the finishing. I would spend hours varnishing the completed ornaments and putting the little final touches on each one.

For our first project, we chose to make tiny houses decorated for the Christmas season. We managed to create eight little houses complete with peaked roofs and chimneys. I decorated them with windows and doors and glued a miniature wreath on the front and back of each house.

Every Christmas, picking out the perfect Christmas tree became the job that Dad and I enjoyed together. The two of us would head out in search of the perfect tree. It had to be a nice big tree, full and lush enough to hold all of our ornaments. But most importantly, the tree had to have a good thick trunk that would provide enough lumber to create decorations for the following year.

Most years we could get about eight ornaments from the previous year's tree. And as soon as they were finished, together we would hang them on the tree where they were admired by everyone else in the family. Friends and family could not believe that we could make such beautiful ornaments from a Christmas tree trunk, and holiday guests would inevitably head over to our tree to admire the latest creation.

Year after year, we continued our tradition. After the inaugural houses, we created Santa's sleighs, piled high with wrapped gifts. Another year, we made little tables that were set for the Christmas season. Each year was special because we did it together. We carried on the tradition for ten years until I moved away to go to University.

That final year Dad created the topper for our family tree, which represented our family perfectly—a sailboat.

I cannot imagine a Christmas tree that is filled with more love and meaning than my family's tree. Each ornament has been made with love, and the memory of the Christmas trees past. And even now that I am grown with a family of my own, I still cherish our family tree, and the memory of what my Dad and I created together.

~Elena Aitken

O Tannenbaum

Never worry about the size of your Christmas tree.
In the eyes of children, they are all 30 feet tall.
~Larry Wilde, The Merry Book of Christmas

Today, I am going to share a story with you. It's the story of a perfect family—Mom, Dad and son—who go into the forest to chop down the perfect Christmas tree. They sip hot cocoa as they wander through the trees, searching for a fabulous nine-foot specimen with lots of branches to hold their heirloom ornaments. When they find just the right tree, they stop, pose for pictures and then saw it down. They tie the tree to their truck and sing Christmas carols all the way home.

And once they get there, the family strings popcorn and lights throughout the tree. Then they hang their precious ornaments from its branches, telling the history of each one as it is hung.

The words above are complete fiction. I don't know who that family is, but I do know one thing: those people aren't related to me. You see, in my family, getting the tree is a little bit different.

Actually, it's a lot different.

First there's that whole cocoa thing. Sure, we've got cocoa to sip. But we have two thermoses—one that holds my special blend so that I stay happy through the entire trip and don't notice that it's raining, cold and/or windy. No, once I have a few sips of my special cocoa, I'm happy and warm, sometimes even a bit silly.

Then there's the search for the tree. I don't know about you, but the perfect tree has never just popped up in front of me. Instead, we wander for what seems like days looking for a tree we can all agree on. Finally, someone will need to use the restroom and, at that point, we just pick the tree we're closest to and cut it down.

Which brings us to the saw. The minute Junior sees it, he grabs it and runs through the tree farm yelling, "Watch out! It's Freddy vs. Jason!" By the time we catch up to him, I'm out of breath and nearly out of my special hot cocoa.

And once the saw is confiscated and the tree is cut, there's the question of which way the tree will fall. Look, maybe it's me, but if the person doing the sawing is saying, "look out on the left" wouldn't you wonder whose left that person is talking about? Is it my left or Harry's left? I usually have it figured it out by the time the tree falls on my head. All I can say is thank goodness for my special cocoa since it dulls the pain.

Once the darned tree is tied down to the truck, it's time to drive home. Okay, at this point we could sing carols, but honestly, not one member of my family can carry a tune. And besides, we're too busy making sure that the tree doesn't fall out of the truck and onto the highway to remember the words to "Silent Night."

Once we get home, we drag the tree into the house and jam it in the stand. That's about the time we discover that 1) driving home removed every single needle from the tree; and 2) the trunk is crooked and the tree looks like a nine-foot tall, bald, question mark.

Let's not even get into heirloom ornaments. Suffice it to say that on Junior's second Christmas—the one where he had just started to walk—he discovered the tree. He would stand next to it, watching the lights and gazing at the collection of handmade crystal balls that I had lovingly collected. And then one day, Junior removed several of those lovely crystal ornaments and used them to demonstrate his newly discovered throwing skills.

And we've had plastic ever since.

And that is the true story of how a true family goes out and cuts down a tree. Of course, this true family got a little tired of the tradition—so this year we bought a fake tree. Its trunk is straight and it has most of its little plastic needles clinging to it. But I still sipped my special cocoa when we set it up in the living room.

After all, there are some traditions you should never abandon.

~Laurie Sontag

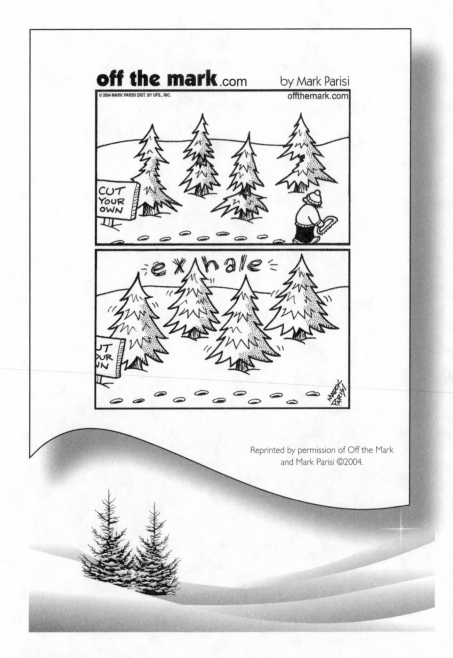

Touched by Love

In the night of death, hope sees a star,
and listening love can hear the rustle of a wing.
~Robert Ingersoll

"Can I have this one, Connie?" my ten-year-old stepson, Conan, asked in reference to a Christmas ornament I was unpacking. It was the second Saturday before Christmas and Conan was visiting us for the weekend. We had just brought our freshly cut Christmas tree inside the house and my husband had lugged several boxes of decorations from the basement. Our four-year-old son, Chase, along with Conan, was helping me unpack them. Our one-year-old daughter, Chelsea, was watching intently from her playpen.

We had several "special" ornaments. I wasn't certain a ten-year-old child would appreciate the intricacies of hand-sewn beads and sequins on the Santa ornament, or the fragility of the painted sand dollar from our favorite beach vacation spots. Some of the ornaments held special memories of the people who made them, or the places we had visited while on vacation. I wanted to keep them and protect them until he was older.

Besides, if I let him have one now, I might never see it again.

Suddenly I got a bright idea. "Conan, how about if we start a new tradition?"

"Like what?" he asked.

"How about this: every year we will buy you a new ornament.

You can use a permanent marker to write your name and the year on it and we'll keep all of them together here, in a box. And then when you're eighteen years old, you'll have lots of special ornaments for your own tree."

His smile told me he liked the idea. I handed him an ornament of a miniature Christmas storybook and he immediately clasped it in his hands, enthralled by it. He took it to the couch and flipped through the pages of the tiny, two-inch *'Twas the Night Before Christmas* book, pleasantly surprised by its cute size and by its timeless endearing message.

Bright for his age, I should have anticipated his next question.

"Well, how about this?" Conan began, with a pensive look on his face. "Since I'm already ten, how about if I pick out ten ornaments now, one for each year I've been alive, and write my name and a year on them? That way I'll have eighteen ornaments, one for each year, for when I'm grown up."

By now I had hung up all the fragile ornaments. I dug out the box of unbreakable ornaments, tickled by his quick thinking. I sat the opened box in front of him and said, "Sure, go ahead and pick out ten."

Conan's face lit up as he carefully carried the box to the kitchen table. He very slowly and intently made his selections. And just as carefully, he printed his name and a year on his prized ten, each representing a year in his young life.

For the next couple of years we remembered the pact and my husband and I purchased an ornament for him, but as he entered his teenage years we all forgot.

And then, in the middle of his seventeenth year, on a beautiful day in May, the unthinkable happened; Conan was killed in a car accident.

The first few months following his death were a painful blur—we went through the motions of living. The grief counselor warned us that the holidays would be especially difficult and he was right. I don't think any of us tasted the turkey at Thanksgiving, and I, personally, struggled with giving thanks that year.

Normally, at the first sign of frost, I would get excited about

Christmas. I'd start singing Christmas carols and pull out my favorite recipes so I could bake cookies and freeze them for gifts. But that year it was all I could do to go through the motions of decorating the house for the holidays.

Chase and Chelsea, who by now were eleven and eight, were not interested in helping decorate the tree, obviously struggling, too. So, late on a Saturday night after my husband had put the tree in its stand and everyone was in bed, I lugged up the trimmings for the freshly cut tree, including the boxes of ornaments.

After first checking all of the strands of lights to see if they worked, I carelessly flung them on the tree. Then I pulled out the stepladder and climbed the few steps to the top of the tree, gingerly attaching the angel to its designated place of honor.

I turned to the box of fragile ornaments. I quickly unwrapped the timeworn beaded and sequined Santa ornament along with the sand dollars and others, going through the motions of hanging the ornaments so I could quickly get it over with.

As soon as I had emptied the box of my favorite fragile orna-ments, I turned to search for the box of inexpensive ornaments. As I did so, I suddenly recalled an excited ten-year-old. I swallowed hard.

Locating the box, I gingerly lifted the lid, and right on top was the tiny little Christmas book ornament. On the front was the title, 'Twas the Night Before Christmas, and on the back, scribbled in a child's excited handwriting, was the name CONAN, in capital letters, as if to lay claim for all eternity.

I wiped the tears from my eyes and dug out the other dozen or so ornaments with his name on them. Some were handmade, some were store-bought, but they suddenly became irreplaceable to me.

Bittersweet memories comforted me as I realized that sometimes the traditions we end up treasuring the most in life have nothing to do with expensive fragile items. Rather, sometimes the most precious memories we can have are those involving ordinary items that have been forever touched by love.

~Connie Sturm Cameron

A Joyful Surprise

Every day may not be good, but there's something good in every day.
~Author Unknown

The year was almost over. November had vacillated between holding onto autumn and allowing winter in, but winter finally came to stay. December brought a raw chill and the clouds delivered a mixture of ice and rain that was more mush than snow. The deciduous trees finally released the last of their leaves and the sky seemed exposed without their moderating cover. There was a sudden dreariness in the yard. Even the evergreens seemed to have lost their vigor. The needles of the black pine appeared sparse and joyless.

I went out bundled up in a sweater and jacket to feed the birds and scooted back inside instead of standing and watching the birds mass on the feeders as I like to do, welcoming them as they light on the sunflower seed-filled cylinders. Today they would have to find the meal without my encouragement.

The lit-up store windows, usually the harbinger of the holiday season, only pointed out the grayness of the weather. Where was the holiday spirit that traditionally energized the end of the year?

I went about my December days shopping, working, cooking, and cleaning in the gray blandness. Nature tried to help me. The sun peeked through the clouds occasionally. The starlings were out in force layering first one tree, then another, with their speckled feathers and raucous cries. I laughed to see them take flight as if they were one huge bird. The house finches, too, swooped en masse onto the feeders. Their dusty red chests added tiny touches of color to the day.

My neighborhood cheered itself up with Christmas decorations. Some houses were subtle, with spots of white glowing softly in windows. Others had lawns decorated with reindeer and sleighs, blow-up Santas, and swirly light trees that were more like paintings than trees. One display had a snowstorm encapsulated in a plastic globe! Nothing much natural about it, but certainly a lot of fun.

The days got colder as the holiday approached. Clouds of white escaped with each breath. I took fast walks in the frigid air to keep my spirits energized. But day after day blended together and I longed for something to shake me out of my lethargy. Each day I wished for a joyful surprise, not even imaging what that might be.

Then it happened. I was going out to my car and heard a lot of squawking in my front yard. It came from the direction of the flowering plum tree I so loved. What I saw was incredible. Underneath the tree was a flock of iridescent grackles, thick as a blanket, pecking for seed. On all the branches were speckled starlings, masking the tree's bareness with dots of white as if a delicate snow had fallen. A blue jay here and another there stood out like a blue ornament. At the very top was a male cardinal lighting up the tree with his red brilliance as if he were a shining star. And each bird was singing in its own voice — the starlings raucous as usual, the grackles loud and brash, the blue jays sounding like squeaky doors, and the cardinal chip-chipping away, all creating a cacophonous but beautiful carol.

I gasped and tried not to move, afraid that the spectacle would disappear. It was a Christmas tree decorated by Mother Nature herself. A joyful surprise indeed.

I don't know how long I stood there transfixed by what I was seeing but when I finally edged toward my car to get out of the cold, the birds took off. In one whoosh, they were gone. The tree was barren once more, only not really, not to me. Whenever I looked that way I no longer saw bare branches; I recalled the birds, plumped against the cold, covering them. I could hear the uninhibited singing vibrating the frosty air. I sensed the limbs invigorated with vibrant, feathery life.

I was rejuvenated, eager to set aside the gray doldrums. All I had to do was think of that incredible Christmas tree and remember that joy is a frame of one's mind, not a state of the weather.

~Ferida Wolff

72

A Child's Gift of Love

A daughter is a gift of love.
~Author Unknown

It always seemed like having traditions was a good thing. They create memories that will last a lifetime. So when our children, David and Darla, were preschoolers we started a family Christmas tradition. It was our tree-trimming party and it would be complete with eggnog and pfeffernüsse cookies.

The kids were excited as we hauled the freshly cut tree into the house. It smelled so good. The ornament boxes were brought up from the basement. We would turn on the Christmas carols and the tree trimming would begin. The routine was always the same: First the lights—oh, how they'd sparkle; then the ornaments—each child had favorites. This was followed by the precise (or not) draping of some beads, and topped off with delicately hung tinsel.

Our hearts seemed to dance to the merriment of the Christmas carols. The kids' eyes twinkled with excitement and anticipation. It was a heartwarming, cozy evening. When finished, we would sit sipping the eggnog and snack on pfeffernüsse cookies as we admired the beauty of the radiant Christmas tree.

Years later, when my daughter, Darla, was home from college, she offered to help trim the tree. I was so grateful. My husband and I were empty nesters now and I wasn't looking forward to trimming the tree alone. With our daughter, the tree trimming was delightful. We turned on the Christmas carols. It was just fun being together, laughing and sharing the latest news of friends and what was happening in our lives.

Before we knew it, the tree trimming was finished. It was a beautiful tree and its fragrance filled the room as its trimmings majestically reigned and heralded the advent of another Christmas. As we had every year before, I brought out the eggnog and the pfeffernüsse cookies for our traditional celebration. It was always the highlight of the evening and having my daughter home in itself was a Christmas present to celebrate.

Then, amidst the laughter, Darla suddenly got very serious and said she had something to tell me. From her hesitation and body language, I knew she was dreading it.

I sat down on the couch to prepare myself for whatever this college student was about to say. She sat down next to me. I could feel my heart pounding in anticipation. Then very gently and caringly, Darla looked me in the eye and proclaimed: "Mom, I've never liked pfeffernüsse cookies."

Whew, at first I was relieved. Then I realized the absolute magnitude of what she had just said. Why didn't she ever tell me? All those childhood years, rather than hurt Mom's feelings and spoil Mom's tradition, she had endured the cookies in silence. From preschool through teenager years she never said a word. I hadn't realized it at the time, but from a child's heart, year after year after year she had given me the gift of love!

The meaning of Christmas really touched me that year. I've always remembered that very special tree-trimming night when the Christmas tree lights twinkled and our hearts glowed and my daughter taught me life's very important lesson: The best gifts aren't always found under the Christmas tree.

~D. Kinza Christenson

Chapter 9

Christmas Magic

All I Want for Christmas

73

In Anticipation of Doll Beds

I loved their home. Everything smelled older, worn but safe;
the food aroma had baked itself into the furniture.
~Susan Strasberg

The weathered old farmhouse had sat for generations near tall poplars lining the cinder driveway. The dining room was on a slant, perfect for sliding in sock feet on the worn wood floor. I was seven years old and had been told to stay out of the kitchen because my grandfather was making Christmas presents. I could hear the saw and see the sawdust fly between the uneven cracks of the old casing. Speckles of sawdust even got in my eyes but it didn't matter. Christmas was coming and when you're seven, anything can happen. And that year, it did.

We always visited our grandparents on weekends, and that year every weekend leading up to Christmas was full of extreme anticipation. What was that tall, lanky man making? Even at a young age, his hands told his story to me—strong yet gentle, worn yet kind. He farmed surrounding fields yielding hay and oats and gardens bursting with freshness that would then be canned or put in the root cellar. He relaxed by reading a *Saturday Evening Post* or a Zane Grey novel. Grampie loved to read.

This Christmas he'd spend whatever time he could creating things in the large kitchen, with its woodstove providing both heat and the means to bake Grandmother's famed Christmas bread and molasses cookies. After the main meal was over and the dishes were put away, the dining room became a playroom for my cousins and me. Although we played quite hard, our ears and eyes were on alert to the commotion on the other side of that closed door.

What was he making? I knew it was something made from wood. Besides the saw, we heard the hammer; we also smelled a heavy lacquer mixed in with chewing tobacco he'd take from a checkered pouch. I remember thinking there was nothing on my Christmas list that was made from wood. The only thing I wanted was a little doll with small blond braids all over her head. Maybe it was a doll bed! I convinced myself it was a doll bed. By the time I was finished it was doll bunk beds complete with little quilts made by my grandmother. If I was really lucky there'd be doll clothes too. I knew where I'd put the beds: to the right as you go down the few stairs leading into my bedroom. I didn't tell my two cousins that I'd figured it out. One was a boy. He probably wouldn't care.

My mother always made oyster broth on Christmas Eve. She'd set the dining room table just so—with linens and china, tall-stemmed, etched crystal glasses and a silver soup ladle. My grandparents would join us. I wasn't surprised that there were whisperings among the adults. I was on high alert, aware of fresh boot tracks leading from Grampie's old pick-up into our side porch off the kitchen.

To say the wait from Christmas Eve to Christmas morning was the longest wait ever, in anticipation of the doll of my dreams, does not suffice. It was sheer agony. I'd been so wrapped up in thoughts of this doll and her bunk beds that I hadn't thought what else might be under that tinseled tree. That's when I fell asleep.

I heard my brother race down the front stairway. I smelled cinnamon coming through the register near where the bunk beds would soon sit. The morning had dawned despite my doubts that it would ever arrive. How should I react? The moment had come. It was time to see what had gone on behind that closed door.

I heard my mother telling my brother he had to wait for me. I heard my father walk in from the kitchen. And then it was quiet, except for the wind moving the freshly fallen snow into little heaps and the stairs creaking as I reached the bottom step. I stopped for a second. I knew when I turned my head it might be sitting there, waiting for me. Probably wrapped with a big, red bow.

The smell of that lacquer confirmed my suspicions. Slowly I peered through the archway. The tree was lit; the stockings were overflowing. Standing in a single line were three smiling faces. They didn't say a word. They didn't have to. I knew they were blocking my view of the bunk beds.

Into Christmas morning I rushed. My brother was the first to move aside, anxious to get to his own surprises. That was when my eyes became set on what has remained my most favorite Christmas present ever. There were no bunk beds. Not even a doll bed with a big, red bow. It was a desk, a simple pine desk with a single drawer and a stool with a carved design.

Something happened to me at that moment. No other gifts mattered, not even the ones wrapped in red or green tissue paper, held together by stickers that never stuck. They were the ones from Santa. I slowly approached my desk. I danced my fingers along the lacquered boards. Visions of my grandfather in that farmhouse kitchen measuring and sawing filled me with an appreciation of this labor of love. Pulling the stool back I sat down. Opening the single drawer, I was overwhelmed by what my grandfather had left for me. There—unwrapped—was a pad of white, lined paper and one yellow, #2 sharpened pencil. How did he know? How did my grandfather know that at that young age I knew I wanted to be a writer, that I spent hours cutting and folding paper into little books? How did he know that the smell of crayons and pencils and pages of words put together stirred my imagination?

I did get that baby doll with blond braids all over her head that year. My cousin received the bunk beds. There were no matching quilts. The pine desk became the focal point in my bedroom, sitting to the right as you go down the little stairs. We became the best of friends.

My grandfather is gone now. So is that farmhouse with the slanted dining room. I think I've figured out why I was the one who received the pine desk. I never realized at age seven but I am certain my grandfather did. We shared a bond for the written word. I'd sit in his chair near the window where the afternoon sun flowed through like a waterfall and pretend to read his *Saturday Evening Posts* and favorite Westerns.

Grampie gave more than just pine boards smelling of lacquer that year. It seems he knew what I really wanted, despite dreams of doll bunk beds with little quilts.

~Barbara Briggs Ward

One Good Gift

I've seen and met angels wearing the disguise of ordinary people
living ordinary lives.
~Tracy Chapman

My brother Louis had charm. So what if he also had Down syndrome? A former coworker once summed up her view on the hidden talents of the developmentally disabled this way, "God may take away from one part, but He gives a gift in another part." Louis had that gift. Friendly and outgoing, he knew how to tell a joke or give a compliment and handed both out freely. My brother instinctively knew the value of a smile or a helping hand and didn't skimp where those were concerned, either. When his charm wasn't enough, Louis found he could supplement it with pure tenacity. Anyone could be won over by my brother, even those possessing the hardest of hearts.

In an effort to teach Louis, then in his teens, that it was equally as important to give as it was to receive, my parents decided he would select and buy one small gift for each of us that Christmas. That required money, however, which he was expected to earn by performing a few household chores. Desperately trying to fit into a world where Louis always felt "different," he eagerly agreed to this opportunity to prove his worth.

All new experiences were a source of fascination to my brother and the act of placing the garbage at the curb was no exception. Every Monday, Wednesday, and Friday Louis would wait for the sounds of the town sanitation truck, then pull the brown plastic garbage pail to the curb where he handed it to the trash collectors like the baton in a well timed relay race. My mother would peek through the living room curtains as Louis stood, his eyes fixed in amazement as the truck's mighty jaws clamped down on his cache, only returning indoors when the job had been completed to his satisfaction.

"Thanks! Have a nice day!" Louis called out each time as the workers quickly turned toward the next waiting pail.

"Would it kill one of them to say hello back?" my mother griped. "It would mean so much to him to get a kind word from someone."

Undaunted, my brother continued his thrice weekly routine with increased fervor, occasionally adding, "Good job!" or "I like your uniform!"

One day as my mother watched, the surliest of the workers stepped to the curb and quickly spoke to Louis. My brother extended his hand and the man reciprocated with a shake.

"What was that?" she asked Louis as she adjusted the evergreen wreath on the front door.

"That's my friend Johnny. Next week, I'm the garbage man."

"You're the garbage man? Now what?" Mom asked herself out loud.

All weekend Louis waited for Monday morning. When it finally arrived, he positioned himself at the curb early where he awaited his sanitation debut. The truck pulled up and Johnny stood guardian as Louis extracted the black garbage bag from its receptacle and tossed it into the back of the truck. There were high-fives all around; even the driver stepped down from the cab to offer his congratulations. It had been confirmed; my brother was now an honorary member of the sanitation department.

For weeks after, the routine continued and my mother eventually left her post behind the living room curtain. Then one morning the doorbell rang and my mother found Louis and Johnny standing at the door together.

"I'm sorry," she apologized. "He's bothering you. I'll keep him inside."

"No," Johnny responded, "I just wanted to say goodbye. I'm getting married in a few weeks and my fiancée and I are moving out of state right after Christmas. This is my last day on the job."

"Well congratulations on your marriage," my mother answered politely.

"I just wanted to say it was real nice to know Louis. We don't usually get so much appreciation for our work, you know?"

"I can imagine. It's not an easy job." She looked at her son and then at Johnny, "Thank you."

Johnny turned to Louis, "Keep it up Lou," and they high-fived for one last time.

Deep into December, Louis continued to take out the trash yet he soon followed the habit of our other neighbors and placed the pail at the curb the night before pick-up. Though he didn't say so, my brother clearly missed his friend Johnny and without him, garbage day had simply lost its luster. He blamed this change of procedure on the weather. As Christmas approached, the climate turned blustery and it was too cold, Louis said, to wait at the curb. Too cold also, it seemed, for Louis to go to the mailbox and retrieve the mail, another of his chores.

"Didn't you check the mailbox today?" my father asked him that Christmas morning.

"It's Christmas," Louis answered. "No mail today."

My father peered out the window, "But there's something in the mailbox. I can see it from here."

Louis breezed past our father, through the door toward the mailbox to further inspect the package that peeked from its winking hatch. "It's a garbage truck!" Louis held the model truck in his outstretched hand for all to see as he galloped back to the house, his slippers flopping against the pavement.

"Check the card, Lou," my father said as he took the box from his hands.

My brother read its simple sentiment aloud, his face shining brighter than any Christmas star: "To my friend Louis. Merry Christmas, from Johnny."

Merry Christmas to you too, Johnny, wherever you may be. And thanks.

~Monica A. Andermann

Playing with Dolls

Even as an adult I find it difficult to sleep on Christmas Eve.
Yuletide excitement is a potent caffeine, no matter your age.
~Carrie Latet

I t was such a magical night, and I just could not fall asleep! My mind went through the list of everything that needed to be done — the stockings were filled, placed lovingly in front of the Christmas tree with lights glowing in soft reds, greens, and blues, waiting for the early-morning excitement; the refrigerator was packed with favorite Christmas foods; the children were all snug in their beds.... Yes, everything seemed in order, but yet, sleep escaped me. My insides seemed to smile, and giggles would bubble up.

We were a young couple with three little girls: a tough diesel mechanic and his busy little wife — a stay-at-home mom. Sometimes it was tough to make ends meet on only one paycheck, but this Christmas we were trying to make dreams come true for our three precious little girls.

It was Cabbage Patch doll time, and a new one that could talk and sing, with a special name, birth date, and different hair color, had just been released. Even better yet, if you owned more than one, they would sing in rounds! It was unbelievable! The ultimate in wonderful!

By some miracle, and by shopping early, we were able to get these greatly coveted new dolls, three of them, one for each of our angels.

That night, my husband and I stayed up late and took the dolls out of the package to test them. One didn't work!! Luckily there was still time to go back to the store. The next morning, the clerk and I took the replacement doll out of the package to make sure it worked, and placed it loosely in the box inside a bag as I left the store. "Do you want to play?" it called from the bag as I walked to the car. A man paused, looking puzzled. "Row, row, row your boat," she started singing. Women turned to look. "Shhh," I playfully chided the doll with a smile, "People are looking!" But already I could feel the fun.

December is the perfect time for all good children to go to bed early. Peeking in and seeing them peacefully sleeping, I gleefully showed the dolls to my husband. We took them out of the boxes again to "test." We talked with the dolls, and sang with the dolls, and finally regretfully, put them away again.

The next night after the children were sound asleep, I looked at that tough mechanic, and he looked at me. "Do you want to play with the dolls?" And we both ran to get them out of the hiding place. Night after night, our secret activity continued, and we played with delight, picturing how happy these toys would make our darlings.

Finally it was Christmas Eve. It was hard for our over-excited little sweethearts to fall to sleep. It was getting later and later, but at last their even breathing filled their rooms. It was safe to get the dolls out one last time. They talked, and sang in rounds, and we joyfully placed them in the boxes, this time wired in tightly, turned on, ready to delight our children.

Dreams of thrilled little girls danced in my head. I couldn't sleep! This special night was too filled with joy and excitement as I envisioned the happiness of our girls. That is what Christmas is really about — the magic, the love — bringing joy to others. That mechanic and I had played night after night, picturing the reaction of our children. They would be so excited — the perfect Christmas surprise.

The hours dragged by; I tossed and turned. I realized that the big tough mechanic was tossing and turning too! Our anticipation was killing us! Finally, around 4 AM, he sat up and left the room. When he came back, he had loud sleigh bells, and started shaking them. I giggled. No sound from the children's room. I jumped up out of bed, and together we stomped loudly around our bedroom, as if someone was walking on the rooftop—smothering our smiles and laughter. Nothing—no sound. We cried in our lowest bass voices, "Ho, ho, ho!" Did we hear a child stir? It was now almost 4:30. Were they awake? Quickly we jumped back in bed, and pretended to be asleep as little footsteps entered our room.

Some pretense of responsible parenthood had to be maintained. So with three little girls, eyes sparkling with excitement, peering into my half open eyes, little hands caressing my cheeks awake, that tough mechanic and I took turns in mock complaining, "It is SO early; we're tired! It is only 4:30! It is still nighttime!"

Being such obedient children, they sighed, turned around, and started back to bed! Quick! I had to do something! "NO!" I called frantically, halting them in their tracks. "We're already awake now. Let's see what Santa brought!"

As the girls dashed to the tree surrounded by the boxed dolls, one doll called out, "Do you want to play?" And the girls gasped, frozen in place, eyes wide. Joy and excitement filled that day—three little "dolls" singing together, playing together. The giggles and laughter continued throughout the weeks to come. That Christmas was everything we hoped for.

Now these beautiful girls are all grown, and the greatest happiness they have is to make dreams come true for their own loved ones. But I will never forget the December when a tough mechanic and his little wife spent the days before Christmas playing with dolls.

~Barbra Yardley

76

I've Got Your Number

The best of all gifts around any Christmas tree:
the presence of a happy family all wrapped up in each other.
~Burton Hillis

My sister Marilyn loves Christmas more than any other holiday. When we were kids, she managed to make it last as long as possible by opening her presents at a ridiculously slow pace… especially for a child. Simultaneously, our parents, my three older brothers, and I would rip into our packages, whooping and hollering across the room to thank whoever had gotten us just what we wanted. For us, it was all over in minutes.

While I would pick through the debris scattered throughout our living room hoping there might be one more package addressed to me, a neat tower of unwrapped presents surrounded Marilyn where she sat. She carefully pulled at taped corners, unfurling ribbons, and logging each gift into a notebook so she would remember to write thank you notes later that afternoon.

Now, as an adult with her own family, Marilyn still manages to savor every moment of Christmas. But her children didn't inherit her patience, so it has taken a little extra effort to keep the magic in the season. Her kids count their presents—and those of everyone else in the family—to see how things stack up, literally and figuratively. A good bit of shaking goes on those last days of December, and the anticipation is downright maddening. When Marilyn's three children started figuring out the contents of their presents before Christmas morning, my sister, a former elementary school teacher, drew on her creative side. She threw them a curve by not putting nametags on their gifts. Which presents were Robert's and which ones were William's or James'? They didn't know until Christmas morning that their mother had allotted a different gift wrap to each person. Robert's presents were the ones wrapped in snowmen print, William's in stars, and James' in reindeer.

The next year, a tag with a specific Christmas motif denoted each recipient's gifts: jingle bells, gingerbread men and candy canes. Again, no names on the tags, and only Mom and Dad knew the secret code. The year after that, gift tags marked with one of three numbers represented each child. The number matched the same number of letters in the recipient's name: six for Robert, seven for William and five for James.

Marilyn and her husband Kenny enjoyed eavesdropping on the discussions taking place around the Christmas tree. Using deductive reasoning, the boys would pick out packages they thought were something they asked for and then work backwards trying to come up with an answer to the code that would make that gift theirs. "James always tries to come up with something that makes the biggest package his," chided Robert.

As the kids got a little older and their names got shorter (Robert became Rob, William preferred Will), Marilyn and Kenny came up with even trickier tactics. The boys thought they had cracked the code the year the tags were labeled with Texas, Arkansas, and Kentucky, the states in which they lived when they started school. Not so fast. The state actually signified where they made their First Communion.

Another year, when a number was the only identifying symbol, the single digit represented the last numeral of the year each boy would graduate from high school. Marilyn said they probably would not have figured this one out, except she and Kenny included themselves that year.

My nephews are clever but they usually haven't deciphered the system before it's time to open the presents. And it's certainly not my sister's style to tell them. No, no, no! She puts her teaching experience to work. On Christmas morning, she and Kenny take turns doling out clues until someone puzzles out the mystery.

This past year, the code was short but still cryptic: S1, S2, and S3. The family visited Universal Studios a few years ago where the boys mugged in front of cutouts of the Three Stooges. A souvenir photo hangs in the den. It laid the groundwork for S1—Stooge 1, S2—Stooge 2 and S3—Stooge 3.

What began as a means to keep the magic in the season has become something much more meaningful. Marilyn said, "This year it was really fun for me to watch all three boys at different times come in and sort through the packages. They made notes and put them in their pockets and wallets, and each one of them called another one to run an idea by him, their eyes twinkling as they spoke to each other."

The boys are almost grown now. Rob is in college and living away from home. Will is a senior in high school and James is in the eighth grade. When Rob brought over his gifts for the family this year, he had devised his own coding system. Correlating the alphabet to numbers, he used the number of the first and last letter of each family member's name. For example, J and S for James became 10-19. Will was the first one to figure that one out. Rob said, "My favorite thing about it is that it is a bond that I share with my brothers."

I have a feeling this family's inimitable Christmas tradition is going to be carried on for a long, long time. Like mother, like sons.

~Martha Miller

"What makes it even more exciting is
that I forget what's in half of them."

A Christmas Glove

The manner of giving is worth more than the gift.
~Pierre Corneille, Le Menteur

Mom didn't want much that first Christmas after she and Dad were married. Which was just as well. It was the end of America's Great Depression, and there wasn't much to be had.

"All I want," she told Dad, "is some nice black gloves."

"But you have black gloves," he protested. "Nice ones. I gave them to you last year."

"I sort of lost one," she said. "The left one. So I've just been wearing the right one."

"Those were expensive gloves," Dad sighed. "And I know how much you liked them."

"I did," Mom said. "So if you could get me some new ones, I don't need anything else."

"I don't know," Dad said with a slight smile. "If you're just going to lose them..."

Mom was pretty sure Dad was teasing. Still, she didn't know what to expect when at last the time came to exchange Christmas presents. She would have been pleased with anything, but she really did need the gloves—especially for her left hand. She carefully removed the ribbons and paper and opened the box. There they were! Beautiful new black gloves!

"Oh, Bud, they're perfect! Just exactly what I..." She paused. "There's only one glove."

"Yes, that's right," Dad said, smiling proudly.

"But gloves usually come in pairs, don't they?"

"That's true. You'd be surprised how hard it is to find one glove. But there it is!"

"So where did you get it?" Mom wanted to know.

"I got it at Stanley's," he said forthrightly, almost proudly—and certainly stupidly.

"Stanley's!" Mom recoiled as she pulled the glove off her hand. "You bought my Christmas present at Stanley's?"

Immediately, Dad could see that he was in trouble.

"Well, I looked at some other places," he said, apologetically. "But that's the only place I could find the right glove. Er, left glove. Er..."

"That's my present—a glove from a second-hand store? What did it cost—a dime?"

"Twenty-five cents!" he blurted.

The fire shooting from Mom's eyes told Dad that revelation hadn't helped his situation.

The drive to Mom's parents' house for Christmas dinner passed without a word being spoken between them. When they arrived, Dad went with Mom's father and her little brother, Jack, to do some target shooting. Mom went straight to the kitchen to get some sympathy.

"Mother," she said, "you won't believe what Bud got me for Christmas."

Her mother smiled and nodded. "Wasn't that something?" she asked.

"You mean... you knew?" Mom asked.

"Darling, we've been immersed in it! He was here for hours, looking for your lost glove. Then he started going to every store in town looking for an exact copy. Whenever he found one that was close, he'd buy it and bring it to me to approve. He must've bought twenty left-hand gloves!"

"But that's... so..."

"Silly? Yes, I thought so, too," Mom's mother said, shaking her head. "And I told him so. But he said, 'Wanda loves these gloves. I'm sure I can find another left glove somewhere.'"

A lump began growing in Mom's throat.

"Now there's just one problem," Mom's mother said, picking up a stuffed pillow case. "What do we do with these?" Laughing, she emptied a pillow case full of black left-hand gloves.

The next hour passed slowly, as Mom awaited Dad's return. When at last he walked up the sidewalk she was standing at the door, her arms outstretched, a black glove on each hand.

Which, it turns out, was exactly what she wanted all along.

~Joseph Walker

A Writer's Christmas

Goals are dreams with deadlines.
~Diana Scharf Hunt

'Twas the night before deadline, when all through the house,
Not a keyboard was stirring, not even the mouse.
The drafts were all filed in the hard drive with care,
In hope that final versions soon would be there.

The muses circled, all up out of bed,
While visions of story lines danced in my head.
And me in my nightgown, with notebook and pen,
Had just settled down to write prose in the den.

When out in the kitchen arose such a clatter,
I sprang from my chair to see what was the matter.
Right to the cookie jar I flew like a flash,
After seeing my offspring raiding the stash.

The light on the pile of dirty pots and dishes,
Added worry to my dreams and writing wishes.
When what to my wondering eye should appear,
But my daughter with algebra questions to share.

Entered my husband, so lively and cute,
I knew in a moment my efforts were moot.
Louder than usual, his reprimands came,
He whistled and shouted, and called them by name.

Now, Tara! Now, Jake! Now both of you two!
Stop fooling around and let's get on the move!
To the top of the stairs; to the top of your beds!
Now dash away! Dash away, pillow your heads!

Dangling participles before edits are done
Must be scrutinized, as should sentences that run.
While on to their bedrooms my children they flew,
Arms heavy with homework and cookie plates too.

And then, in a twinkling, I heard up above
Jake asking for supplies, attention and love.
As I put down my papers, and turned back around,
In came my husband with laundry he found.

He was dressed in pajamas from his head to his foot,
And his hair was all tarnished with gray streaks like soot.
The basket of laundry was flung on his back,
"Will you please do this now; it's clean clothes that I lack."

My eyes didn't sparkle, my thoughts were not merry,
My fingers were clenching my pen; I felt weary.
I didn't then care about clean clothes to wear.
Quite distressed, I was ready to pull out my hair.

A stump of cigar he held tense in his teeth,
The smoke so heavy it made my thoughts seethe.
Ideas, revisions, punctuation all tossed,
Dialogue, characters, plot development lost.

Please Santa, my wish for a jolly old elf!
I blinked when I saw him in spite of myself.
A glint of his eye and a twist of his head,
Soon gave me to know I had nothing to dread.

He belched not a sound, but went straight down to work,
Did laundry and dishes, then turned with a jerk,
"I know you need quiet and more time to write,
The house is now clean, and I'll fix you a bite."

He sprang from the den with a quick goodbye call,
And suddenly flew down the brightly lit hall.
But I heard him exclaim, as he went out of sight,
"Happy writing to all, and to all a good night!"

~Marian Gormley

The Samaritan's Table

Be content with what you have, rejoice in the way things are.
When you realize there is nothing lacking, the whole world belongs to you.
~Lao Tzu

One autumn I was accepted into a yearlong leadership program designed to recognize and build community leaders, or trustees of the community. The program was planned with an intense curriculum, educating participants about our local systems and the county area. It included everything from economic development to the justice system, with the yearlong program ending in community projects.

I looked forward to this opportunity for my growth although I realized that this was certainly a large undertaking and commitment of time and energy. At that particular time of my life, I was searching to expand what I thought to be my calling and responsibility in my community.

December's program day dealt with human services, both needed and already available. Upon receiving my advance instructions, I immediately envisioned many sad stories of impoverished families, hungry children, and abused women. I anticipated that the human services day would have a serious impact on me. My assumptions proved correct.

We started the day listening to a very articulate young mother who had graduated from high school some years ago but, at that time, could not read with any comprehension. She spoke of the wonderful literacy program that she was attending and was proud to say that she had improved her reading ability to a ninth-grade level. "This I can handle," I thought to myself. Sure, it was a sad story but it seemed to have a happy ending.

After a welfare simulation and the debriefing, we were off to lunch. The program committee had suitably selected a nutrition center (to some, known as a soup kitchen) for lunch that day. We were asked not to wear our nametags or carry a purse. We were also asked to disperse ourselves among the tables and talk to those who were lunching at the Samaritan's Table. Okay, so I envisioned a cafeteria-style line with plastic gloved volunteers dishing out shredded chicken on biscuits or something of the like.

Much to my surprise, what the Samaritan's Table proved to be was not at all what I had expected. As I walked in, an elderly lady with an enormously happy smile greeted me. She, in turn, directed me to the "maitre d'" who escorted me to my table. I was up front by a stage beautifully adorned with hand-crafted Christmas decorations and gleeful carolers from a nearby elementary school.

There was no cafeteria line. I was served soup, salad, and a full plate of deliciously hot food. In addition, another elderly person presented me with a dessert cart so I could choose from a vast variety of pastries, cakes, and puddings. The atmosphere was so welcoming and open that I had no difficulty in striking up a conversation with my tablemates.

Seated next to me was a small imp of a child with tattered clothes and in need of a good bath. But this small child's delight in the performance of the carolers brought a spontaneous smile to my face. Next to this little wonder was her grandmother. After my initial "hello" the grandmother began speaking of how much she enjoyed her granddaughter. She had seen that I, too, was greatly enjoying the little girl singing along and clapping her hands.

As the conversation progressed, I learned that the little girl's name was Sam. Sam stayed with her grandmother throughout the week because Sam's mom had been lucky enough to be hired as holiday help in a discount department store. I was somewhat surprised at how much of this family's life was being disclosed to me, a total stranger. Yet, being somewhat taken aback by the Samaritan's Table's welcoming atmosphere, there was little wonder that people felt respected and not at all ashamed.

The grandmother and I continued our conversation during our meal. We talked a lot about Sam. Sam was missing her mom terribly this Christmas season. Her mom was working quite a bit and Sam didn't get much time with her. Although everyone knew that the work hours weren't permanent, three-year-olds don't typically have a tremendous amount of patience to wait until after the holidays for Mom to be home more often.

As I noticed that my time was drawing to a close, I asked the grandmother what special thing Sam was wishing to get for Christmas. Expecting a plush purple dinosaur or a baby doll of some sorts, I was totally surprised to hear her respond, "Sam wants a quarter for Christmas."

A simple quarter. One little quarter.

I thought of my own daughter's two-page wish list.

Sam's grandmother continued, "Sam wants to visit her mommy at work and she knows from riding the bus that she needs to give the driver a quarter."

And here I was without a purse.

That simple little quarter, and little Sam who wished so dearly for that simple little quarter, had a tremendous impact on me. Too often we begin to take for granted those small yet wonderful experiences and even the people who share our lives. We begin to disregard the everyday beauty in the world, the smell of a holiday meal cooking, the crackle of a fire, or the warmth of holding a hand.

Whenever I find myself rushing through this life without giving due consideration to those I love, I remember the quarter. It has now become a tradition in our home. Each Christmas stocking's toe is rounded with one shiny quarter to symbolize how very lucky we all are to have each other close throughout the holidays (and every day for that matter). And I always remember Sam and wish her a very Merry Christmas.

~Lil Blosfield

Danny's Christmas Gift

Every child begins the world again....
~Henry David Thoreau

Each time Mrs. Swanson looked down at her class list, I was sure that I would be the next one she called to bore the class with my oral report about my Christmas vacation. I had been sure I'd be the next one through the last twenty-two names, but now it was down to just Danny and me.

What could I say that was of any interest to anyone? Clare had flown away with her family for their annual ski trip and had received so many presents that they had to ship them home because the airlines couldn't take all their boxes. Jack had celebrated a fun and old-fashioned Christmas at his grandmother's farmhouse. He and his cousins had skated on her pond, sang carols on a sleigh ride, pulled taffy, and opened the gifts his grandmother made for them every year: multicolored scarves and mittens that she knit from her leftover yarn scraps. Every year Jack told us about these scarves and mittens, but we had never seen him wear them.

Then there were the same things over and over again: inline skates, snowboards, CDs, turkey dinners, relatives, puppies, kittens and bikes.

Mrs. Swanson looked up from her class list, "Danny, you're next."

Whew, I thought, if Danny talked long enough, there'd only be a few minutes left for my report. That wasn't likely though. Danny was the quiet one in our class. He was shorter than the rest of us, wore clean but obviously hand-me-downs and his hair was home-bowl-cut-styled.

Danny walked slowly to the front of the class. His hands shook and his voice squeaked as he began to talk. "For Christmas, I got three packs of baseball cards and a Hacky Sack."

We waited for him to go on. He shifted his feet, cleared his throat a few times, but he didn't say another word. Could that be all Danny had to say? Was that all he got for Christmas? Three packs of baseball cards and a Hacky Sack?

"Well, Danny," said Mrs. Swanson, "I'm sure there's more to share about your Christmas."

Unease rippled through the class. Mrs. Swanson was usually so kind. Why hadn't she just thanked Danny and let him sit down? Couldn't she see that there might not be anything else for him to share?

Danny looked over at Mrs. Swanson. She nodded her encouragement.

"Well, we didn't go out of town or anything, but on Christmas Eve, we did go to the living nativity outside our church. My brother was a shepherd and one of my sisters got to be Mary. It looked real; right in front of us there were live donkeys, cows and sheep. There weren't any camels, though. The only thing not real was the baby in the manger. It was too cold for that.

"When we got in the car to go home my mom really surprised us. She said we were going to pick Grandma up to stay overnight with us because she and Dad were going to be gone."

Now Danny had our attention. Why would his parents leave on Christmas Eve?

"We all squished over to make room for Grandma in the car. She smelled like her nightly heat rub so we knew that this trip to our house was as much of a surprise to her as it was to us.

"Dad didn't even pull into the driveway when we got home, he just stopped at the curb and we all hurried out of the car. They were in a rush to leave. It was time for our new baby to come."

Oohs went around the classroom. Danny seemed to have forgotten that he was standing in front of all of us and that he was the shy one in the class. The tension eased from his face as he stepped into the happy moments of the story he was telling us.

"None of us slept much that night. It was Christmas morning before we heard the garage door open and Dad's car pull in. We all ran to wait for him on the entry porch. He came in grinning and shouting Merry Christmas. He tried to hug us all at once. He said, 'On the very day the world celebrates the gift of God's son to us, God has gifted this family with another son. You have a baby brother!'

"Man, we were happy. We gobbled down some pancakes, grabbed the presents from under the tree and went to see our new baby."

We were all smiling at Danny. As shy as he was, he was smiling and talking about his little brother.

"You should see him. He's so little and cute. We all got to hold him. No one wanted to put him down to open our presents. He yawns and tries to suck his thumb."

It was then that our feelings about Danny's Christmas gifts shifted. We had felt sorry for him when we thought he had only received three packs of baseball cards and a Hacky Sack, but he didn't feel slighted at all, he only felt the fullness of his baby brother in his arms.

We all wished we had gotten as much.

"Our family will never forget this best Christmas ever. Other families may have had big dinners and lots and lots of presents to celebrate the birth of Jesus, but our family got to hold the baby."

~Cynthia M. Hamond

The Butterscotch Bear

Generosity is not giving me that which I want more than you do,
but it is giving me that which you want more than I do.
~Kahlil Gibran

A h-ha! I finally found the perfect gift for Eric's stocking. The butterscotch bear sat perched in a display near the store's front window. In one hand it held a football, complete with the white laces, and a helmet in the other. To top it off, the bear wore an Ohio State scarlet and gray sweater—perfect for my young OSU football fan! After spotting the bear, I knew I'd have to sneak down there later to get it without any little people. I was so excited!

Each year, our family traveled an hour to the mall to gather our Christmas gifts for one another. My husband, David, and I would split up, taking one or two of the kids to buy for the other members of the family. Then, we'd meet at a designated time and switch kids to complete their lists.

After a fast food meal, the three kids finished their lists. David took the tired, but pleased, children to the car, where I would meet them after completing my specific task. The kids had been so good, but that would soon turn to grumpy bickering if they were forced to wait an excessive length of time. Thankfully, it wouldn't take long because I knew exactly what I wanted and where it was.

Upon entering the little shop, the salesclerk greeted me with a cheerful smile. "May I help you find something?"

"Oh, no thanks," I said confidently. "I was just in here, and snuck back without my kids to get what I needed."

I hurried toward the shelf, ready to grab the little guy and go. Imagine my surprise! The bear was not there! I rummaged through all the other stuffed animals in the display—no butterscotch OSU bear anywhere.

I questioned the clerk, who replied, "Oh, I'm sorry. Someone bought that bear a little while ago, and we don't have any more."

Now I felt defeated. It had only been a couple of hours. Who could have bought that bear? Every person I passed became a suspect. I could search for something else, but I had already been in almost every store in the mall without seeing anything come close to the ideal gift. Besides, my kids were waiting in the car.

With a huge sigh, I scurried out of the mall to my expectant family.

On Christmas morning the kids opened all of their presents. Now it was time for Mommy and Daddy.

"Mommy, open mine first," Eric beamed, carrying over his kid-wrapped gift.

"Okay. What'd you get me?"

"I'm not telling." That was a great accomplishment. This was the first year he didn't tell, or get tricked into telling every Christmas secret he knew.

I opened the package slowly. "Hmm... I wonder what it is," I teased him.

He giggled, "Just open it and find out!"

As soon as the paper fell open, tears filled my eyes. Before me was the butterscotch OSU bear that I wanted for him. He purchased it for my bear collection.

"Do you like it?" His little face was so eager and proud. "I really wanted that bear, but I thought it'd be a good present for you."

Choking back tears, I hugged him and said, "I love it, honey. Thank you. It really is the perfect gift."

~Paula F. Blevins

The Gift

Kids spell love T-I-M-E.
~John Crudele

It was just an ordinary Christmas card, disappointingly plain to my eight-year-old eyes. I noticed first the dark colors and then the snow-covered scenery with a horse pulling an open carriage. It was a card that adults would give to other, not very interesting, adults. I couldn't see its relevance to me.

My siblings and I each received a card, close to the end of our family Christmas celebration. I don't remember much of what we had received earlier. I remember that I was wearing my favorite soft blue sweater, with a royal blue skirt, ruffled at the bottom. For our family picture I was even allowed to wear my hair down and unrestrained, a rare treat for one with naturally wavy and unruly hair. I remember that Mom was wearing a bold pink blouse, with ruffles encircling her neckline. The Christmas lights glistened off her wire-rimmed glasses. I also remember how excited we were to watch her open her gift, a brand new set of copper-colored canisters. They were perfect for her kitchen.

Earlier, our family had celebrated Christmas Eve at a German service at our church. This was the annual Christmas torture. While the rest of the year the services were in English, on this night—the night of unbearable waiting—the service was in a language we didn't understand. "Lo How A Rose E'er Blooming," sung in German, seemed to drag on forever. And then we went home for a traditional light supper of buns, cheese, cold cuts, and squares.

Finally, it was time to open our gifts. It is perhaps one of life's ironies that the only gift I remember from that Christmas is the one that didn't seem as exciting at the time. The only one that I couldn't hold and play with.

The gift I remember is the card. Each of us — my sister, brother, and I — received an envelope with our name on it. I was puzzled. I had never received an envelope as a gift before. This was before the era of giving money or gift cards, and so I had no context in which to place this strange, white, two-dimensional gift box.

I opened the envelope and saw the picture. A picture clearly designed for adults and not for children. Inside was a generic Christmas message, its typed words as irrelevant to my eight-year-old mind as the picture on the cover. And below was my dad's scrawling handwriting, his words a gift. "For your Christmas present, this year I promise to spend an hour each week with you, doing whatever you want to do."

I looked up, not certain what this meant. Dad explained that each of us would have time with him each week — time that was all ours to plan. We could do something alone with him or could include our siblings. We could play table games, Barbies, or do an outside activity.

Over the next couple of weeks, we incorporated Dad's gift into our lives. We played *Sorry*, Chinese Checkers, and *Parcheesi*. I picture these times as being idyllic, with our family calmly sitting around the coffee table and patiently taking turns. I suspect, however, that they were as noisy and chaotic as most of family life is.

We only managed to each take Dad up on his promise a couple of times. Three weeks after Christmas, my mother and I were in a car accident that killed her and left me in the hospital for three months. The promise of a structured one hour per week was quickly replaced with Dad single parenting three children, while simultaneously mourning his wife.

But while the structure changed, the gift remained — and remains with me still. In some ways, that Christmas promise has become more important with the passing of time. Dad's gift was highly unusual in its time, showing a commitment to spend time with us and to get to know each of us individually. It dared all of us to step away from the usual practice of Christmas and to move closer to its true intent. It dared us to remember the importance of relationships and the depth of his love for us. As I prepare for Christmas with my son, it prompts me to find ways to incorporate the same love and presence into my celebrations with him. To give to him what my dad gave to me... the gift of time.

~Heather Block

Chicken Soup for the Soul®

Winston's Boy

It isn't the size of the gift that matters, but the size of the heart that gives it.
~Eileen Elias Freeman

By late December in Anchorage, Alaska, the streets are sheeted in bumpy ice with crusts of snow mounding at the road shoulders. It made for tricky driving and tiring night shifts at work. I was eager to fall asleep, glad to be almost home. Just before turning off the main road for the final blocks to home—I saw the body.

The little dog was at the edge of the street and appeared undamaged except for the smallest bit of dried blood on his nose. Undoubtedly, he'd been hit by a car and there his life had ended. His coat was a lovely cinnamon, with thick rich fur that suggested a Chow ancestry. I checked the tag on his collar and learned that "Winston" had only been a couple of blocks from home when he died. He was small enough that I could have picked him up, but something made me hesitate and instead I left him there and drove alone to the address inscribed on the tag.

The front yard of the house had sleds and balls and assorted bright plastic toys. I went past these things with a lowered head, held my breath while I knocked, and sighed with relief when no young faces, nor any adults, came to the door. I thought about leaving a note, but again hesitated, not knowing what to write. How could a note let the parents know what had happened and yet not tell the children?

Winston's tag had the phone number as well, so in the end, I simply left a message on the owners' answering machine, giving my name and number, asking that they call me about their dog. Before going to bed, I called the animal shelter and asked that they pick up the body.

The sad situation was gone from my mind as I awoke and went back to work, but when I came home again, there were messages waiting on the answering machine. A young boy was calling over and over, wanting to know if I had a dog.

Yes, I had a dog. Jack was a large, strikingly beautiful Golden Retriever, feathered in every shade of yellow from the palest silvery gild to a honey red as burnished as Winston's coat. With the dawning realization that the family must have called the shelter, I felt my mind lurch. Suppose the boy thought that I was the one who had hit his dog? I called him back with reluctance, dreading talking about his loss at all, hesitant to see his sorrow.

His voice sounded as shaky as I felt. "I was wondering if you have a dog," he asked. "And if so, if I could give Winston's Christmas presents... to your dog?"

Jack and I went over right away. The boy was older than I thought he'd be, maybe ten or eleven and he was alone at home. With the friendly enthusiasm typical of his breed, Jack went right up and plunged his face into the large grocery bag the boy was holding. Wrapped present after wrapped present came up, clasped gently in Jack's jaws. Dog treats, a rawhide chew toy, a ball. With tears on his cheeks, the boy helped Jack pull the paper off each gift and inspect them one by one.

I don't know if the boy told me his name. I couldn't have remembered, could hardly trust my voice not to crack when I thanked him and drove Jack home with his new belongings. That boy's profound sense of Christmas, wanting to give gifts in his grief, was an experience to keep in the heart forever and so, while it was a brief encounter and I was sad for his loss, I'll always treasure that time I had with Winston's boy.

~Lisa Preston

Christmas Magic

Santa Claus
Is Coming to Town

Santa's Key

Childhood is the most beautiful of all life's seasons.
~Author Unknown

Bounding down the stairs of our new home, Lucas and Hanna, with a sudden realization of a potential catastrophe, sought me out, clinging to me desperately with panicked eyes and urgently questioned, "How will Santa deliver presents to our new house if we don't have a fireplace with a chimney?"

"Don't worry," and "He's magic," didn't quite cut it. I needed an answer. An answer that would satisfy two very curious young minds. An answer that is grounded in reality yet clings beautifully to mystery. An answer that invites childhood to live in our home for as long as it wants to stay.

The room seemed to spin as my mind reeled back to those wonder-filled holiday memories from my own childhood: opening the little doors on a calendar one by one until the night Santa would arrive; composing my letter to him more thoughtfully than any school assignment. I'd even start prancing through the house singing "Santa Claus Is Coming to Town" before the Thanksgiving table was cleared. So many of our traditions revolved around this eagerly anticipated arrival, I felt I must attend to the urgent query of my little ones.

And so the search began. First stop: our local library. I plopped myself down on the floor, surrounded by an avalanche of Christmas stories. Almost every book I perused displayed a bright, colorful illustration of that jolly old elf landing in the living room in a pile of soot. Great, no help there. Next, I braved the crowded department stores searching aimlessly for this elusive answer. What was I thinking? I was elbow to elbow with last-minute shoppers loaded down with their bags full of goodies, and there I was mumbling to myself, "Macy's ain't got any. Nobody's got any." No miracle on 34th Street for me.

I returned home empty-handed. Out of pure desperation, I finally found myself rummaging through, of all places, the sock drawer—a haven for all missing things. I don't know what inspiration I expected to find there, but buried in the corner, I caught a glimpse of promise. It was an old key from the house in which I grew up.

I carefully threaded a red satin ribbon through the top and adorned it with a tag engraved "Santa's Key." When I presented this solution to Lucas and Hanna, their wide eyes and satisfied smiles assured me I had successfully granted their Christmas wish. They scurried around the house, dodging decorations, searching their stockings, and rooting through gift wrap until they found the perfect box in which to safely store the key until that special night. Now every year, the children dangle "Santa's Key" outside on our doorknob with faith that it will turn for his magical hand on Christmas Eve, unlocking the doorway of tradition.

I'm glad I finally found a fitting use for that old key I had sentimentally stashed away all these years—that very same golden key which used to open the door to my parents' house: the house full of Christmas past; the house where magic lived; the house in which the Santa of my childhood dwelled. So indeed, it truly is Santa's key.

~Erin Solej

85

Too Many Santas

Blessed is the season which engages the whole world
in a conspiracy of love.
~Hamilton Wright Mabie

There was no snow at all that day,
Though Christmas was just days away.
The trees were bare, the grass was brown,
In short the kids were feeling down.

A rumor floated round the room,
That added to the frigid gloom.
This new idea was tough to hear,
And stole some of their Christmas cheer.

The rumor said with mocking tongue
That Santa was just for the young,
For little ones with lists all made
Not for big kids in the second grade.

So they were depressed in room 124
When the man in red walked through the door.
Should they resist the urge to now believe,
It being so close to Christmas Eve?

His cheeks were rosy, his dimples merry,
The usual beard and a nose like a cherry.
He smiled at them all and he moved toward the chair
And he sat as the whispers were filling the air.

Some hesitated and some gave a shrug,
But then as a group they all moved toward the rug.
"It's him," stated Zack, with commitment and zeal,
"I've seen lots of Santas, but this one is real!"

"How do you know?" whispered Rachel, unsure —
"He's not like the Santa I saw at the store —
"I thought he was real, at least it seemed so,
With so many Santas it's so hard to know."

Santa talked to them all as they sat on the floor,
And he spoke of behaving and giving and more.
And they listened intently and then watched him stand,
But before he could leave, Nathan put up his hand.

"Yes?" Santa asked as he towered above,
And he pointed at Nathan with gleaming white glove.
"Santa," asked the child with an uneasy grin,
"What we want to know, is — are you really him?"

And like a sudden shattering glass,
A silence fell upon the class.

The teacher was shocked as she stared at the child,
A question like that could send the class wild.
But a quiet remained and the children all waited
The question, they felt, was very well stated.

Briana was the first to speak
As she pointed gently toward his cheek.
"I've seen you Santa, in other classes,
But I don't remember you with glasses.

"And yesterday your eyes were brown,
When I saw you in a store downtown
And now I see your eyes are blue—
So tell us Santa, which one is true?"

Then up spoke Chris with impish grin,
"I have to ask about your skin.
One day I saw you with your sack
In another place and you were black!

"How can Santa be both black and white,
With eyes of blue and brown, what's right?"
"How can it be?" the children mused.
They were stumped, and angered and a bit confused.

"The real Santa," stated James,
"Wouldn't play these kinds of games.
So tell us, Santa—are you real or fake—
This is not a chance we'd like to take."

"Oh my," sighed Santa. "What a position!
I'll answer you on one condition—believe anyway."

And he sat back down upon the chair
And met them with a loving stare,
"I may not always look the same,
But Santa is my one true name."

Said Kaij, "We mean no disrespect,
But I'm afraid that we suspect
That not all Santas can be real
And you're in on this impostor deal."

"Mom says Santa," said Stefanie,
"Is not one that you ever see,
You and others in disguise
Are merely Santa's helper guys."

"If that's the case," Dakota said,
"How can we trust any man in red?
You must admit there is a danger,
When sharing wishes with a stranger."

"Ah," said Santa, "A point well taken
I can see that your faith's been shaken.
You want to know if wishes are heard
By the one true Santa? You have my word.

"No matter which man plays the part,
Your wish goes straight to Santa's heart."
And here he softly tapped his chest
The very part that kids know best.

"It's not a question of real or fake
Believing is a choice you make."

So once again the large man stood,
And reminded them firmly to be good.
He left them there to sit and think,
But through the doorway gave a wink.

So quietly they left the floor,
Eyes still on the classroom door.
After all, it gives a person pause
To think they'd just met Santa Claus.

So was he the real one? They'll never know,
But outside the window fell flakes of snow.

~Michelle D. Halperin

86

Reindeer Magic

Christmas waves a magic wand over this world, and behold,
everything is softer and more beautiful.
~Norman Vincent Peale

I t was magic. The Christmas etched indelibly in my mind was the type of Christmas that greeting cards depict and poems are written about. As a young child I was being driven "over the hills and through the woods" to my grandmother's home in Sussex, Wisconsin. We slipped and slid over icy roads. My dad, the determined driver, managed to maneuver us out of a snow bank as my mom sat by his side.

There I was, the Mississippi-born girl, bouncing in the back seat asking, "When will we be there, when are we ever going to be there?" This was to be my first Christmas in Wisconsin with my mom's family.

We were to arrive early afternoon on Christmas Eve but because of the ice and snow we were much later than planned. The skies darkened early as the weather worsened. There was tension in the car between my parents. They worried for our safety. My excitement couldn't be contained, for this was pure adventure.

Hugs, screams, and shouts of welcome met us as the door opened and my aunts, uncles, and grandmother rushed to greet us. We unloaded the car and my family began piling food and goodies on the table for us to eat. There was "soft talk" in the background. "Grown-up" talk about roads being closed and how thankful they were we'd traveled safely. Uncle Bud broke out his special dominos—a favorite activity for him and my dad. My mom huddled with her mom and sisters catching up on all the news.

I realized that my family had very different speaking voices than I did. There were things in this unique home I'd never seen before. The quiet and calm of the rooms seemed filled with expectation. Christmas was almost here.

Outside the snow grew heavier. The sights, smells, and thoughts I experienced that night would be part of this Christmas memory forever.

Cuddled down after some hot chocolate and my grandmother's one-of-a-kind "lifelike cut-out cookies," I yawned. Meme's antique couch cushioned every inch of my body. My uncle sat down beside me and I snuggled into his arms. The family drifted into the room, dimmed the lights, lit the tree, and whispered their words.

I heard things like, "Where should she sleep?" I knew they meant me.

I'd not considered sleeping in this strange place but guessed that was in the plan. A bed was readied and I was snuggled into warm pajamas. The biggest, fluffiest blankets covered me. It was to be a cold night. The snow continued to deepen.

"Reindeer." I heard that word from my uncle. I'd been a little concerned about Santa. We were eight hundred miles from home. Would he find me? Would I get any Christmas gifts? My parents assured me they'd left a note for him and he'd know exactly where to leave my presents. I wasn't at all sure he would find this house.

My uncle Dave had a sleigh. I'd been told he'd hook up the horse and I'd get to ride in a one horse open sleigh complete with bells. How could I go to sleep with the prospect of Santa coming and my own sleigh ride the next day?

"Reindeer bells." My ears perked up. I was told, "If you go to bed soon you will probably hear the reindeer tonight. Children do hear them every year. In fact, not only will you hear their bells, you will see their footprints in the snow tomorrow morning!"

It was hard to catch my breath at the thought of hearing the bells and then seeing their footprints. I tried "not" to sleep. I lay in the bed listening, waiting, and straining to hear every creak and groan of the house. Fatigue took over my body and while listening to adults talking and getting themselves ready for bed, my sleep came.

The room was dark as my eyes opened. The house was quiet. It was hard to remember where I was. My eyes became accustomed to the dark and my breathing stopped as I heard a bell. The ringing was a gentle, mellow sound and it was not inside the house. It was assuredly outside. It was the sound of reindeer bells.

My mom and dad were asleep. Would they hear the bells? Wide awake, I lay perfectly still, for as long as I could. Sleep soon came again.

Sunlight streamed in the window. Even the curtains that hung there are etched in my memory. My family woke me with shouts of, "Merry Christmas! Santa visited us last night! Did you hear the reindeer?"

I remember jumping up and my uncle ushering me to the window.

"Look! Look right out there! Do you see the hoof prints? There they are!"

They were there. Hoof prints were clearly in the snow.

Breakfast couldn't have been better. The tree could not have been more beautiful, the day couldn't have possibly been more wondrous. It was the Christmas a little girl would only dream of and I would experience once in my life. The ride in the one-horse open sleigh with my uncle Dave and my cousin Donna was all I'd hoped. We were all snuggled down in the blanket and the horse decked in bells. The ride through the hills and dales of the family farm was like a fairytale.

I have held the memory of the bells and the hoof prints in the snow all these years. Christmas brings a sense of sweet nostalgia and the little girl inside my soul will always recall the Wisconsin Christmas filled with reindeer magic.

~Marilyn Ross

Some Assembly Required

There are no rules of architecture for a castle in the clouds.
~G.K. Chesterton

There is a phrase that strikes terror in the heart of any parent, especially on Christmas Eve. It's those three little words—just three. But say those words to parents and you will see fear in their eyes. They may scream. They may cry. Some will instantly turn into blubbering idiots. And what are those three words of horror?

"Some assembly required."

You see, when a toy box says "some assembly required," it doesn't mean that you might have to spend ten minutes or so putting together a plastic castle complete with knights and a moat. No, it means you need a degree in architecture, an entire toolkit scaled to the castle's proportions and the ability to read and understand 392 pages of instructions written in Sanskrit.

And that's just to get the castle parts out of the box.

Now there are people—men—who believe that they don't need the instructions. No, they will run around, beat their chests and yell, "Instructions? I don't need no stinking instructions!" Then they will dump the 1,528 castle pieces in a pile on the floor and proceed to assemble something that looks like a cross between an Easy Bake

Oven and a Labrador Retriever—but which in no way resembles a castle.

Women, on the other hand, love to read instructions. We don't actually want to assemble the stupid castle, but we want to tell the man making the castle exactly how to do it. This doesn't endear us to the man who is putting the castle together. In fact, castle assembly arguments are the leading cause of divorce in this country.

Occasionally, more than one man will attempt to build the castle. This is a very, very bad idea. For some reason, men see castle assembly as a challenge. They must win against the castle, no matter what. And if another man steps in to help with the castle, it becomes an even bigger challenge. The first guy is no longer just battling a castle with 1,528 pieces; he's also battling his best friend who just had to stick his nose into the castle assembly process. Soon, the battle escalates into a full-blown testosterone war, and a challenge is issued.

Man 1: I can build that castle in two hours.
Man 2: I can build that castle in an hour.
Man 1: I can build that castle in fifteen minutes, without once glancing at the instructions.
Man 2: Build that castle!

And that is how the drawbridge ends up on the wrong side of the moat.

Once the drawbridge is fixed, the men will circle the castle, thumping their chests with pride for a job well done. Unfortunately, they aren't finished. You see, no castle is complete without teeny, tiny decals that have to be stuck onto the castle pieces. Some of these decals are so small they are not visible to the naked eye. You need special glasses and tweezers just to apply them.

And the decals are always either too small or too large for the castle part they need to be stuck on. Even if you are lucky enough to find a castle part and decal that are perfectly sized, the decal always ends up crooked. Or upside down. Or ripped and then painstakingly pieced back together.

About this time, one of the chest thumpers discovers that the decals are supposed to be put on before the castle is assembled. So now the entire castle has to be taken apart, decals put on and then reassembled.

Many men have failed at this point. They may try to block the pain by drinking large amounts of alcohol. Unfortunately, women will step in and try to help. They'll mix drinks or maybe call customer service. Neither works. For one thing, customer service is only open on weekdays from 9 to 5 when no one in the entire world is trying to assemble toys. And you should never drink and assemble. You don't even want to imagine what the castle will look like after the assembler has a few Mai Tai's under his belt.

So what is a parent to do? First, throw the decals away. And then don't worry about the castle. Because once it is set up in the playroom, your kid will move the knights around and make sure the water in the moat is real. And then he'll be bored and want to play with something else.

And, of course, that toy needs just a little assembly. Relax. Have a hot cocoa with schnapps—you'll feel better.

~Laurie Sontag

"SOMETHING WITH COMPLICATED INSTRUCTIONS TO KEEP MY DAD BUSY SO I CAN PLAY WITH MY OTHER TOYS BY MYSELF."

88

The Voice of Santa Claus

No road is long with good company.
~Turkish Proverb

Driving after midnight was always peaceful. The midnight sky in West Texas after a Christmas Eve service, well, that is in a class all to itself. The deep navy sky punctuated with stars shining like crystals hanging from a chandelier was nothing new. Driving along a highway in far West Texas, we might as well have been the only people in the world. There were no lights, no other vehicles, no towns. Just absolute dark pierced by the stars and our car lights. No sound other than the hum of tires on the highway and the soft sounds of my daughters.

Usually my daughters slept the thirty-five miles back to the ranch. This night was different. Six-year-old Mitty was uncharacteristically fussy and tired. She wanted to be home in her bed. Her big sister, Sarah, tried to dissuade her, but there was no distracting Mitty from her thoughts, and disappointment was sure to follow. Suddenly, I thought of the CB radio. I plucked the mike off the seat and handed it over the back to Mitty, suggesting she try calling Santa. She looked doubtful but at least it would keep her occupied. Her older sister Sarah wanted a little peace and quiet as well, so she too encouraged her to call Santa.

"Breaker one nine, this is the Little Peanut calling for Santa."

"Santa? Are you there?" The only sounds were the humming of tires and static on the radio. Tears came to my eyes at the innocence of this precious child. We waited. She repeated her call.

"Breaker one nine for the Jolly Elf. This is the Little Peanut. Over."

Soft static from the radio and the soft hum of night driving. Nothing else.

"Aw, Mom. There probably isn't really a Santa Claus." Disappointed silence.

As she handed the mike over the seat there was crackling of static and the sound that comes with thumbing the mike.

"Come back Little Peanut. This is the Jolly Elf. What are you doing up so late?" Mitty gasped. Sarah sat up straighter in the backseat. I felt a huge lump in my throat.

Mitty took back the mike and stammered, "This is the Little Peanut. Where are you Santa? What's your twenty?"

"Well, Little Peanut, I'm somewhere overhead and I can't finish my evening until you are in bed asleep."

"I've been to midnight mass, Santa. We are almost home. Please wait. Over."

"This is the Jolly Old Elf. You go straight to bed. I'll wait, Little Peanut. Out."

By then I was unashamedly crying. I had thought I knew most of the voices on our tower, but that night it was a stranger's voice.

It was the voice of Santa.

~Sally Baggett Griffis

89

Chicken Soup for the Soul

A Trip to Santasy Land

Santa is very jolly because he knows where all the bad girls live.
~Dennis Miller

I've celebrated Christmas exactly one day in my life. No, make that twelve hours. It was Christmas Eve day in Sausalito, California and I was breakfasting with my friend Steve when we started talking about the Christmas hubbub.

"Miami Beach wasn't the Mecca of Christmasville," I said recalling my childhood. "Aside from being eighty degrees, all of my friends and I were Jewish. Still I loved how Christmas made people friendlier, more open, more giving. What about you?" I asked.

Steve, a prominent attorney, whose nickname was "Tubby," wiped the cream cheese from his lips.

"I always thought it was cool that Santa could get the girls to sit on his lap." His blue eyes twinkled. "Wanna be an elf?"

"What?"

"You could be my elf and I could be Santa."

"And…?"

"We could hitchhike into San Francisco and see what Christmas is like."

No stranger to Steve's antics, I had a decade worth of stories with him.

"Hmm, well we don't have any plans," I said. "I can easily do elf."

After all I was 4'10", I had tights, and this was the 1970s. "Sounds good," I said. "I'm in."

We called a local costume shop.

"We've got one Santa suit left. If you can get here in thirty minutes, it's yours."

The next thing we knew, we were fully suited up: Santa, his beard, and his bag of goodies, a hastily assembled assortment of toys picked up at a drugstore, and I in green tights, a leotard and streaming scarves. We walked to Bridgeway, the main street in Sausalito. Feeling suddenly conspicuous in the glaring sunshine with a crowd watching, we realized there was only one thing to do—stick out our thumbs.

A gleaming BMW screeched to a halt.

"Lost your sled Santa? Where are you going?"

"Anywhere in San Francisco."

"Hop in," he said, "and watch out for your sack of toys. Hey, my advertising firm is hosting a party on a yacht. Do you want to come?"

"Wherever Santa and his elf can bring the most joy is where we'll go," Santa replied.

He was fully and deeply into his Santa-sy, I thought. This was going to be some ride. I stifled the laughter, but the glances we exchanged shared our unspoken promise to remain Santa and elf for the duration of our journey.

We arrived at the yacht and were escorted aboard. A collection of elegantly attired executives turned towards us. Unbeknownst to us we were with the owner of the poshest advertising firm in San Francisco. All eyes were on us, expecting a show, a showering of gifts, a something, but feeling a little peckish we headed to the hors d'oeuvre table.

"So really, who are you? What are you going to do?" dogged the tall Armani-clad man inspecting Santa's face.

"Well, I'm going to have a little snack right now. I've got a big night ahead," said Santa, swallowing his gravlax and caper canapé. "I'm in the toy business. Tonight's our busy night." Santa continued munching. "Brought one of my best elves to help." He gestured towards me as if it were necessary. Thoroughly confused by our non-performing performance, the adman skulked away. We schmoozed, scarfed down some more hors d'oeuvres, said a few "Ho Ho Ho's," and disembarked as mysteriously as we'd arrived.

Once on the street, we stuck out our thumbs. As if we'd summoned Rudolph, within seconds, a limo was chauffeuring us to our next party. The entire night a fleet was at our disposal: limos, sports cars, pick-up trucks and we selected our "sleighs" solely on whim.

After a few parties we felt stuffed. Needing fresh air and a new plan we started walking the streets. The Christmas lights twinkled. The air was chilled. We were basking in the wonder of it all when an elderly woman suddenly walked up to Santa, grabbed his arm, and looked him square in the eyes.

"I have always loved you, Santa."

"And I have always loved you," said Santa giving her a warm and gentle hug. By now Santa's sack weighed heavy. "We've got toys to deliver," he said with a grin.

Perhaps security measures were different in the 1970s, or maybe Santa's always had carte blanche clearance, or perhaps someone at the hospital just believed, but somehow we were welcomed onto the pediatric ward. We joked and giggled with the sick children, who lit up at the sight of Santa. Toys were pulled from Santa's sack and as it emptied out, our hearts filled up.

We wished everyone "Sweet Dreams" and headed for the exit. The automatic doors released us into the cold night. We stood, still and speechless, trying to take in everything we'd experienced. Though our hearts were warmed, our hands were freezing.

"Let's go to the Wharf for Irish coffee," I said shivering.

Just then a family walked by engaged in a lively conversation peppered with Yiddish expressions. Without missing a beat, Santa raised his arms as if ordaining a blessing, "A gesund auf dein keppeleh," (A blessing on your head) he winked. Stunned at first, the parents returned the good wishes with a hearty laugh.

"Zie Gesund, Santa!" (To your health!)

We arrived at the overflowing Buena Vista Bar. Santa had an

inkling he was about to have his dreams come true. Though the patrons were three deep at the bar, it was as if Moses had parted the Red Sea and a path opened for us to walk through. A man popped up offering us his seat as he ordered a round of drinks. As soon as Santa was seated the parade began. Women in varying degrees of intoxication clamored to sit on Santa's lap.

"So, have you been naughty or nice?" Santa would ask, penning their names and numbers in their appropriate categories. He was clever and quick and whether it was his lawyering skills or his alluring blue eyes, those women confessed everything. While Santa's book filled with dating data, I chatted with the men who had obvious elf fantasies.

Noticing the time, Santa leaned over and said we had one final stop.

"Come by tonight and have eggnog with my kids and friends," Santa's recent date had suggested. Carrie had only been on two dates with Steve, so she had no idea what her invitation might bring. We had to get across the Golden Gate Bridge, and there was no time to lose.

"Ho ho ho," Santa quieted the noisy bar. "I've got a bit of an issue. My sleigh's been towed by SFPD and we'd hate to disappoint the children of Marin, would…"

Before he could finish his sentence we had three offers to whisk us across the bridge. We arrived around midnight. "Merry Christmas!" We rapped at the door. Recognizing Steve's voice, Carrie opened the door.

"Santa!" she gasped. Her children stared in amazement. Even the adults were intrigued. Was it a miracle? Not exactly, but the room was aglow with sheer wonder and magic.

Maybe I've only celebrated Christmas for twelve hours once in my lifetime, but if you ask if I believe in Santa, oh, I do. And as for Santa's black book? It never got much play, because not too long afterwards, Santa's girl, Carrie, said, "I do" and became Mrs. Claus.

~Tsgoyna Tanzman

Santa Sent Me

How beautiful a day can be
When kindness touches it!
~George Elliston

"Mom, look, there's Santa!" my six-year-old son, Jordan, shouted. "Can I sit on his lap and tell him what I want for Christmas?"

Jordan's three-year-old sister, Julia, grabbed my hand. "Please, Mommy?" Her huge blue eyes seemed to plead with me to say yes.

I sighed. It had been an incredibly rough year. I'd gone through a divorce I hadn't wanted, the kids and I had subsequently lost our home, and making ends meet as a single mom was proving a lot more difficult than I'd anticipated. And here I was at the mall, just three days before Christmas, hoping and praying to find a few toys on sale so that my children would have some semblance of a Christmas.

Slowly, I shook my head at the kids' question. "I'm sorry, guys, but I don't think we're going to be able to sit on Santa's lap this year."

Both of their faces fell. "Why not?" Julia asked. And Jordan said, "But I wanted to tell Santa about the Lego set I want him to bring me."

I bent down and looked into their sad little faces. "When you sit on Santa's lap, they take your picture and it costs money." I felt my eyes fill with tears as I added, "And we just can't afford it right now."

"But, Mommy, it's almost Christmas," Julia wailed. "How will Santa know what we want if we don't sit on his lap and tell him?"

At her words, my tears threatened to spill over. My heart ached for all that my children had lost in the last year. They'd already given up so much, and now they couldn't even tell Santa about their Christmas wishes. Not that I could afford to make them come true anyway.

I was stumbling through another explanation when I noticed that the line of children waiting to see Santa was gone. He caught my eye and motioned us over to him. I shook my head and shrugged my shoulders, ashamed that even Santa seemed to know that I was broke. Santa waved us over a second time. When I ignored him, he got out of his giant velvet chair and walked toward us. "Hello, children," he boomed when he reached us. "What would you two like for Christmas?"

My kids' eyes lit up. Julia started to describe her wish list, but Santa interrupted her. "Oh, no, young lady," he said. "If we're going to do this, we've got to do it right. You have to sit in my chair and tell me. And we'll take your picture, so your mom can always remember you at this age."

"Santa, we're not going to get our picture taken this year." Quietly I added, "Things are a little tight right now."

He turned to me and said with the kindest smile, "This one's on me, dear."

I began to protest, but my kids looked so happy that I just couldn't say anything. Each of my children took a turn on Santa's lap and then the three of them posed for a picture. Their smiles were like beacons of light during the darkest time in my life, and I was incredibly grateful for Santa's kindness.

But he wasn't finished yet. While his helper developed our photo, Santa gave my children the customary coloring book and candy cane. And then he handed me a note card. I glanced down at it and read the words, "Santa Sent Me."

Before I could ask the question, he explained, "My son is the manager of the toy store on the second floor. Let the children pick out anything in the store and then give this note to the clerk at the check-out. They'll know what it means."

I was about to say, "But I don't know what it means," when Santa patted my shoulder. "I said this one was on me, and I meant it."

My eyes filled with tears as I looked into his kindly face. The thought occurred to me that his bushy white beard and jelly-belly tummy were probably not part of his costume. "I can't thank you enough for this," I said. "I am overwhelmed by your generosity."

"It's part of the job." He winked and added, "I'm Santa, you know."

On the car ride home, both children chattered non-stop about their new toys. Listening to them made my heart feel lighter than it had in months. Finally, Julia said, "Mommy, you know how sometimes the Santas at the mall are just the real Santa's helpers? Well, I don't think it was like that this time. Tonight, we saw the real Santa."

I smiled at her in the rearview mirror. "I think you're right about that, honey."

"And he even gave me my present early." She hugged her new doll and said, "And it's the best present ever."

I felt the constant weight finally lift from my shoulders and I knew that Santa's gift to me was even more precious.

~Diane Stark

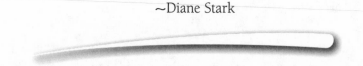

Santa's Secret

There are three stages of a man's life: He believes in Santa Claus,
he doesn't believe in Santa Claus,
he is Santa Claus.
~Author Unknown

"He's here! He's here!" I shouted as the sound of ringing bells approached our front door. I jumped down half a flight of stairs to open the door, but my brother beat me to it. He threw it open, and from the threshold Santa shouted, "Ho, ho, ho. Merry Christmas!"

My other siblings gathered from around the house — the younger ones, like me, beside themselves with excitement, with the older following more slowly behind. I eagerly watched as Santa handed father a sack of Christmas goodies, then made his way to the living room. He sat on the sofa where each of us would get a turn to sit on his lap and share with him our most earnest Christmas wishes.

When my turn arrived, my father lifted me onto Santa's knee.

"Have you been good this year, young lady?"

"Yes, sir!" I looked to my parents for confirmation.

"What would you like for Christmas?"

"I want a Cinderella Barbie doll."

"Well, we'll see." He winked at me, making no promises.

I slid off his lap to let my brother have his turn.

Santa shared pleasantries with my parents before wishing us

all a final "Merry Christmas!" Then as suddenly as he'd arrived, he jingled his way down the stairs and out the door.

It never bothered me that Santa arrived through the front door instead of the chimney. My mother said it was because we had a wood-burning stove instead of a fireplace. But I knew he was just a nice man pretending to be Santa Claus. The real Santa wouldn't be so obvious.

As I grew older, I became less eager to sit on his lap and more interested in discovering his true identity. Ours was a small town, so I thought that if I looked hard enough past the beard, I would figure it out. I never did.

My junior year of high school, with college admissions applications looming, I decided to join the Youth Town Council. Twice each week we would gather for meetings and service projects. Christmastime was no exception. We spent hours screwing light bulbs into the giant tinsel candy canes that hung from the light posts on Main Street. And we stripped down the Fourth of July floats to redecorate them for the Christmas Light Parade. But it was at our last meeting before Christmas that we received my favorite assignment.

"All youth council members old enough to drive should arrive with your vehicle at 6 PM on Christmas Eve at this address." Our advisor indicated an address written on the board.

"What? We're doing a project on Christmas Eve?" someone asked.

"What's the assignment?"

She smiled before answering. "You're going to drive Santa around town for his annual visits."

A murmur of anticipation spread at her announcement. It wasn't until after the meeting adjourned that someone thought to ask, "Why does she need all of us?"

After enduring the trepidation on my parents' faces as they placed the keys to the family car into their teenaged daughter's hands, I drove to the address. It was an unassuming warehouse on the outskirts of town leased by the local Lion's Club chapter. I parked the car and walked into the building.

About twenty men milled around a table heaped with Santa Claus costumes—some wearing beards, others wearing red pants and boots—as they dressed for their roles. They bantered and chatted, clearly looking forward to the night's events.

As I stood there, I began to wonder. Why would twenty men give up their Christmas Eve to put on a red suit and drive around town? I imagined one man might be willing to do it, but twenty?

Someone tapped me on the shoulder, and I turned. A Santa Claus stood there with a box of goody sacks under one arm. I looked at him for a minute before I realized I knew him. Santa was the church choir director... or at least this one was.

"I guess you're my driver," he said, smiling.

He handed me the route he'd been assigned, and I looked it over. It seemed somewhat haphazard until I realized that it had been carefully constructed so that this particular Santa would not likely be recognized at the houses he visited.

He buckled his seatbelt as I pulled out of the parking lot, and we exchanged small talk on our way to the first stop. I waited in the car while he grabbed a goody sack and jingled his way up the sidewalk to the front door.

"Ho, ho, ho. Merry Christmas!" I heard him shout. I smiled to myself at the memories the sounds evoked.

Ten minutes later he came back, eager to share everything that had happened—how the boy's face lit up with wonder when he arrived, and how the younger brother was too shy to sit on his lap. It surprised me that he would be so excited—a grown adult. You'd think Santa had visited him!

The night passed quickly. I drove him to each house, and after the visit he would tell me what happened inside. It seemed to me that our car had been magically altered to spread Christmas joy in its wake. We'd pull up to a quiet house, Santa would make his visit, and we'd leave the same house, now full of life and holiday spirit.

After three hours we finished our route. I drove him back to the warehouse and joined my fellow youth town councilors at the hot chocolate table. We listened to the stand-in Santas swap stories about their visits ("She asked me for a pony for Christmas. What was I supposed to say to that?") and laugh together.

As I stood there taking in the scene, it occurred to me that I was now privy to one of the biggest secrets in our small town... and I would never tell a soul.

~Rebecca C. Emrich

Reprinted by permission of Off the Mark
and Mark Parisi ©2000.

92

Three Little Girls

Love is what's in the room with you at Christmas if you
stop opening presents and listen.
~Author unknown, attributed to a 7-year-old named Bobby

Three little girls in the evening's light,
Ready to climb into bed for the night.
They gaze at the tree they hate to leave,
For this is the magic of Christmas Eve.

Three little girls who have tried to be good,
Minding, reminding each other they should
Thinking that Christmas must surely be late
Because it came slowly, and they couldn't wait!

They're hoping that Santa had been sleeping sound
Last week when they left all their clothes lying 'round.
Hoping that, too, he had been fast asleep
When one hit the other and caused her to weep!

Hoping that Santa just wasn't there
When Daddy had made them sit on a chair
The time that their dinner was left on their plate,
And hoping that they hadn't been good too late!

It's so hard to move them away from the glow
Of tinsel and bright lights and glistening snow.
But think of their dreams as they sleep through the night
To again in the morning, awake to this sight!

Despite all their protests and giggles of glee,
And after a warning that St. Nick might flee
If maybe he found them awake in the night,
They rush off to bed and are snuggled in tight.

As parents we know that St. Nick will be here,
For happiness blessed us throughout the year
With the magic of children, their faith and their love.
We whisper our thanks to the good God above.

Three little girls in bed for the night
Sure to arise with the morning's first light.
Lord, help them to gain all the joys that they can
From this season of Love and Good Will toward all men.

~Beverly F. Walker

Christmas Magic

It's the Most Wonderful Time of the Year

93

The Twelve Days
of Christmas

A fellow who does things that count, doesn't usually stop to count them.
~Variation of a saying by Albert Einstein

From the minute our neighbor and best friend's daughter, Olivia, was born, my son Bailey thought of her as his little sister. Bailey, being an only child, took her under his wing right from the start and loved to watch her grow and change. As Olivia began to talk and see the world through toddler and then little girl eyes, she looked up to Bailey as if he were her big brother and friend. With Bailey being thirteen years old and Olivia only four, there is quite an age gap. But I watch in awe as my son patiently plays kitchen with her, allowing her to prepare fake food for him. He knows how much enjoyment she gets from that and that gives him enjoyment, too. He even gave her his favorite swing set when he thought he'd outgrown it, only with the hope that he can still be a "little boy" again and swing on it when we go to her house.

With each holiday that approaches Bailey tries to share with Olivia the excitement that is to come... especially at Christmas. As Christmas was approaching last year Bailey talked to Olivia about how exciting it is when Santa arrives. He knew this Christmas she really understood and loved everything about the holiday from building gingerbread houses together to playing in the snow. Snow is definitely an unusual occurrence in Southern California but my husband drove up into the mountains, filled the back of his truck with snow and drove it home. He then dumped it out onto our lawn. The snow didn't last that long but the memories did.

Bailey really wanted to make the upcoming Christmas special for Olivia. He came up with a plan to surprise her by placing a small package on her doorstep each morning leading up to Christmas. He wanted to be her Secret Santa. We modified the words to the "The Twelve Days of Christmas" to reflect some of the things in her little world. So, the fun of shopping began.

On the first morning we printed the lyrics to the song, modifying the theme just a bit, to match his special gifts. We only gave her the lyrics for that specific day so as not to spoil the surprise. On the first day, he delivered a bag of pears and a partridge ornament for her tree. On the second morning instead of two turtle doves, he delivered a turtle bath toy and Dove chocolate. The third day, coming up with the three French hens, was a bit harder but we did find what we thought looked like a hen ornament. The fourth day we found a bird plush toy that made real bird sounds when you squeezed it.

What fun he was having each morning! I stood in the window in the early morning and watched him cross the street, drop the package at her front door, ring the doorbell and then run away as fast as he could. Each morning I watched as Olivia would swing the door open trying to catch her Secret Santa.

By day five we were having a ball and looking forward to delivering the glazed donuts symbolizing the five golden rings. The geese-a-laying and swans-a-swimming on days six and seven were hard for us but when we stumbled upon a Mother Goose book and a swan story book we felt proud of ourselves. By day eight trying to outsmart the cutest little girl ever was becoming more difficult. She was watching out her window! Bailey waited. When she finally left the window he was able to deliver the surprise for day eight… a bottle of Nestle's Chocolate Milk and French Maid Barbie. As her love for Barbies and all things girly was obvious, day nine of ladies dancing was easy. Her gift was a ballerina Barbie. Lord's a leaping on day ten stumped us, but what better gift to give than a frog pool toy that winds up and swims through the water. On the eleventh day, eleven pipers piping, he left a Christmas pipe cleaner craft kit.

We had made it... day twelve had arrived and it was time to deliver the final gift and reveal his identify. For twelve drummers drumming, the best gift to give your "little sister," especially when she doesn't live in your house, was a drum set. Instead of drummers drumming we could hear Olivia pounding on the drums. And she started screaming with excitement and delight when she discovered it was Bailey who had been her Secret Santa. She knew that it meant he cared so much about making Christmas magical and fun for her.

Although the age gap seems huge now, as adults I don't think it will be so bad. And since my friend and I are secretly hoping this friendship will blossom into something more in time, I only hope his future mother-in-law can find it in her heart to forgive him (and me) for the drum set that got plenty of use by a beautiful little girl.

~D'ette Corona

No Hostess Gifts Please

Christmas is the season for kindling the fire of hospitality in the hall,
the genial flame of charity in the heart.
~Washington Irving

For the past eleven years, friends of mine have hosted a Christmas party that for the most part resembles what you might expect at any gathering of friends and family during the holiday season. There is always a wonderful assortment of good food, never an empty glass, and plenty of great company. However, the Trafford Family Christmas Party is one-of-a-kind.

First and foremost the instructions are clear. "Please, do not bring a hostess gift." Not that the hostess doesn't deserve one — it's just that long before hostess gifts were in vogue the Trafford Family asked guests to bring canned goods for the local food bank. The entrance to their home often looks like a small distribution center on the eve of December 23, but once you're past the boxes of canned goods stacked outside it is always warm and inviting inside and filled with the promise of what is still to come.

Secondly, you are encouraged to bring whoever happens to be staying with you during the holidays. The more generations of family you bring, the better. There have been occasions when three generations of a family can be found at the Trafford's Party.

Thirdly, and certainly a key factor contributing to the spirit and joy of the evening, is the music. Along with your canned goods and your relatives you are encouraged to bring an instrument. Many people bring guitars, some bring flutes, mandolins, trumpets, drums, tambourines, maracas—even the occasional penny whistle. Voices are always welcome!

The first time my family attended, December 23, 1997 to be precise, was actually the Second Annual Trafford Party. I'm sure they had no idea they were starting a tradition that continues to bring generations of families and friends together year after year.

I've known my friend Dave, the host, since I was twelve, but we had lost touch with one another for a number of years. In 1997 our families moved into the same neighbourhood and in November we received an invitation to the Second Annual Trafford Party. Having missed the first I didn't quite know what to expect. With my wife and children joining me, I took our donation for the food bank—I had no desire to take my relatives and we would probably leave early anyway—we still had a closet full of presents to wrap. I certainly wasn't going to take my guitar—it had been years since I'd played it.

When we arrived, we deposited our canned goods in the appropriate bin, took the opportunity to catch up with some friends we hadn't seen in a number of years, and were just settling in by the fire when Dave announced it was time to go caroling. While we were initially a little uncertain about what to expect, we decided to bundle everyone up (with three kids under the age of eight, this is no easy task) and accompany him along with many other brave souls who chose to venture out into the cold. That night we stood and sang Christmas carols for people who opened their doors to us. Dave played his heart out; we all sang and anyone who opened his door in our neighbourhood that night over twelve years ago remembers and will tell you how wonderful it made them feel. It was a magical night—one I will never forget.

This year, over a decade later, the invitation arrived late in November and started with the same message as it had in years past: "No Hostess Gifts Please." The difference this year was there was no request for canned goods. It read: "Let's fill a stable." The Traffords had decided to ask friends and family and their community to help provide a family in some remote part of the world with essential animals that would, in turn, allow that family and their community to sustain itself. As I reread the invitation I couldn't help but recall the story of a baby named Jesus born over two thousand years ago in a stable surrounded by animals. A baby whose birth started a tradition that has lasted just as long and had an incredible influence on history and brought hope throughout the world.

Each year my children, now in their late teens, start asking about the Trafford's Christmas Party sometime just after Halloween. If the invitation for December 23 hasn't arrived by the end of November they start to get a little antsy. Our friends Anne and Dave and their children Erin and David Jr., whether they like it or not, have created a tradition that has become one of the most important parts of my family's and our community's Christmas traditions.

Like a little kid who lies awake in bed waiting for Santa, I can't wait for tomorrow night. It's December 23!

By the way—my mom and dad are really looking forward to the party, a couple of cousins have arrived from Europe and will be joining us and… I'm taking my guitar!

~Tom Knight

Love and a
Christmas Fruitcake

Open your heart — open it wide; someone is standing outside.
~Mary Engelbreit

My foster mother stooped in front of me and slicked back my hair. "We want you looking real nice when you go to meet these people today. They're thinking about adopting you, you know."

I sighed and looked over at my younger brother and sister. Even though I was only nine, I was old enough to know that this day could be the most important one of our lives. Whether we would be better off after this day, though, or worse, I had no idea.

By any standard, our lives had already been tough. Raised by impoverished Native Americans, we had moved more times than I could count. By the time I finished second grade, I had attended seven schools. We had even lived on an Oklahoma reservation for a time. Both of our parents were alcoholics.

We learned early in life that nothing could be counted on, that no one was dependable. Sometimes our parents would take us to the afternoon matinee at the local theater, then not return until after the final evening show was over, if then. We sat and watched the same movie over and over until the theater manager told us we had to leave. Then we'd go outside and sit on the curb until our parents finally came.

There were already six of us when my mother went to the hospital to have another baby. Only, she came back without the child. We found out later that she had given the little girl away to someone at the hospital.

Then my father left. We didn't understand why. We just knew that he was gone, and I, as the oldest boy, thought it must be my fault. Why else would a father leave his family, unless the children were just terrible?

After that, two of our sisters were taken away. We didn't know they had been given up for adoption. We only knew that everything around us was falling apart, and we were terrified of what would happen next.

We were headed for disaster, and it seemed that no one had the power to prevent it. All crammed into one bed, we often fell asleep crying with hunger.

Then one day, my mother met a man who said he loved her but didn't want a ready-made family. I don't know if the decision was hard or easy for her, but at the end of my second-grade year, she signed us over to an adoption agency and walked out of our lives.

Life in the foster home wasn't too bad at first. Although we missed our mother, at least we had beds to sleep in and got three meals a day—plain, unadorned food, yes, but when you've gone to bed hungry as often as we had, you learned to appreciate the basics. Our foster mother was nice enough, but we soon discovered that our foster father also had a "drinking problem," along with a violent temper.

And now this. What could we expect to happen this day? Would the family like us? Would they want us? What if the adoptive family had "drinking problems" too? Worst of all, what if they only wanted one or two of us, but not all? I didn't think I could stand losing any more of my family. As we bundled into the car with the adoption worker, my stomach knotted in apprehension.

We were supposed to meet the family at a church in a small neighboring town. As we pulled into the church parking lot, I saw a man and a woman get out of a car and walk toward us. They looked nice, but I had already learned that looks could be deceiving.

We met the people, whose names were Don and Dixie Hill. I don't remember much that was said, but after a while, Mrs. Hill suggested that since it was almost Christmas, we should all go over to their house and have a snack. The adoption worker agreed, so we climbed into the car once again and followed the Hills to their home.

I'll never forget the moment I walked into that house. An intoxicatingly sweet aroma permeated the house and assaulted all my senses. What was it? My mouth watered and my stomach growled a pitiful request. Mrs. Hill looked down at me and smiled.

"I'll bet you've never had Christmas fruitcake, have you? I just baked one fresh this morning. Would you like a piece?"

Would I? As we sat at the table and waited for our treat, I looked around the warm, comfortable house and realized I would like to live there. But life had been filled with so many disappointments already that I knew not to get my hopes up.

Then the fruitcake was placed before me. I could see the dried fruits and nuts oozing out of the rich brown cake, and the smell was even more tantalizing now that it was so close.

I looked up at Mr. and Mrs. Hill, who were smiling encouragingly. I looked at my younger brother and sister, who were already eating ravenously. I picked up my fork, cut a piece carefully, and slipped it into my mouth.

I had never tasted anything so delicious in my entire life—the sweetness was beyond anything I had ever imagined. How could people who didn't even know us share such an incredible treat with us? Surely they had important grown-up friends they could have saved this for. Each bite I took filled a need in my stomach but opened a bigger one in my heart.

These people didn't know how bad we were, I remember thinking. They didn't know we had driven our own father away or that we were so terrible that our mother chose some strange man over us. They were probably just being nice because the adoption agency worker was there.

But as our visit ended and we prepared to leave, I knew I wanted to live with this family forever. Oh, how I hoped they wanted us too!

It turned out that they did want us—all of us. That Christmas, a childless couple in northern California opened their home and their hearts to three little Indian kids who had no concept of unconditional love.

In the days and years to come they would teach us about Jesus, the first and best Christmas gift, and the God who loves us all, no matter what side of the tracks we come from. They gave us a home and a hope, and pointed the way to God and His eternal love. And it all started with a fresh-that-morning Christmas fruitcake!

~Robert Hill as told to Dawn Shipman

96

The Best Gift of All

If you want others to be happy, practice compassion.
If you want to be happy, practice compassion.
~Dalai Lama

During the holiday season, it sometimes seems like the whole world is wrapped up in presents and material possessions. Kids are writing their wish lists to Santa, adults are trying to find the "perfect gift" for their special someone, and mall parking lots are jam-packed with eager shoppers. I had always been just as guilty as the next person of harboring this fraudulent yuletide spirit, until a few years ago when my dad taught me what the holiday season is truly about.

While my mom usually spends the twenty-four days of December leading up to Christmas stressing out about what to buy for my many aunts, uncles, and cousins, my dad has always tried to instill the spirit of giving in my brother and me. Every year, we stop by the local fire station and drop off two brand new basketballs, one from each of us, for their annual toy drive for underprivileged kids. It always makes me smile to think of the special holiday we're giving a few kids, and I like to picture them happily dribbling their new basketballs around all year long.

A few years ago, my dad went even further and started his own Holiday Ball Drive to collect sports balls for children. He figured sports balls don't break, don't need batteries, and stand a chance to last all year long. He is a sports columnist and informed the public about his project through his newspaper column. Five years later, he has collected and donated 3,257 new balls to less fortunate kids.

I always enjoyed helping him collect, sort, and distribute the sports balls. It gave me a great deal of satisfaction to think I helped so many kids have a little-bit-brighter Christmas. So, a few years ago, following my dad's example, I decided I would start a project of my own. I have always loved to read and write, so it was only natural that I would hold a book drive for my community. After all, toys get broken and clothes get outgrown—but the magic of books lasts forever. Think about it: have you ever met a person who doesn't vividly remember his or her favorite book as a kid? Or someone who can't think of at least one book, that one special book, that suddenly, for an instant, brought the world into focus, clicked his mind into gear, helped shape who he is?

No, right? Me neither. Books are a common thread that links us all together.

So, with my dad's help, I passed out flyers to local bookstores and schools, and made a website (www.writeonbooks.org) with essay contests, reading lists, author interviews, and details about how to donate to my cause. That first year I collected 126 books that I then gave to the local library to distribute to underprivileged children.

I felt a happiness brighter than all the Christmas lights in my city when I saw that one smile on the librarian's face—a stranger's face—as I gave her the box of books I had collected. I felt happier than any present has ever made me. Happier than I have ever felt giving my friends and family the "perfect gifts" I spent hours searching for. I didn't know who would receive the books, but I knew they would be appreciated. I had the distinct feeling that I really helped make a positive difference—if not in the world, at least in my little community—and I tried to hold it inside me and savor it, because that is one of the best feelings in the world.

Eight years later, I still relish that feeling. I have now collected and distributed more than 11,000 new books to underprivileged kids in my community. My annual Holiday Book Drive has not only given books to disadvantaged children—just as importantly, it has shown them people care. I have also found that many, many people want to help others, but often don't know how. My book drive has given them a way. From a one-person effort it has evolved into an entire community of volunteers, including forty student helpers, with collection boxes at local bookstores, post offices, and fourteen area schools. I have learned that together, we can help give sad tales a happier storyline.

Shortly after Christmas in January 2003, my dad was driving home from covering the Super Bowl in San Diego when his car was rear-ended by a drunk driver. Dad was driving through the parking lot on the way out of the stadium, pausing before making a right-hand turn, when the drunk driver, going sixty miles per hour, slammed into his Honda Civic—skid marks trailed back for fifty meters along the asphalt. The Honda was totaled, but blessedly Dad walked away from the terrible wreck. He did, however, have to undergo painful spinal fusion disk surgery, and still today suffers from neck pain and numbness in his fingers. Still, my family feels very fortunate that he is alive at all.

When news about Dad's accident spread among our hometown community, words of comfort and sympathy and prayer poured in from neighbors, friends, former teachers and classmates—even some people we had never met before but had collected balls for Dad's ball drive or received books from my book drive. Suddenly kids who I had given books to were giving back to me, literally—cards and letters and drawings that brought tears to my eyes. When I was laying the groundwork for my foundation to give back to others, I never realized that I was also laying a safety net of friends and supporters beneath me, to help me through my own difficult or scary times.

Indeed, while my Holiday Book Drive is a project that helps countless other people, it really is my own Christmas present to myself—and the gift I most look forward to every year. Dad taught me the old adage is true: giving really is better than receiving—and selfless giving will come back to you in ways you never would have imagined.

~Dallas Woodburn

Keeping Things in Perspective

Sometimes someone does something really small,
and it just fits right into this place in your heart.
~From the television show My So-Called Life

Standing precariously on a stool in my office, I found the Christmas boxes high on a back shelf. It was time to transform our home into the magic colors of the "love season." Somehow I never can enter into the spirit of things until I set my own stage, so I slid the boxes to the carpet and knelt to explore once again the scented candles, satin balls and sparkling ornaments that have hung every year upon our tree. Separating the strings of tiny colored lights, I leaned to plug in the first strand. On it came! Glancing at the box once again, my eyes fell upon something tucked in the bottom corner. There was a red candle. Next to it, folded in yellow tissue, were four dimes and, underneath these things, lay an old magazine. I rocked back on my heels and, while the lights burned on, my mind relived the events that led these things to be in my possession.

I once knew a woman who had very little in the way of material possessions. Her clothes were clean but faded. She ironed other people's clothes to make money for her children. There was no car so she walked everywhere, and thus her shoes were worn and cracked. She and her two children lived in a tiny corner house that had once been white and they all slept in one bedroom.

I met her through her little boy who used to come into my pet store after school. He loved animals and I would pay him a little to "help me" by sweeping the floor. He brought his mom around to see me one wintry day and I liked her and, since I was nice to her child, she liked me. Mothers are like that.

When Christmas came, she appeared in my store, smiling and red-cheeked, with a gift for me. Wrapped in a newspaper were three things—a red candle never lit, four dimes wrapped in tissue and a magazine. She asked if I would open it so she could explain it to me. Blinking back tears, I listened as she said that the red candle would bring light in my life. The four dimes were to be distributed to my four children, and, in the magazine was an article she'd found about the true meaning of giving and loving one another. Never had I received such a wondrous gift as this or one with as much heart. She stood silently, hoping I'd accept her humble offering of friendship. I could not close the space between us quickly enough and, with my arms around her, I told her I was honored and would keep them always.

And I have. Every year, I lovingly place the red candle, the four dimes and the magazine under our tree to remind us of the value of relationships and of giving of ourselves. And I can tell you that amid all the gaily wrapped gifts piled high each year, these precious gifts from my friend so long ago help to keep Christmas in its proper perspective for me. It is too easy to fall prey to materialistic advertising, too easy to get entangled with spending "enough" on each person on your list, too easy to get tight as a rubber band on a slingshot because you've spent yourself and your pocketbook too thin. It is too easy to forget that this is the "love season."

So, once again this year, I have placed these three gifts under our tree to remind us that the true reason we celebrate Christmas has nothing to do with money. These are really hard times and, more than likely, there will be fewer gifts under your tree and mine but that is okay. Maybe, just maybe, it will turn out to be a blessing, not that we have less but that we may celebrate Christmas this year with a clearer perspective.

~Jean Brody

The Gift of Forgiveness

Forgiveness does not change the past, but it does enlarge the future.
~Paul Boese

The last group of guests bumped merrily out our front door and down the steps. I stood in the open doorway answering the final round of good wishes as our visitors, walking down our front sidewalk to their cars, turned back to wave. Their voices sounded crisp in the newly arrived frigid air of early December. A full moon climbed high in the dark slate sky. I eased the glass storm door shut, and it instantly frosted up as the warm air of our living room hit the icy cold surface. Now, all I could see outside were the hazy gleam of headlights flashing on as our friends started their cars, and the brightly hued blur of Christmas bulbs on the bush just outside our door.

I shut the heavy inside door and turned into our living room. My husband, Mike, bit the leg off a gingerbread man and grinned at me as he sank down onto the couch. "Well," I said as I plunked down beside him, "it's beginning to look a lot like Christmas." A decorated tree next to the fireplace shimmered with tiny white lights, and a row of candles glowed along the mantel. Gifts wrapped in gorgeous holiday paper and tied with red, green, cobalt blue, or fuchsia metallic ribbon were piled beneath the tree. On some packages, I'd attached a jingle bell or two. Candlelight flickered on the dining room table, glinting off shiny glass Christmas bulbs placed among crystal pedestal cake plates and silver platters that still displayed an abundance of holiday cookies. The scent of cinnamon and cloves from hot apple cider perfumed the air, and the coffee urn emitted its own pleasant and comforting fragrance. Since I am enthralled with all things Christmas, this was bliss. We sat close and relished the quiet.

"Hey, how about some fresh air before we start cleaning up?" asked Mike after a time, breaking the spell.

"Good idea," I responded, happy to put off the job of restoring order to our kitchen. He rose from the couch and offered me his hand. We pulled coats, hats, gloves, and scarves out of the front closet. "My mother would have liked our party tonight. You know how much she loved all the Christmas hoopla," I told Mike as we suited up in our warmest winter attire and headed out for a late-night walk. Mike nodded silently, waiting for my cue on the direction of our conversation. My mother died three years ago, in her nineties, and what grieving I did was not so much about losing her, as about never having had her. Burdened with a melancholy outlook for most of her life, she was difficult to please. In my childhood I worked relentlessly, but ineffectively, to satisfy her. Then I worked just as hard in my adulthood to distinguish myself from her and to diminish any similarities between us, in an effort to convince myself that her disapproval of me mattered little.

Only with her death has our reconciliation begun. A cynic would say that I have fashioned this truce to meet my own needs, a convenient and thoughtful gift from an optimistic mind. However, I know otherwise. I sense her hand in the peacemaking, as I have been inspired to ponder the events of her childhood, a time of which she rarely spoke. Those few memories she chose to share about her youth were never pleasant. My concern has slowly turned from the ways in which she broke me, to the ways in which she may herself have been broken in the decades before my life began.

As Mike and I hiked through one neighborhood and into another in the brisk air, I absentmindedly led us into the area where I grew up. Hand in hand we traversed the sidewalk bordering the golf course in my childhood neighborhood. We traded stories of earlier Yuletides. "Is there a reason you're so nuts about Christmas?" he asked.

I considered the source of the giddiness and sentimentality that overtake me every year as soon as the carcass of the Thanksgiving turkey hits the trash. "I don't know," I said. "I'll have to think about that one."

I glanced over at the golf course, which is one block from my childhood home. I described to Mike how, when I was in early grade school, I begged my older brother to take me sledding there on winter afternoons. And how at dusk on Christmas Eve in my youthful years, our parents would send him and me over to these hills with our sleds. On that night we generally had the snowy slopes all to ourselves. We'd make several runs down the double hill, facing a magical spectacle of brightly lit, snow-frosted evergreens in front yards all up and down the blocks bordering that corner of the golf course. My excitement reached a higher level with every speedy descent because I knew that while we were gone, Santa was at our home loading heaps of presents under our Christmas tree. The short trek back to our house after sledding never seemed longer than it did on Christmas Eve.

It didn't matter to us that many of those gifts were necessities masquerading in bright gift wrap as luxuries: new underwear, socks, wool gloves, and school supplies. We were all the more jubilant when one of the boxes contained a toy train or a doll.

As Mike and I reminisced on our stroll, I realized for the first time the origin of much that I treasure about Christmas. The singing: my mom. The candlelight: my mom. The gift wrapping: my mom. Those tiny white twinkle lights: my mom.

And so my mother and I continue our reconciliation. As the weather gets colder, I become warmer.

~Beverly A. Golberg

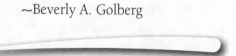

Christmas on Lawrence Street

I will honor Christmas in my heart, and try to keep it all the year.
~Charles Dickens

Our family changed the day we drove to Lawrence Street. Not any day, mind you — Christmas Day. Determined our three suburban-raised boys would not grow up naive and spoiled, we decided to serve up a slice of real life before feasting on the rest of our holiday. Instead of the early morning race down the stairs to the bulging tree, we dressed, loaded up the car, and took off for the forty-five-minute drive downtown to the rescue mission. Perhaps a look at the homeless would temper the bickering over too many Christmas presents? Maybe stepping into a different life for a few moments would make us more appreciative of our own? The disappointed look on little boy faces told me otherwise.

I've always been a fan of the rescue mission, "fan" being the key word. Like a spectator who never steps on the field, I felt real good about sitting in the bleachers, clapping my hands and cheering them on. Good organization! Great mission! Go, team, go! Somewhere along the way, however, I'd grown dissatisfied with rah-rahing from bleacher seats. I wanted to be in the game, do my part to make a difference.

Watching my young boys struggle against materialism probably had something to do with it. We live in one of the most affluent communities in Colorado, where the high school parking lot looks like a new car dealership and weekly allowances rival my salary. Trying to withstand the lure of wealth tested each of us. Whether watching TV shows littered with must-have commercials or hanging out with friends boasting an endless collection of toys and gadgets, greed bombarded my children day after day. I want what he has! Why can't I do what he does?

Even I felt the pressure to keep up. Materialism seemed to be dragging us down its slippery slope. If I wanted our family to have a heart for the world beyond self and stuff, I needed to do something drastic to counteract the culture. I couldn't wait for compassion and selflessness to bloom without planting a few seeds of generosity.

Thus our Christmas morning trip to Lawrence Street. After recovering from their initial disappointment, my boys soon resumed their normal Christmas morning chatter in the backseat. They weren't happy about the detour, but they tried to make the best of it. I sat in the front seat, thinking about my pajamas and warm cinnamon rolls back at home. I missed the slow pace of our normal Christmas. It surprised me how easily I turned to thoughts of my own comfort. Is giving up one morning of leisure that much of a sacrifice? Had I become consumed with only thoughts of myself?

My questions were silenced the minute we pulled onto Lawrence Street, for nothing could have prepared our family for what we saw there. In front of beat-up storefronts, loitering below a glowing sign proclaiming "Jesus Saves," more than one hundred of Denver's homeless gathered in tattered jackets and worn-out shoes. Hungry. Forgotten. Cold. On Christmas Day. And as I took in the crowd of displaced souls, it hit me: Although Christmas Day is the pinnacle of our year, to the homeless December 25th is simply another agonizing day to fill an empty stomach and warm a cold body.

With this revelation ringing in my ears, the cacophony of little boy voices in the backseat quieted to a whisper, eventually deadening to silence. A few scruffy-looking men approached our car, probably hoping we had food or a spare blanket. My husband looked at me with a question mark in his eyes: "You ready?"

Mute, I nodded once and then opened my door. A few feet away a man leaned up against the brick wall of the mission building, his worn clothes layered and filthy. He mumbled something nonsensical, oblivious to our presence. Another man pushed a beat-up cart, full of his treasures, likely someone else's garbage. I glanced back at the car to see the faces of my boys pressed against the window, looking more like men than children as they took in the scene themselves.

My husband rang the bell for the mission while I opened the back of our truck. Anxious to help, my boys handed me bags and gifts as I set them on the sidewalk. Soon a couple of mission volunteers arrived to help us unload. Bags of clothes, winter coats, toys, as well as a couple of frozen turkeys including all the makings for a large Christmas dinner. Not nearly enough to meet the needs of the multitude surrounding our car. I felt foolish. Our gift was far too small.

After emptying our car of everything but ourselves, we offered our warmest "Merry Christmas" and biggest smiles. But like the too-small gifts, even that kindness felt hollow. Our version of "Merry Christmas" differed vastly from that of those on Lawrence Street. After all, in an hour or two we'd be sitting indoors around a tree, opening gifts and stuffing ourselves with enough food for two families. The faces on Lawrence Street would still be searching for a home.

I climbed back into the front seat and glanced over my shoulder to see quiet boys with sober eyes, serious faces that likely mirrored my own. Nothing needed to be said. The vision on Lawrence Street hit its mark, piercing the heart of every last one of us.

Yes, our family changed that day. And every December 25th since, as we continue the tradition initiated that first year. While our own gifts sit wrapped and untouched at home, we drive to Lawrence Street to remember those who are too often forgotten and to deliver gifts to those who need them far more than we do. It's a small effort. We realize that now. But it's now an expected part of our Christmas celebration, perhaps changing us far more than it changes them.

We've been transformed in other ways, too. Our tree doesn't bulge as it once did. Our desire for more stuff isn't as powerful as it once was. At times we've left the comfort of home to love the poorest in Africa and Haiti, for a week or two instead of a single morning.

Still, there are moments when my boys would prefer to sleep in on Christmas morning. And sometimes I think about closing my eyes to the needy and staying home to eat warm cinnamon rolls in my pajamas. But then the faces of Lawrence Street pierce my heart once again. And I realize afresh there is more to Christmas—more to living—than a bulging tree and full stomach. For my greatest satisfaction wasn't found in stuff or things, but in the gift of an average day spent loving someone else.

~Michele Cushatt

This Christmas Is Different

If I had known how wonderful it would be to have grandchildren,
I'd have had them first.
~Lois Wyse

This Christmas is different. For so many Christmases past, as our kids grew older, a feeling of bah-humbug was usually experienced. This was especially true when they entered high school and college. Boring and predictable adequately described their wish lists.

It's been a long time since we danced down Santa Claus Lane as we watched our giddy little girls sit on Santa's lap asking for the perfect doll or other must-have toy that we couldn't wait for them to open on Christmas morning.

This Christmas is different thanks to the arrival of our very first grandchild. A very Jolly Old St. Nick will be making a stop at our house this year and it doesn't even matter that the future little believer is still way too little to believe.

Grandpa and I took a trip to Toys "R" Us the other day because now we have reason to peruse the tot-sized merchandise. What a treat! The rows and rows of toys seemed to stretch for miles, taking us on a jingle bell journey back to yesteryear where the kid in us was once again reborn.

We headed straight for the infant aisle. I was ready to do some browsing. Oh what fun it is to shop in a great big kiddie store!

This new grandma was bent on buying my dear grandbaby a toy chest. I settled on a darling pink and purple one with a bench for sitting on.

My daughter thought my gift idea was a good one as long as I promised not to go on a merry mission to fill it. I promised—with fingers crossed, of course.

This Christmas is different. Our family has grown by one and she is the reason our hearts are alive with wonder. She has no clue the giddiness her grandparents feel at sharing her first Christmas with her.

The only thing better than being a kid at Christmas is being a grandparent at Christmas.

It's been quite a long time since Santa and toys have been part of the same sentence at our house.

Avery will be decked out in a pretty red party dress and black patent leather shoes. She'll drool between giggles and the smiles she'll make us work extra hard to coax from her.

My very best gift this Christmas will come after the presents are opened and the feast of turkey has been eaten. It is then that I'll steal a quiet moment with my angel of a grandchild. As I rock her in front of the twinkling lights on the Christmas tree, I'll hum a little lullaby in her ear, as I always do, and from my heart I'll sing the praises of a loving God who has given us the greatest gift of all—a baby to love, and the opportunity to see life through the eyes of a child once again.

~Kathy Whirity

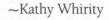

A Christmas Surprise

It is Christmas in the heart that puts Christmas in the air.
~W.T. Ellis

There is a Christmas I won't soon forget. It's not a Christmas with lots of presents, and it's not a Christmas where large miracles happened, or even where hard circumstances were greatly changed. But it was a Christmas that changed my life, and allowed me to witness firsthand the spirit that lives within many of us.

This Christmas I speak of, my family and I were far from home, or at least the home I'd known all of my young life. I was eight years old, and a few months before Christmas we had been living in Texas. Times had been tough for us, and try as she might, my mom could not find a way to make a go of it where we were. It was time, she said, to pull up stakes and try our luck somewhere else. So we packed and got ready to leave Texas behind, to build a better life for our family in California.

California? The name of the place didn't seem as down to earth as the places I had known and loved. What could be better than the home I had grown up in? Were we going to live near the ocean? Every picture I'd ever seen of California showed a beach and the ocean and the pounding, foaming surf. I couldn't even swim. Plus I had heard that California was a place where they had earthquakes and mudslides and raging fires. What kind of a place were we moving to?

Then there was the fact that we didn't know anybody in California. My mom knew only the name of the person who had hired her by long distance for her new job. We were moving to a place where we had no family, no friends, and no friendly neighbors. The tiny apartment we lived in wasn't much, but it was home, and I dreaded leaving it behind. Not only that, but we pulled up stakes in the middle of a school year, which meant I was leaving all my old friends. What would California kids be like?

The job my mom had gotten was in Oakland, and we soon found ourselves in an inner-city apartment in a neighborhood that was very different from our old one. We made the best of things, and tried to fit in both in our new home and at the school we attended. The neighborhood around us didn't have many kids, and our school was a tough one, where you had to learn how to survive. It was not the easiest place to live.

But in our small apartment we managed to make a good life. The beach wasn't too far by bus, and we explored the sand and surf with wide-eyed wonder. Though we didn't have many friends, my brother, sister, and I had each other. We were very frugal, and my mom counted our pennies carefully while we settled in and tried to make a go of things. At first everything seemed all right. My mom's job allowed her to support us and just make ends meet. We were still poor but she managed to put food on the table and take care of us.

But the move took a lot out of our finances, and by the time that first Christmas in our new home came along we were practically penniless. Christmas in Oakland, California didn't bring a lot of cold weather, and even though stores were decorated for the season it was hard to create that Christmas feeling that seemed so easy to capture in our old home. It didn't help that we didn't have money for a Christmas tree, presents, or even a Christmas dinner. It was hard for us to feel that Christmas spirit.

My mom tried to help us find it. We made homemade decorations, sang Christmas carols, talked about our favorite Christmas memories and took walks to see the Christmas lights in the city. Even though we wouldn't have presents, we colored pictures and wrote stories and poems to give to each other. My mom scraped enough money together to plan a simple Christmas meal. Being alone in this new place was very hard, and I think especially hard on my mom, but we tried to make the best of it.

Then something magical happened on Christmas Eve. There was a knock on the door and we opened it to see two people, a man and woman, who seemed oddly familiar. It took a few minutes for me to realize that I was staring at the two people who were the local television news anchors on the station we watched on TV. The pair came in and explained to us that our mom had written to them after she had seen a story about how the TV station was collecting toys for needy children to give out at Christmas. They explained that her letter had come very late, only arriving the day before, after all the toys had been given away.

"Well, almost all of them," the woman explained to me. "We wanted you to have these presents that Santa asked us to give you."

Then they handed each of us a toy. They weren't fancy toys. My brother got a pinball game, my sister got a chocolate-colored stuffed bear, and I got a small football. They also gave my mom a bottle of perfume. The couple smiled at us.

"We hope you like them and have a Merry Christmas. Remember, you have friends here in your new home."

Then they were gone. I stood looking at the little plastic football in my hands. It felt like the greatest gift I had ever gotten. I looked at my mom, knowing how hard she had tried to make this Christmas a happy one for us, and at the two people as they drove off waving at us. I didn't know their names, but they seemed like members of our family. They hadn't asked for anything, not a story for the news, nothing, just the chance to let us know someone cared about us.

That Christmas we all celebrated as if it was the most wonderful Christmas we ever had. In a way it was, because our little family was together, here in this strange new place, holding the surest sign of the Christmas spirit, delivered by a pair of angels whose job it was to let us know that there would always be those who were ready to reach out to remind us that this truly is a season of love.

~John P. Buentello

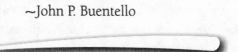

Christmas Magic

Meet Our Contributors
Meet Our Authors
Thank You
About Chicken Soup for the Soul

Meet Our Contributors

Elena Aitken lives in Okotoks, Alberta where she spends her time hanging out with her eight-year-old twins, training for various athletic events, running her own copywriting business and writing fiction. She's currently looking for a publisher for her first novel. She can be reached via e-mail at elena@inkblotcommunications.ca or www.inkblotcommunications.ca.

Pamela Underhill Altendorf lives in Wisconsin with her husband. She is currently a volunteer tutor in English as a Second Language, and enjoys traveling throughout the United States and abroad. Her stories have appeared in the *Chicken Soup for the Soul* series, and several other magazines and newspapers.

Monica A. Andermann writes and lives on Long Island where her brother, Louis, is a frequent inspiration for many of her essays. More of Monica's work can be found both online and in print, including several credits in the *Chicken Soup for the Soul* and *A Cup of Comfort* collections.

Paula F. Blevins and her husband, David, live on a farm in southern Ohio with three wonderful kids. She is the author of the *For Hymn Mystery* series, a variety of *Chicken Soup for the Soul* stories, and enjoys writing for children as well as adults. Contact Paula through her website at www.paulafblevins.com.

Heather Block squeezes in writing between raising her charming eight-year-old son, a job in a Winnipeg Family Centre, good friends, good books, and a character home that constantly needs upkeep. She writes for personal growth, publishing in her spiritual reflections blog, http://spiritsflight.wordpress.com.

Lil Blosfield is the Chief Financial Officer for Child & Adolescent Behavioral Health in Canton, Ohio. She has been writing stories and poems pretty much since she first learned to write which was many, many years ago. In addition to writing, Lil enjoys music, working outdoors and spending time with family and friends. She can be reached at LBlosfield40@msn.com.

Jean Brody has a BS degree in Journalism and Education plus graduate work in Animal Behavior. This is her seventeenth story in *Chicken Soup for the Soul*. She writes a weekly newspaper column and a monthly magazine column. She and her husband Gene live on their horse farm.

John P. Buentello is a writer who has published essays, fiction, and poetry. He is the co-author of the novel *Reproduction Rights* and the story collection *Binary Tales*. He is at work on a new novel and a picture book for children. He can be reached via e-mail at jakkhakk@yahoo.com.

Connie Sturm Cameron is a speaker and author of the book, *God's Gentle Nudges*. She's been published dozens of times, including several *Chicken Soup for the Soul* books and other compilations. She and Chuck have three children and three grandchildren. Contact her through her website www.conniecameron.com; or via e-mail at connie_cameron@sbcglobal.net.

Kathe Campbell lives on a Montana mountain with her mammoth donkeys, a Keeshond, and a few kitties. Three children, eleven grands and three greats round her herd. She is a prolific writer on Alzheimer's. Kathe is a contributing author to the *Chicken Soup for the Soul* and *A Cup of Comfort* series, *Rx for Writers*, and medical journals. E-mail her at kathe@wildblue.net.

D. Kinza Christenson is nationally recognized as The Performance Pro and wellness "Humorist with Heart." A boomer in denial, she combines her love of belly dancing with her business and life experience to help people achieve a standing ovation in life. You can reach her via e-mail at kinza@kinza.net or via her website at www.kinza.net.

Kristen Clark is the founder of His Witness Ministries and contributing author to New Beginnings Marriage Ministry. She is a published author, public speaker, and singer/songwriter, and she lives in Houston with her darling husband, Lawrence. Please e-mail her at kristens@hiswitness.org.

Joan Clayton is a retired teacher. Her passion now is writing. She and her husband have three sons, six grandchildren and two great-grandchildren. Joan has published eight books of her own. She has many stories in anthologies. Currently she is the religion columnist for her local paper.

Bridget Colern lives in Southern California, where she runs a bookkeeping and tax practice. In her spare time, she enjoys reading, writing, and playing with her grandchildren. Bridget has been previously published in *Chicken Soup for the Adopted Soul*. She can be contacted at BridgeBKnT@yahoo.com.

D'ette Corona is the Assistant Publisher for Chicken Soup for the Soul Publishing, LLC. She received her bachelor of science in business management in 1994. D'ette has been married for eighteen years and has a thirteen-year-old son.

Kayla Rehme Crockett and her husband Jared are parents to three daughters, ages seven, four, and one. They love to spend time as a family hiking Colorado's Rocky Mountains. When she's not changing diapers, kissing boo-boos, or pretending to be the evil queen, Kayla enjoys baking, reading, and teaching piano.

Michele Cushatt writes articles, stories and devotionals for numerous publications from a unique collection of life experiences. The director of a local writers group and a speaker trainer, she and her husband and three teenage boys make their home in Colorado. Connect with her at www.MicheleCushatt.com.

Barbara D'Amario is a retired executive secretary who honed her skills writing accommodation letters and personnel evaluations. She belongs to two writing groups, attends workshops and enjoys cooking, reading and painting.

Although blind, **Janet Perez Eckles** thrives as a Spanish interpreter, international speaker, writer and author of *Trials of Today, Treasures for Tomorrow — Overcoming Adversities in Life*. From her home in Florida, she enjoys working on church ministries and taking Caribbean cruises with her husband Gene. She imparts inspiration at: www.janetperezeckles.com.

Rebecca C. Emrich graduated with her Bachelor of Arts in History from Brigham Young University in 1999. She currently lives in Syracuse, New York with her husband and twin daughters. She enjoys serving in her church, exploring state parks, and exhausting the reading opportunities at the local library.

Cheri Eplin received her Bachelor of Science from Cal Poly and Masters in Education from JFK University. She teaches third grade in Danville, California. Cheri feels blessed to do what she loves: be a mom to two amazing boys, teach, write, hike, and travel. E-mail her at ceplin@mac.com.

Susan Farr-Fahncke is the founder of 2TheHeart.com, where you can find more of her writing and sign up for an online writing workshop! She is also the founder of the amazing volunteer group, Angels2TheHeart, the author of *Angel's Legacy*, and contributor to over sixty books, including many in the *Chicken Soup for the Soul* series. Visit her at www.2TheHeart.com.

Jackie Fleming, a native Californian, grew up in the Bay Area and raised three boys on an island in the California Delta. Her hobbies are traveling the world by freighter, yoga, reading and writing. For six years, she wrote columns for two weekly newspapers. She now lives in Paradise, California.

Peggy Frezon is a freelance writer specializing in pets. Her first book, *Losing It With My Dog*, is about dieting with a lovable, chubby Spaniel. Peggy is also a contributing writer for *Guideposts* and *Angels on Earth*. Her favorite Christmas tradition is hanging stockings! Visit Peggy's Pet Place (peggyfrezon.blogspot.com) or connect with her on Twitter @peggyfrezon.

Susan Garrard holds a B.S. in Chemistry from the University of Southern Maine. She currently works in the marketing field. She lives in Scarborough, Maine with her three sons. Susan enjoys running, fitness, writing and long walks along the beautiful Maine coast. Please e-mail her at segarrard@gmail.com.

Beverly Golberg, a resident of St. Paul, Minnesota, turned her energy to writing after retiring from paralegal work. Her essays have appeared in literary journals, *Cottage Life* magazine, *A Cup of Comfort*, and the *St. Paul Pioneer Press*. She reads her work at the Wild Yam Cabaret in St. Paul.

Marian Gormley's writing has appeared in numerous *Chicken Soup for the Soul* books and other regional, national and international publications. She writes primarily about parenting, family life, education, health and the arts. She recently earned a Masters Degree in Education and looks forward to instilling a love of reading in Northern Virginia elementary-age students.

Sally Baggett Griffis, a West Texas ranch girl who finally went to college, received a B.S. in Education, Psychology and a B.S. in Psychology, Counseling from Angelo State University. In agency and private practice for many years, she is now retired. Her first book, *From the Back of the Beast*, is a memoir of a war widow. Contact her via e-mail at sallyg54@gmail.com.

Michelle D. Halperin is a teacher in Elmira, New York, where she lives with her husband, two sons and three dogs. Michelle enjoys working with children and spending time with her family.

Cynthia M. Hamond's in over 100 publications including *Chicken Soup for the Soul*, magazines, Bible study aids and is a King Features Syndicate recurring author. She's received several writing awards. Two stories have been made for TV. She enjoys her speaking and school visits and is founder of Joyful MOMs. E-mail her at Candbh@aol.com.

Bonnie Compton Hanson is author of over twenty-five books for children and adults. Her stories and poems have been published in many magazines and books, including thirty-two in *Chicken Soup for the Soul*. Besides mentoring new writers, she speaks to women, seniors, and student groups. You may contact her via e-mail at bonnieh1@sbcglobal.net.

Carol Harrison earned her Bachelor of Education from the University of Saskatchewan, and her Distinguished Toastmaster designation. She is a motivational speaker and author of *Amee's Story*. She enjoys time with family, reading, scrapbooking and speaking. You can e-mail her at carol@carolscorner.ca or visit her website www.carolscorner.ca.

Jonny Hawkins has been cartooning professionally since 1986. His work has appeared in over 600 publications and on dozens of products. He has five Cartoon-a-Day Calendars on the market: Medical, Fishing, Teachers, Cat and Dog. He lives in Sherwood, Michigan with his wife, Carissa, and their three children. He can be reached at jonnyhawkins2nz@yahoo.com.

Kat Heckenbach, honors graduate of the University of Tampa, home schools her two children while writing speculative fiction and inspirational nonfiction. She also enjoys reading, drawing, and anything that stretches her creative muscles. Please visit her at www.findingangel.com.

Laurie Higgins is an award-winning freelance journalist. She is a regular contributor to the *Cape Cod Times* and *The Cape Codder* newspapers. In addition to writing, her other passion is cooking and she combines both at her website, www.thatsnotwhattherecipesays.com. You can contact her via e-mail at lauriehiggins@comcast.net.

Corinne "Cori" Foley Hill received her B.A. from the University of Virginia and her M.Ed. from James Madison University. She provides personnel training in early intervention in Virginia where she lives with her husband and two daughters. Cori dreams of living in the Caribbean and writing children's books.

Robert Hill lives in Vancouver, Washington, and is very active in church and Native American ministries. In his spare time he likes to travel and spend time with his grandchildren, and after all these years, he still loves fruitcake!

Elaine Ingalls Hogg is an award-winning author and the editor of *Christmas in the Maritimes* (Nimbus Publishing), a book which became a Canadian bestseller in 2006. Elaine shares her office with two Ragdoll cats, Angus and Alex, enjoys writing, music and travel. Please contact her through her website: http://elainehogg.com.

Cindy Holcomb is working toward an Associate of Science in

Interdisciplinary Studies - Communication degree. Cindy's book, *The Reverse Mortgage Book: Everything You Need to Know Explained Simply* was published in 2008. She is working on her first novel. When not writing, Cindy loves spending time with her three daughters and three granddaughters.

David J. Hull has been a teacher for twenty-three years and also writes a monthly column in a local newspaper. He is currently working on creating a book of his collected columns. He enjoys reading, gardening and spending time with his nieces and nephews. You can e-mail him at Davidhull59@aol.com.

Taryn R. Hutchison is the author of *We Wait You: Waiting on God in Eastern Europe* (2008 WinePress Publishing). She contributed to *Chicken Soup for the Soul: Living Catholic Faith* and has published over twenty-five articles. Taryn and her husband live in North Carolina. Visit her at www.tarynhutchison.com.

Cindy Hval's work has appeared in numerous *Chicken Soup for the Soul* collections. She's currently working on her first book *Love Stories From the Greatest Generation*. She's a columnist and correspondent for *The Spokesman-Review* newspaper in Spokane, Washington where she lives with her husband, four sons and one cat.

Bonnie Jarvis-Lowe is a retired Registered Nurse who spends much of her time now working with animals at the SPCA in her town. She just celebrated her fortieth wedding anniversary and is the mother of two and the grandmother of one little girl.

Pat Stockett Johnston is published in a variety of devotionals, print publications, take-home papers, e-magazines, and missions' education books. She received her BA from Pasadena/Point Loma Nazarene University. Pat and her husband Gordon served as missionaries in Beirut, Lebanon; Amman, Jordan; and Papua New Guinea. Please e-mail her at writerpat@att.net.

Mimi Greenwood Knight is one of twelve kids and mama to four. She lives with her husband and kiddos in South Louisiana where she enjoys artisan bread making, her butterfly garden, Bible study and the lost art of letter writing. Visit her blog at blog.nola.com/faith/mimi_greenwood_knight.

Tom Knight is a husband and father who lives and works in Toronto, Canada. After reading *Chicken Soup for the Soul* he realized he had his own stories to share and he hopes that his first published story will not be his last. He is eternally grateful for the love and support of his wife and children, without whom none of his dreams would ever have been realized.

Marla Stewart Konrad is the author of several books for children, including the award-winning picture book, *Just Like You*. She lives with her family near Toronto, Canada.

Nancy Julien Kopp grew up in Chicago and now lives in the Flint Hills of Kansas. Her work is in ten *Chicken Soup for the Soul* books, other anthologies, magazines and newspapers. A former teacher, she still enjoys teaching through the written word. Learn more at www.writergrannysworld.blogspot.com.

Aletheia D. Lee lives with her husband and son in Georgia where she teaches English as a Second Language to elementary school students. They are expecting the addition of twin girls very soon. She has had three poems and three short stories published previously. She can be contacted via e-mail at lee.aletheia@gmail.com.

Glenda Carol Lee is a published author of two bulletin board idea books, numerous magazine articles and poems. Her first story was published in *Chicken Soup for the Soul: Count Your Blessings*. She enjoys writing, reading and spending time with her family. Please e-mail her at nanmom1@gmail.com.

Janeen Lewis is a writer living in central Kentucky with her husband and two children. She enjoys reading, sewing and spending time with her family. Contact her via e-mail at jlewis0402@netzero.net.

God's deliverance from an abusive childhood frames the joy that **Delores Liesner** shares with her readers. God "sightings" have been shared via speaking, magazines, Examiner.com, CBN.com, radio, television, anthologies, devotionals, Bible studies, and her column in *Prime Magazine*. Delores welcomes contact at lovedliftedandled@wi.rr.com.

Brooke Linville and her family moved home in February 2009. She writes about their journey after the fire at www.lifeafterthefire.com and is working on a memoir. Contact her via e-mail at life_after_the_fire@yahoo.com.

Barbara LoMonaco received her BS from the University of Southern California and has an elementary teaching credential. Barbara has worked for Chicken Soup for the Soul since 1998 as an editor and webmaster. She is a co-author of *Chicken Soup for the Mother and Son Soul* and *Chicken Soup for the Soul: My Resolution*.

Nyx Martinez is a travel TV host for Living Asia Channel, and Managing Editor of *Mabuhay* and *Mango* travel and lifestyle magazines. She lived in Uganda as a full-time volunteer and radio presenter for three and a half years. Visit her at www.nyxmartinez.com.

Teresa Ann Maxwell lives in Washington with her favorite fisherman and husband, Richard. She has many fond memories of snowy, white Christmases celebrated, with family, in her home state of Idaho.

Erin McCormack is thirteen years old and lives with her parents and brother, Matt. She is preparing to attend high school in the fall of 2010. Erin enjoys reading, writing, and many sports, including soccer and running. Erin plans to continue writing both fiction and nonfiction stories and books for children and teenagers.

Chantal Meijer is a freelance writer whose articles, stories, and essays have appeared in regional and national magazines, newspapers, and anthologies, including *Chicken Soup for the Soul: Empty Nesters*. Chantal and her husband Rick, proud parents of four grown children, live in Terrace, British Columbia, Canada. Contact her via e-mail at meijer@telus.net.

Martha Miller is a Texas-based, freelance writer. Her work has appeared in *Family Circle, Parents, The Christian Science Monitor* and www.LifeInItaly.com. Her syndicated columns, "Living Greenly" and "Living Online," are published in regional parenting magazines across the country. E-mail her at Martha@MarthaMillerWrites.com.

Susan H. Miller lives in Coldspring, Texas, where she works periodically as an R.N. Case Manager. She lives to draw from her own life experiences for her stories, but hasn't quite figured out what her genre is. Susan loves adventure, and will travel anywhere, anytime. E-mail her at suehmakm@yahoo.com.

Mike Morin co-hosts a morning radio show at WZID-FM in Manchester, New Hampshire. In addition to his forty years as a radio and TV personality, Mike writes humor columns and features for New England newspapers and magazines. He enjoys baking artisan breads for local charity auctions. Please e-mail Mike at Heymikey@aol.com.

Carrie Morris married her high school sweetheart, Chris, who is now a Marine stationed at MCAS New River in North Carolina. They have two furbabies, Lily and Duke. She is currently working on her first novel.

Beth Morrissey is a freelance writer and writing instructor living in Dublin, Ireland. Christmas has always been her favorite time of year, and she truly believes in the magic of the season. Visit Beth online at www.bethmorrissey.com.

Irene Morse is a freelance writer. When not hanging out with her husband Gary and their large family, she enjoys travel in search of adventure and examining the human condition through drama and community theatre. Her column on theatre appears regularly in the local newspaper. Please e-mail her at irene@ingramct.com.

As a journalist and screenwriter in Northern California, **Russell Nichols** likes to travel and write stories that explore the crevices of society. His work has appeared in *The Boston Globe*, the *Los Angeles Times* and *Sactown Magazine*. Contact him via e-mail at thirdeyewitness@gmail.com.

Barbara Nicks grew up in lower Wisconsin and now resides in East Texas. She has been teaching for twenty-five years, spending two of them in Portugal. She enjoys traveling with her husband and two teenage sons, sewing, reading, and learning about technology. E-mail her at barbnicks@gmail.com.

Mark Parisi's "off the mark" comic, syndicated since 1987, is distributed by United Media. His cartoon feature won the National Cartoonists Society's award for Best Newspaper Panel in 2009. His humor also graces greeting cards, T-shirts, calendars, magazines, newsletters and books. See www.offthemark.com. Lynn is his wife/business partner. Daughter Jen contributes inspiration, as do three cats, one dog and an unknown number of koi.

Lisa Pawlak is a creative writer of nonfiction, who stands firmly behind the belief that writing is cheaper than therapy. She received a B.A. in Communication and since has developed a professional background in marketing and non-profit management. In more recent years, Lisa left her career behind to focus on the challenges of motherhood.

Ann Peachman has two degrees in theology, has run a home daycare, and currently works with the elderly. She is a widow with three grown children and one granddaughter, and lives in Mississauga, Ontario, Canada. Ann enjoys family, friends, scrapbooking and knitting. She is working on her first novel.

Julia G. Powell received her Bachelor of Arts Degree, with honors, from Lycoming College (Williamsport, PA) in 1973. She is a federal employee/educator in Tennessee. She enjoys her grandsons, writing, gardening, and painting/drawing. Her plans are to write from her heart. Please e-mail her at navfit@aol.com.

Lisa Preston (www.lisapreston.com) lives in the Pacific Northwest where she kayaks, writes, trail runs, rides fast, and tortures her guitar, fiddle and mandolin. She remembers Winston and his boy throughout the year, every year.

Tracy Rasmussen is an award-winning journalist, essayist, author and stay-at-home mom. She lives in Pennsylvania with her hardworking husband, spirited twin daughters and an over-achieving Standard Poodle. Tracy is currently working on an adoption memoir. Please e-mail her through her website www.tracyrasmussen.com.

Natalie June Reilly is a single mother of two extraordinary teenage boys, a full-time football mom and the author of the children's book, *My Stick Family: Helping Children Cope with Divorce*. Natalie lives and loves in gratitude every day and she welcomes you to reach out to her at natalie@themeanmom.com.

Bruce Robinson is an award-winning internationally published cartoonist whose work has appeared in numerous consumer and trade periodicals including the *National Enquirer*, *The Saturday Evening Post*, *Woman's World*, *The Sun*, *First*, *Highlights for Children*, etc. He is also the author of the cartoon book *Good Medicine*. Contact him via e-mail at cartoonsbybrucerobinson@hotmail.com.

Marilyn (Lynn) Ross, a graduate of Arkansas State University, teaches special education in Prince William County, Virginia. Her other stories appear in *Chicken Soup for the Soul: Celebrating Mothers and Daughters* and *Chicken Soup for the Soul: Empty Nesters*. Marilyn's favorites include writing, photography and album making. E-mail her at lynn.ross96@gmail.com.

Ann M. Sheridan has contributed stories to three other *Chicken Soup for the Soul* books. She founded Bimbo's Buddies in 2002 to distribute her children's book, *Dogs Get Cancer Too*, to pediatric cancer patients. Ann resides in Long Branch, New Jersey. E-mail her at ASheridan529@aol.com.

Deborah Shouse is a writer, speaker, editor and creativity catalyst. Deborah is donating all proceeds from her book, *Love in the Land of Dementia: Finding Hope in the Caregiver's Journey*, to Alzheimer's programs and research. So far, she has raised more than $80,000. Visit her website at www.TheCreativityConnection.com.

Paula L. Silici is an award-winning, multi-published author. She firmly believes in the dictum, "Peace begins with me," and endeavors to practice at least one random act of kindness every day. Contact her via e-mail at psilici@hotmail.com.

Carol Slamowitz is a graduate of the College of Charleston. Currently she practices massage therapy in Richmond, Virginia. She is married with two amazing kids. She enjoys reading, travel, fitness and adventure... she plans to continue to lead an interesting and unconventional life.

Lynetta Smith lives with her husband and two daughters near Nashville, Tennessee. When she is not writing or homeschooling, she can be found at the local community theatre.

Sue Smith shared her story, "The Garbage Can Christmas," with Linda LaRocque. Linda LaRocque is the author of several award-winning plays. Linda is a retired self-employed interior designer. She writes from her South Haven, Michigan home.

Erin Solej teaches Language Arts Literacy at Mountain View Middle School in Mendham, New Jersey. She loves to read and write with her sixth graders and her children, Lucas and Hanna. Please contact her via e-mail at esolej@optonline.net.

Laurie Sontag has been a humor columnist for California newspapers since 2001. Her work has appeared in various books and magazines and her popular blog, Manic Motherhood, has been featured on Yahoo's Shine Network. You can see more of her work at www.lauriesontag.com.

Jean Sorensen's cartoons have appeared in *Good Housekeeping*, *The Washington Post Magazine*, *The Lutheran*, and numerous textbooks. Her work has also been featured in greeting cards for Oatmeal Studios. Jean lives in the Washington, DC area with her high school sweetheart and three children, who always keep her laughing.

Diane Stark is a former teacher turned stay-at-home mom and freelance writer. She loves to write about the important things in life: her family and her faith. She is the author of *Teachers' Devotions to Go*. Diane can be reached via e-mail at DianeStark19@yahoo.com.

Melanie Stiles is an AACC Master Life Coach, award-winning author and speaker who enjoys sharing life journeys and tools that help others to become all God says they can be. Her favorite experience to date is when her granddaughter rushes in yelling, "YaYa I'm here!"

Teri Stohlberg received her bachelor's degree in business from the University of Texas at Arlington in 1996. She now lives in Woodstock, Connecticut with her husband and two children. Teri will always believe in miracles. Contact her via e-mail at teristohlberg@yahoo.com.

Nancy Sullivan has multiple degrees and has written extensively over a long career in the disability arena. Her passion is writing mysteries with a paranormal flair. An animal rescue volunteer, Nancy delights in her own rescued menagerie and her avocation working in energetic healing alternatives. Contact Nancy via e-mail at nancy.writes@sbcglobal.net.

From belly dancer, to fitness trainer, to speech pathologist, to memoir teacher, **Tsgoyna Tanzman** credits writing as the supreme "therapy" for raising an adolescent daughter. Published in four *Chicken Soup for the Soul* books, her humorous essays and poems can be read on more.com, motheringmagazine.com, and in *The Orange County Register*. E-mail her at tnzmn@cox.net.

Jan Vallone was once a disillusioned lawyer. In 2001, she took a job teaching English at a yeshiva—an Orthodox Jewish high school—where she learned what fulfillment means. Jan's first book, *Pieces of Someday*, published in 2010, recounts her yeshiva days and benefits several charities. For details visit www.janvallone.com.

Beverly F. Walker lives in Tennessee, with her retired husband. She enjoys writing, photography, and scrapbooking pictures of her grandchildren. Beverly wrote this poem right after she married her husband and became stepmother to his three little girls. She has stories in many *Chicken Soup for the Soul* books, and in *Angel Cats: Divine Messengers of Comfort*.

Since 1990, **Joseph Walker** has written a weekly newspaper column called "ValueSpeak." Some of his columns were published in three other *Chicken Soup for the Soul* books. His books include *Look What Love Has Done* and *Christmas on Mill Street*. Joseph and his wife, Anita, have five children and seven grandchildren.

Growing up playing in her clubhouse filled with the contents of an abandoned one-room schoolhouse, **Barbara Briggs Ward** realized she wanted to be a writer. Published in *Highlights for Children*; author/illustrator of two children's books, Barbara invites you to go to www.snarlysally.com and www.thereindeerkeeper.com. Please contact her via e-mail at maggieosheacompany@yahoo.com.

Stefanie Wass's essays have been published in the *Los Angeles Times, Seattle Times, Christian Science Monitor, Akron Beacon Journal, Akron Life and Leisure, Cleveland Magazine, The Writer* magazine, *A Cup of Comfort for Mothers, A Cup of Comfort for a Better World*, and eight *Chicken Soup for the Soul* anthologies. Visit her website at www.stefaniewass.com.

Gerri Wetta-Hilger recently retired after thirty years teaching. She received her Bachelor of Science in English from Pittsburg State University in Kansas and her Masters in Education from Wichita State. Gerri now has more time to enjoy her four children, twelve grandchildren, read, write and travel with her husband.

Kathy Whirity is a syndicated newspaper columnist who shares her sentimental musings on family life. Her first published book, *Life Is A Kaleidoscope* is a compilation of some of those columns. Please e-mail Kathy at kathywhirity@yahoo.com.

Ernie Witham writes the humor column "Ernie's World" for the *Montecito Journal* in Montecito, California. He is the author of two humor books: *Ernie's World the Book* and *A Year in the Life of a "Working" Writer*. He has been published in many anthologies including more than a dozen *Chicken Soup for the Soul* books.

Ferida Wolff is author of seventeen children's books and three essay books, her latest being the award-winning picture book *The Story Blanket* and *Missed Perceptions: Challenge Your Thoughts Change Your Thinking*. Her work appears in anthologies, newspapers, magazines, online at www.seniorwomen.com and in her nature blog http://feridasbackyard.blogspot.com. Visit her at www.feridawolff.com.

Sandra Wood received her BA in communications and worked as a marketing executive for twenty-four years. Today, she writes short stories about everyday miracles. Favorite things: Children, chocolate, puppy breath, long talks with loved ones, international travel, and watching God paint the sky with new mercy every morning.

Dallas Woodburn is twenty-three years old and the author of two collections of short stories, a forthcoming novel, and articles in *Family Circle*, *Writer's Digest*, and the *Los Angeles Times*, among other publications. She is also the founder of Write On! For Literacy and Write On! Books youth publishing company. Visit www.writeonbooks.org for more information.

Barbra Yardley is a wife and mother of three delightful young women. She works as a legal secretary in a small town in Utah. She enjoys the outdoors, quilting, biking, reading, spending time with family, and being a grandmother to two active little boys.

Meet Our Authors

Jack Canfield is the co-creator of the *Chicken Soup for the Soul* series, which *Time* magazine has called "the publishing phenomenon of the decade." Jack is also the co-author of many other bestselling books.

Jack is the CEO of the Canfield Training Group in Santa Barbara, California, and founder of the Foundation for Self-Esteem in Culver City, California. He has conducted intensive personal and professional development seminars on the principles of success for more than a million people in twenty-three countries, has spoken to hundreds of thousands of people at more than 1,000 corporations, universities, professional conferences and conventions, and has been seen by millions more on national television shows.

Jack has received many awards and honors, including three honorary doctorates and a Guinness World Records Certificate for having seven books from the *Chicken Soup for the Soul* series appearing on the New York Times bestseller list on May 24, 1998.

You can reach Jack at www.jackcanfield.com.

Mark Victor Hansen is the co-founder of Chicken Soup for the Soul, along with Jack Canfield. He is a sought-after keynote speaker, bestselling author, and marketing maven. Mark's powerful messages of possibility, opportunity, and action have created powerful change in thousands of organizations and millions of individuals worldwide.

Mark is a prolific writer with many bestselling books in addition to the *Chicken Soup for the Soul* series. Mark has had a profound influence in the field of human potential through his library of audios, videos, and articles in the areas of big thinking, sales achievement, wealth building, publishing success, and personal and professional development. He is also the founder of the MEGA Seminar Series.

Mark has received numerous awards that honor his entrepreneurial spirit, philanthropic heart, and business acumen. He is a lifetime member of the Horatio Alger Association of Distinguished Americans.

You can reach Mark at www.markvictorhansen.com.

Amy Newmark is the publisher and editor-in-chief of *Chicken Soup for the Soul*, after a thirty-year career as a writer, speaker, financial analyst, and business executive in the worlds of finance and telecommunications. Amy is a *magna cum laude* graduate of Harvard College, where she majored in Portuguese, minored in French, and traveled extensively. She and her husband have four grown children.

After a long career writing books on telecommunications, voluminous financial reports, business plans, and corporate press releases, Chicken Soup for the Soul is a breath of fresh air for Amy. She has fallen in love with Chicken Soup for the Soul and its life-changing books, and really enjoys putting these books together for Chicken Soup's inspiring readers. She has co-authored more than two dozen *Chicken Soup for the Soul* books and has edited another two dozen.

You can reach Amy through the webmaster@chickensoupforthesoul.com.

Thank You

W e owe huge thanks to all of our contributors. We know that you poured your hearts and souls into the thousands of stories and poems that you shared with us, and ultimately with each other. We appreciate your willingness to open up your lives to other Chicken Soup for the Soul readers. And we loved hearing about how you and your families celebrate Christmas.

We could only publish a small percentage of the stories that were submitted, but we read every single one and even the ones that do not appear in the book had an influence on us and on the final manuscript.

We owe special thanks to our assistant publisher, D'ette Corona, who read the 6,000 stories that were submitted for this book. Our webmaster and editor, Barbara LoMonaco, then stepped in and the two of them narrowed several hundred finalists down to about 120 stories, of which 101 ultimately were chosen and edited for the final manuscript. It was a huge undertaking, and they did a great job. This book could not have been made without their expertise, their input, and their innate knowledge of what makes a great Chicken Soup for the Soul story. We also want to thank Chicken Soup for the Soul editor Kristiana Glavin for her assistance with the final manuscript and proofreading, and Madeline Clapps for proofreading assistance.

We owe a very special thanks to our creative director and book producer, Brian Taylor at Pneuma Books, for his brilliant vision for our covers and interiors. Finally, none of this would be possible without the business and creative leadership of our CEO, Bill Rouhana, and our president, Bob Jacobs.

Improving Your Life Every Day

Real people sharing real stories—for seventeen years. Now, Chicken Soup for the Soul has gone beyond the bookstore to become a world leader in life improvement. Through books, movies, DVDs, online resources and other partnerships, we bring hope, courage, inspiration and love to hundreds of millions of people around the world. Chicken Soup for the Soul's writers and readers belong to a one-of-a-kind global community, sharing advice, support, guidance, comfort, and knowledge.

Chicken Soup for the Soul stories have been translated into more than forty languages and can be found in more than one hundred countries. Every day, millions of people experience a Chicken Soup for the Soul story in a book, magazine, newspaper or online. As we share our life experiences through these stories, we offer hope, comfort and inspiration to one another. The stories travel from person to person, and from country to country, helping to improve lives everywhere.

Share with Us

We all have had Chicken Soup for the Soul moments in our lives. If you would like to share your story or poem with millions of people around the world, go to chickensoup.com and click on "Submit Your Story." You may be able to help another reader, and become a published author at the same time. Some of our past contributors have launched writing and speaking careers from the publication of their stories in our books!

Our submission volume has been increasing steadily—the quality and quantity of your submissions has been fabulous. We only accept story submissions via our website. They are no longer accepted via mail or fax.

To contact us regarding other matters, please send us an e-mail through webmaster@chickensoupforthesoul.com, or fax or write us at:

Chicken Soup for the Soul
P.O. Box 700
Cos Cob, CT 06807-0700
Fax: 203-861-7194

One more note from your friends at Chicken Soup for the Soul: Occasionally, we receive an unsolicited book manuscript from one of our readers, and we would like to respectfully inform you that we do not accept unsolicited manuscripts and we must discard the ones that appear.

Chicken Soup for the Soul®

www.chickensoup.com